# Frame Reflection

# Frame
# Re*fl*ection

Toward the Resolution
of Intractable Policy Controversies

Donald A. Schön
and
Martin Rein

 BasicBooks

*A Division of* HarperCollins*Publishers*

*Designed by John Chung*

**Library of Congress Cataloging-in-Publication Data**

Schön, Donald A.
   Frame reflection: toward the resolution of intractable policy controversies /
Donald A. Schön and Martin Rein.
      p.   cm.
   Includes bibliographical references and index.
   ISBN 0-465-02506-4
   1. Policy sciences. 2. Social policy. I. Rein, Martin, 1928–. II. Title.
H97.S36   1994
320'.6—dc20                                                         94-8589
                                                                      CIP


94 95 96 97 ❖/RRD 9 8 7 6 5 4 3 2 1

# Contents

# Preface

This book grew out of a collaboration that began in the early 1970s, when we were preparing a new course at MIT on the design of social service systems. Not surprisingly, we found that we had to reconcile somehow our two initially divergent perspectives. Donald A. Schön approached the course from an interest in the design process derived in part from his earlier consulting on product development in industry and his studies of service systems such as the system of services to the blind. Martin Rein came to the course with a strong background in social work and social welfare theory, and with a lively interest in the sociology of knowledge, which focused on the constructedness of our knowledge of social reality.

Out of our initial discussions we came to recognize that design, whether of social service systems or social policy, is not a process of problem solving governed by criteria of technical-rational analysis. We became interested in how problems of social policy and service delivery systems are set, and we saw that disagreements over the nature of these problems are not of the same order as disagreements over how best to increase the effectiveness or efficiency of a service delivery system.

In our first efforts to write about the social construction of policy problems, we proposed to make a study of policy studies. We were especially intrigued by the puzzle of understanding how policy researchers made the "normative leap" from the "is" to the "ought"—from research-based statements of fact to statements that contained policy recommendations. At this point we began to think in terms of policy "frames," the taken-for-granted assumptional structures of policy research that seemed to us to derive from generative metaphors, such as *housing blight* or *fragmented services*. We puzzled about the origins and uses of such metaphors in the research process, especially in effecting the transition from statements of fact to judgments of value. These efforts did not lead to a book, as we first intended, but to a series of individual and collaborative articles in which we explored the structures of problem-setting policy stories, the frames and generative metaphors that underlay such stories, and the possibility of a frame-critical approach to policy analysis. We inquired into the process by which we, as researchers, might more explicitly reflect on the frames that underlay our intuitions and convictions as we conducted action-oriented policy inquiry.

Gradually, as we continued to talk, teach, and write about these issues over the years—and the years did stretch out!—our focus shifted from policy research to policy design. We came to recognize two different but potentially complementary traditions of inquiry: the study of the practical work through which policies are designed in action, and the study of the frames that underlie policy controversies—the assumptional structures held by participants in the forums of policy discourse and by actors in policy-making arenas.

As we developed the case studies that provide the material for this book, we sought to bring these traditions closer together, directing our attention to the management of policy controversies in concrete situations of action. We observed, theoretical objections to the contrary, that there is evidence for the belief that policies are sometimes reframed in action, and that their reframing sometimes results from the actors' reflection on frame conflicts that arise in the evolving, politically colored process of policy design. In the search for pragmatic resolution of policy controversies in policy practice, policy analysis and applied social science, as conventionally understood, play relatively minor roles. The major ones are reserved for reflective policy practitioners.

# Acknowledgments

Professor Langley Keyes, our colleague in MIT's Department of Urban Studies and Planning, made detailed and very helpful critical comments on chapter 6, "Homelessness in Massachusetts." But his contributions went well beyond that. As a thoughtful policy practitioner and keen observer of policy making in the political arena, Keyes urged us to pay attention to the ways in which policies and programs actually develop and challenged us to show how our analysis could give him what he did not already know. His concern with the use of frame reflection was of great importance to us.

Together with Professor William Gamson of Boston College, Rein taught for several years a course on policy discourse that focused on the development of a methodology for frame-critical policy analysis. The special emphases Gamson brought to this course have influenced the present work in many ways.

Our discussion of policy negotiation in part I profited from the critical comments of David Laws, a doctoral student in the Department of Urban Studies and Planning at MIT, who has worked closely with Professor Lawrence Susskind in the uses of mediated negotiation for the resolution of environmental disputes.

Professor Rainer Bauback, at the Institute of Advanced Studies in Vienna, and Professor Herman van Gunsteren, at the Law School of the University of Leyden in Holland, played important roles in the evolution of Rein's ideas about policy frames. Especially important in this regard was the course on policy frames that Rein and van Gunsteren taught together at the Institute for Advanced Studies.

The details of the case of early retirement in Germany, discussed in chapter 4, were originally set out in Wolfgang Kohli and Martin Rein, *Time for Retirement* (1992), where the main focus was on the role of enterprises in the production of early retirement. Matthias Beck, a doctoral student at MIT, was of great help in updating the original study and adding to it material relevant to the themes of this book.

Chapter 5, on Project Athena at MIT, grew out of a 1989 study of Athena that was jointly directed by Schön and Professor Sherry Turkle (coauthor of this chapter), with research support from Brenda Nielsen, M. Stella Orsini, and Wim Overmeer. Nielson and Overmeer were, at the time, doctoral students in the Department of Urban Studies and Planning. Overmeer contributed, in addition, a very helpful critique of an early version of this chapter.

Chapter 6 profited greatly from research work carried out by Peter Shapiro and Amory Starr, then graduate students in the Department of Urban Studies and Planning at MIT, and from the suggestions of our colleague, Professor Lisa Peattie.

# Introduction

This book is about the kinds of intractable policy controversies that are all too familiar to readers of the daily newspapers and watchers of the evening television news—controversies about issues such as poverty, crime, environmental protection, the Third World, and abortion, which are highly resistant to resolution by appeal to evidence, research, or reasoned argument.

This book is also about the kind of rationality appropriate to policy inquiry, by which we mean the intertwining of thought and action in the policy-making process. We see policy making as a dialectic within which policy makers function as designers and exhibit, at their best, a particular kind of reflective practice, which we call design rationality. We shall explore how controversies arise and evolve in policy practice, and what it means for practitioners to respond to them in design-rational ways. At the very outset, however, we must observe that the argument of our book swims against the prevailing tide. Reflection in policy practice has very little currency among scholars and practitioners in the policy field.

As we shall see, the scholarly arguments against reflection in practice take several forms. All of them, however, are versions of Hannah Arendt's thesis that "thinking is out of place in action."[1] What Arendt means by thinking is not the ordinary, common-sense cognition that goes on when we recognize and solve problems, whether in everyday life or in the realm of practical policy making. On the contrary, she posits a state of "intramural warfare" between thought and common sense. Her thought is a kind of reflection that deals with "essences"—

with what is most abstract, general, and theoretical—and it involves "withdrawal from the common-sense world of appearances."

For Arendt, the theoretical belongs not to those who participate in the drama of life but to the spectators:

> From the Greek word for spectators, *theatai,* the later philosophical term "theory" was derived, and the word "theoretical" until a few hundred years ago meant "contemplating," looking upon something from the outside, from a position implying a view that is hidden from those who take part in the spectacle and actualize it. . . . [As] a spectator you may understand the "truth" of what the spectacle is about; but the price you have to pay is withdrawal from participating in it.[2]

Hence thinking is essentially a withdrawal from action. In practical life, it is always out of order. It "interrupts all ordinary activities and is interrupted by them."[3]

Arendt's paradigmatic thinker is Socrates. The Socrates she chooses to portray, however, is not the gadfly of Plato's early dialogues, who buttonholes Sophists in the streets of Athens, peppering them with questions about the nature of the good, and not the one who then, before the assembled citizens, defends himself against the accusation of impiety on the ground that his irreverent moral dialectic is the highest form of political action.[4] Her Socrates is the one Xenophon describes as having remained in complete immobility for twenty-four hours in a military camp, "turning his mind to himself . . . deep in thought."[5]

Like Xenophon's Socrates, anyone who would truly think, in Arendt's sense, pays a formidable price: withdrawal from "the festival of life," even to the point of "homelessness": "The thinking ego, moving among universals, among invisible essences, is, strictly speaking, nowhere; it is homeless."[6] But those who do take part in the game of life also pay a heavy price: they must give up the possibility of understanding the deeper meaning of the events in which they are involved. For, according to Arendt, it is "withdrawal from direct involvement to a standpoint outside the game [that is] not only a condition for judging, for being the final arbiter in the ongoing competition, but also the condition for understanding the meaning of the play."[7]

In the realm of policy, we understand the kind of thinking that Arendt excludes from the common-sense world in terms of a "ladder of reflection," in which objects of policy-making thought are ordered by their abstractness and conceptual distance from concrete situations. The rungs of this ladder proceed, from low to high, roughly as follows:

1) policy practices, such as regulation, screening, and verification;
2) policy itself, conceived as a set of rules, laws, prohibitions, entitlements, or resource allocations;
3) the policy-making process, including its debates and struggles;
4) the particular positions and accompanying arguments held by advocates and opponents in policy debates and struggles;
5) the beliefs, values, and perspectives held by particular institutions and interest groups from which particular policy positions are derived (we shall call these *institutional action frames*); and
6) the broadly shared beliefs, values, and perspectives familiar to the members of a societal culture and likely to endure in that culture over long periods of time, on which individuals and institutions draw in order to give meaning, sense, and normative direction to their thinking and action in policy matters (we shall call these *metacultural frames*).

Neither scholars like Arendt nor practitioners in the policy sphere assert that reflection as such is out of place in policy making or in any situation of practical life. Everyone seems to take for granted that policy makers can and do reflect on such lower-level objects as policy practices and policies themselves. Policy makers are ordinarily assumed to think about such things in the course of their day-to-day lives with at least some chance of a constructive outcome. But when it comes to higher-level reflection—by which we mean reflection on such "invisible essences" as the beliefs, values, and perspectives implicit in policy struggles—this assumption is frequently called into question. Indeed, the view that prevails among scholars who think about such things at all is that higher-level reflection in policy-making practice is neither feasible nor desirable.

For example, the contemporary sociologist, Joseph Gusfield, has written that "the clinician, the practitioner, the official, cannot afford to stand outside the frameworks within which action occurs, to examine their institutions and beliefs as only one among a number of possible worlds."[8] If practitioners were to do this, Gusfield believes, they would have to give up that wholehearted commitment to a single set of institutions and beliefs that is indispensable to their effective action.

Albert Hirschman, the perceptive economist and social thinker, has proposed another version of the argument that reflection may paralyze action. He suggests, in the context of economic development, that if we knew in advance how difficult the problems of ambitious development projects were going to be, we would not be foolhardy enough to tackle them. He believes that we can muster the courage to undertake such projects only with the assistance of a "hiding hand" that "beneficially hides difficulties from us," protecting us through "ignorance of ignorance, or uncertainties, and of difficulties."[9] One might elaborate on Hirschman's view by pointing out that action is always embedded in a broader context that limits the scope of action. Practitioners tend to assume that the factors essential to the goals they pursue lie at least partly within their control. With their taken-for-granted assumptions, they tend to ignore the factors that lie beyond their control and the shifts of context that may distort the hoped-for outcomes of deliberate action. In Hirschman's view, such early ignorance is beneficial. It protects us from the profound discouragement that follows from an awareness of uncertainties and difficulties beyond our control, thereby unleashing the creativity we need in order to solve the design problems that come up later on.[10]

Renata Mayntz has suggested a variant of Hirschman's argument for the necessity of a hiding hand. She considers a situation in which policy antagonists begin to become reflective about the controversy in which they are engaged. They imagine what they might do on the basis of their interests and powers, how their opponents might respond to their actions, and how they might respond to their opponents' response. If all relevant actors were to pursue such a line of thought, she claims, they might easily conclude that any action is likely to lead to a hopeless stalemate. That recognition could paralyze them and lock them into the status quo. In short, the more policy antagonists become aware of one another's perspectives and strategies of action, the more likely they are to bring themselves to an impasse.[11]

Yet another version of the argument against reflection in practice is to be found in the writings of Jon Elster. Elster focuses on "byproducts," which he defines as "states that cannot be brought about intelligently and intentionally" but can only arise as unintended consequences of actions undertaken for the sake of other ends.[12] He sees it as contradictory to attempt, deliberately and directly, to bring about such "inaccessible" states. For example, he argues that success in psychotherapy does not depend on which theory the therapist uses but only on his having *some* theory. Most theories instruct the therapist to try to bring about some intermediary state—usually, a form of insight—as a precondition for realizing the final goal of mental health. Elster suggests, however, that success in therapy is not realized instrumentally through the intermediary state, but as a byproduct of the attempt to bring about that state. Personal change arises, in other words, only as a byproduct of the search for insight.

If Elster makes this argument about personal change, he might well make an analogous argument about change in the policy-making sphere: that a fundamental rethinking of policy comes not as a direct result of insights gained through reflection but only as a byproduct of the search for such insights. Paradoxically, then, he might argue that practical policy makers, though they gain no direct benefits from reflective insight, should nevertheless pursue it.

It is very striking that scholars who argue that higher-level reflection is out of place in action do not argue that it is out of place in scholarship. On the contrary, they clearly believe it is the main business of scholarship, illustrating their belief in the very process of reflecting on reflection's mismatch to situations of action. The scholars' stance toward reflection is reminiscent of the distinction Thorstein Veblen made, in the second decade of this century, between the proper business of the "higher" schools (the research universities) and of the "lower" professional schools, which had begun, at the time of Veblen's writing, to seek their place in the universities.[13] The lower schools, in Veblen's opinion, should be schools of "applications," devoting themselves to the task of applying to problems of practice the systematic theoretical knowledge whose development is proper to the higher schools. Practicing professionals, in turn, should make use of the applied knowledge developed by the lower schools.

Veblen's intellectual descendants, the scholars and scientists who reside in the great research universities, have tended, on the whole, to maintain an attitude rather like Veblen's.[14] Members of the faculties of the professional schools who have, despite Veblen, found their ways into the universities tend to mirror the attitude of their counterparts in the higher schools. In the field of policy, researchers tend to believe that their brand of social-scientific or policy-analytic reflection would be out of place in the world of practical policy making.[15] We should hasten to add that many policy makers agree with them.

Many practitioners believe, on grounds of hard-headed practicality and in view of the pressures and distractions of real-world experience, that higher-level reflection is the prerogative of university scholars and out of place in the world of practice. It is true that not all practitioners share this belief. Some of them appear to believe that it may be appropriate to think about what they are doing while doing it, even in ways that bear on the assumptions and values embedded in policy positions, and that it is important, perhaps essential, for them to engage in such activity together with their fellow policy makers. Nevertheless, it is not uncommon to find policy practitioners arguing that such reflection is profoundly impractical and distracting, that there is no time for it, and that (as Arendt would say) it is out of order in the real world.

What can be wrong with such a position, when most scholars and many practitioners agree with it?

There are, as we see it, two main difficulties. First, the Veblenian bargain has not paid off very well for policy makers. As the following chapter argues, the policy-analytic movement begun by Harold Lasswell in the early 1950s has largely failed. Policy researchers have tended to be co-opted by one side or another in policy controversies and have done more to fuel such controversies than to resolve them. More importantly, perhaps, there is something about the *kind* of reflection practiced by scholars in the universities—those who, in Arendt's words, seek to understand the meaning of the game by withdrawing to a standpoint outside it—that is ill-suited to the production of usable knowledge. Gusfield is eloquent on this very point, even though he also argues, as we noted, that practitioners "cannot afford . . . to examine their institutions and beliefs as only one among a number of possible worlds." He suggests that the academicians, who do aspire to examine life "through the prism of alternative perspectives," tend to do so in ways that are either "Utopian" or "Olympian." In the first case, he claims, the agents of reflection tend to see the unmasking of a dominant perspective as "the occasion for the creation of a newer and better one," but in ways that tend to ignore the constraints of action in some real institutional world. In the second case, they tend to be "more detached, more skeptical of *all* perspectives."[16] In both cases, the results of their reflections are minimally useful to practitioners.

A second troublesome feature of the argument that higher-level reflection is out of place in action is that it is based on questionable assumptions about the nature of both reflection and practical action. Arendt, for example, appears to believe that thinking is irretrievably seductive—that once one has withdrawn from action to engage in what she calls a "stop and think," one can never return to participate, perhaps more wisely, in the drama of life. Hirschman's discussion of the hiding hand seems to assume that awareness of complexity and difficulty on the part of those who contemplate ambitious projects must have the effect of discouraging them rather than inducing them to proceed with greater care and thoughtfulness. Mayntz assumes that reflection can only function as an instrument of win-lose competition; she seems not to consider the possibility that it might also lead to an awareness of the benefits of cooperation. Like the writers in the field of mediated negotiation, whose work we will consider in later chapters, she seems to assume that reflection can only serve the instrumental purpose of furthering our existing interests, leaving untouched our views of what our real interests are.

Gusfield, finally, appears to believe that it is quite impossible for practitioners to achieve what Lisa Peattie has happily called "double vision," the ability to act from one perspective while, in the back of our minds, we hold onto an awareness of other possible perspectives. Double vision is, in effect, an ability to muster the commitment essential to action in the face of the doubt that grows out of our having passed through the valley of despair. It is an antidote to Utopian thinking, and it is the very capability that William Perry identifies, in his study of the cognitive and ethical development of college students, with the achievement of ethical maturity.[17]

It is perhaps worth considering that those who have chosen to withdraw from the drama of life in order to contemplate it and extract its meaning (in our time, mainly from the vantage point of the research universities) have thereby acquired a peculiarly disabling way of imagining the nature of both reflective policy inquiry and practical politics. As this book argues, even the few scholars who advocate a more nearly ideal discourse among the holders of conflicting perspectives or paradigms do so in a way that suffers from their divorce from the experience of concrete practice.

Stubborn policy controversies do seem essentially unresolvable when they are divorced from the concrete problematic situations in which they arise, and the idealized discourse imagined by some philosophers does seem disconnected from, perhaps unconnectable to, the world of policy-making practice. On the other hand, as we shall argue, the concrete situations of policy making, some of whose features militate against higher-level reflection, also offer the most fertile soil for it.

So the scholarly arguments that higher levels of reflection are out of place in practice have the ring of a catch-22: reflection of a kind that might hold potential for help in the resolution of intractable policy controversies is deemed to be out of place in policy making, where it might be most fruitful, while in the academy, which is seen as its proper locus, it tends to unfold in a way that is useless to those who are engaged in policy practice. On both counts practice loses out.

In contrast to this rather dismal picture, we shall stress both the feasibility and the potential benefits of higher-level reflection on the part of policy practitioners—though we shall also suggest that the very idea of reflection is in need of some rethinking. We shall illustrate how policy makers sometimes do bring higher-level reflection to bear on the controversies that crop up so frequently in their practice, and suggest how they might more fully and systematically accomplish this. In order to make a legitimate place for such practically useful reflection, we believe it is helpful to view policy practice as a kind of distributed designing, undertaken by multiple actors in the policy environment, and to think of policy rationality in terms not only of rational choice, or even rational politics or negotiation, but of a more encompassing kind of rationality, inclusive of higher-level reflection, that we shall call "design rationality." We shall argue that when controversies are situated in messy and politically contentious policy arenas, they may actually lend themselves, through design rationality, to pragmatic resolution.

The argument of this book is presented in three parts. Part I sets the problem of policy controversy. Chapter 1 shows that such controversies exist, are consequential, and are neither well explained by the prevailing scholarly approaches to the policy-making process—policy science, politics, and negotiation—nor well addressed, from a normative point of view, by the models of rationality associated with these approaches.

Chapter 2 introduces the ideas of frames, frame conflicts, and reframing. We assert that the parties to policy controversies see issues, policies, and policy situations in different and conflicting ways that embody different systems of belief and related prescriptions for action, often crystallized in generative metaphors. These frames determine what counts as a fact and how one makes the normative leap from facts to prescriptions for action. We distinguish action frames from rhetorical frames, and identify three levels of action frames in order of increasing generality and abstraction: policy, institutional, and metacultural frames.

Chapter 3 argues that awareness of the frames that underlie policy positions leads to an awareness of the relativist trap. If policy controversies are rooted in conflicting frames, immune to evidence, on what basis can we say that one frame is preferable to another? What happens to such notions as validity, truth, and objectivity? The relativist trap has been widely recognized, especially by scholars influenced by the sociology of knowledge, but the approaches scholars have taken toward it— in terms of frame criteria, reality's resistance to framing, and idealized models of discourse across frames—tend to be vacuous in the sense that they offer no practical embodiment of their highly abstract speculations. What is needed, we argue, is empirical study of the careers of policy controversies in actual policy practice.

Part II traces, in three case studies of policy making, how situated policy controversies arise in practice and how they are dealt with there. In chapter 4, which tells the story of the evolution of a de facto public-private policy of early retirement in Germany from the end of World War II to the present, we show that policy evolves dialectically through the unfolding of a policy drama, a partly cooperative, partly antagonistic interplay of institutional actors in the policy arena. Policy controversies arise in this process when shifts in the situation, internally or externally generated, trigger conflicts of interests rooted in the actors' divergent frames.

Actors in the policy drama design policy much as architects or engineers design material artifacts. They compete and cooperate to set policy problems, and they invent policy solutions that evolve as a result of the actors' transactions with the policy situation. When policy objects are put out into the larger environment, they tend to take on meanings unanticipated by their designers, as other actors see and respond to them in the light of their own frames and, often, in a changing policy context. Design rationality is a form of reflective policy practice that closely follows this sketch of policy designing. It is distinct from the types of rationality associated with policy science, politics, and negotiation, though it may include them as special cases.

Chapter 5 presents the story of Project Athena, MIT's large-scale experiment in the educational use of computers. We observe within the boundaries of a single institution how individual actors engage in policy design. Here we see designing as a communicative, "conversational" process. Athena's designers put their system out into the larger environment, generating "back talk"—disjunctions between intentions and outcomes—to which, at first, the designers are blind. The back talk grows in volume, culminating in a controversy that blocks further designing, at which point the designers search for a "marketing" approach to pragmatic resolution of the controversy. We identify four paths they might have taken—contention, marketing, negotiation, and codesign—noting for each the kind of reflective inquiry design rationality entails.

Chapter 6 presents an example of what we take to be a reflective conversation with the policy situation, elaborating the meaning of design rationality, the conditions favorable to it, and the sense in which it breaks through the relativist trap. In this case, set in Massachusetts, we tell the story of the evolution of statewide policy toward the homeless between 1982 and 1991, showing how controversies emerged between state bureaucrats and advocates for the homeless and within the state system itself. Controversies were pragmatically resolved at two different "policy windows." A statewide program was initially hammered out to incorporate elements of the views of many contending actors. Later in the decade, discovery of the program's perverse effects combined with shifts in context and "background learning" to produce a political/policy crisis, at which point a coalition of agency heads reframed the policy problem, invented a solution, and implemented it. Their situated frame reflection resulted in a synthesis of conflicting frames that unblocked the policy stalemate.

Part III summarizes the argument of the book and draws out some of its implications. Chapter 7 brings together in one account the strands of design rationality identified in our three cases, and takes up several of the issues it raises: how situated policy controversies may lend themselves to pragmatic resolution, in what sense practitioners may engage in frame reflection, under what contextual conditions they are more likely to do so, and how their doing so is compatible with an understanding of the relativist predicament. We also consider to what extent our model of design rationality can be applied generally.

Chapter 8, finally, explores how design rationality may be fostered through education, assistance, and research. We propose an approach to education for reflective policy practice and a form of collaborative action research in which policy analysts join with practitioners in "optimally distant" settings to pursue frame-reflective policy inquiry.

# PART I

# Setting
# the Problem
# of Reframing

# CHAPTER 1

# Intractable Policy Controversies

## DISAGREEMENTS AND CONTROVERSIES DISTINGUISHED

In matters of public policy, disputes are endemic. Whatever the issue may be—the costs of public pensions, the inadequacy of our system of public education, the protection of our natural environment, the causes of and remedies for homelessness—the public process of considering and coping with that issue is marked by contention, more or less acrimonious, more or less enduring. We believe, however, that it is critically important to distinguish between two kinds of policy disputes: those that may be settled by reasoned discourse and those that are stubbornly resistant to resolution through the exercise of reason.

We use the term *policy disagreement* to refer to disputes in which the parties to contention are able to resolve the questions at the heart of their disputes by examining the facts of the situation. These sorts of disputes can be settled by recourse to evidence to which all of the contending parties will agree. Suppose, for example, that we want to know how many youths are enrolled in drug rehabilitation programs. If we agree on the definition of "youth," the time period and geographic location we wish to consider, and what it means to be enrolled in a rehabilitation program, it is clear what "facts" are relevant. If these facts are accessible to investigation, the contending parties should be able to reach agreement on the question. Should a further disagreement about it arise, they have a good chance of settling it by searching out new information.

In contrast, the policy disputes we call *controversies* are immune to resolution by appeal to the facts. Disputes of this kind arise around such issues as crime, welfare, abortion, drugs, poverty, mass unemployment, the Third World, the conservation of energy, economic uncertainties, environmental destruction and resource depletion, and the threat of nuclear war. Disputes about such issues tend to be intractable, enduring, and seldom finally resolved.

Although the distinction between policy disagreements and controversies is conceptually clear, it may not be easy to determine, in a given instance, which type of dispute is in question. Often, a disagreement about "facts" turns out to mask an underlying controversy, and such apparently straightforward questions such as How many? Can we afford to? and What are the causes? may be difficult or impossible to answer by recourse to empirical investigation alone. Consider, for example, such questions as the following: How large is the population of homeless people in the United States? Is it true that we can no longer afford to maintain the welfare state? What are the principal causes of drug dependency? As we try to address such apparently neutral questions of "fact," we rapidly slip into the morass of controversy. Moreover, the boundaries between controversy and disagreement may be blurred as one historical period gives way to another. Sometimes, disagreements about matters of fact escalate into controversies, while at other times—though perhaps less often—controversial questions, such as those surrounding agricultural productivity in the Third World, may be reinterpreted as disagreements.

Although the boundary between disagreement and controversy may be blurred or elusive, controversies often arise in a way that is unmistakably clear. When they do present themselves, they are marked by their stubborn resistance to resolution by recourse to "the facts." "Facts" play a very different role in policy controversies than in policy disagreements.

First, the parties to a controversy employ different strategies of selective attention. Depending on their views of the issue, they differ as to what facts are relevant. For example, in debates over the alleged decline of the welfare state, political conservatives tend to focus on data that pertain to economic competitiveness. They argue that welfare expenditures erode the comparative advantage of industrialized countries and undermine their ability to compete with Third World industry. Liberals, on the other hand, tend to dismiss the "can't afford" arguments of the conservatives; they focus on data that demonstrate either the need for income support or the inequity of income distribution.

Second, even when the parties to a controversy focus their attention on the same facts, they tend to give them different interpretations. For example, a secular trend that shows an increase in the proportion of men not working may be seen either as evidence of a decrease in opportunities for work or as a deterioration in the will to work. In the War on Drugs, a decline in the rate of interdiction of drug-runners at the borders of the United States and Mexico may be seen either as a sign of the ineffectiveness of the policy of interdiction or as evidence that the strategy is functioning as an effective deterrent.

By focusing our attention on different facts and by interpreting the same facts in different ways, we have a remarkable ability, when we are embroiled in controversy, to dismiss the evidence adduced by our antagonists. We display an astonishing virtuosity in "patching" our arguments so as to assimilate counterevidence and refute countervailing arguments. Of course, this sort of virtuosity has its limits. In most forums of policy discourse, we usually feel some obligation at least to appear reasonable and meet prevailing standards of debate. We know that we cannot simply make up the stories we would like to tell. Some policy stories are more faithful to reality, as reality may be commonly understood, and more congenial to conventional criteria of validity. Yet it is a hallmark of policy controversy, in contrast to policy disagreement, that these minimal standards of reasonable discourse are insufficient to enable us to resolve our disputes by recourse to evidence and argumentation.

Let us consider two examples of controversies that have proved stubbornly resistant to resolution by appeal to evidence. In the early 1980s, Charles Murray's *Losing Ground* claimed that the programs of the War on Poverty, waged by the Kennedy and Johnson administrations, had actually caused poverty rates to increase.[1] Murray argued that policy is its own cause, creating the very conditions it seeks to redress. This is how he saw the "fact" of persistent or increasing poverty. Not surprisingly, his book triggered an acrimonious debate. Riding a wave of resurgent conservative ideology, policy intellectuals associated with the new conservative regime found that Murray's book suited their attempt to recast the intellectual foundations of the welfare state, and they gave the book their full support. Squared off against them were scholars and practitioners, mainly liberal or radical in their political orientation, who claimed that the poverty programs of the Kennedy and Johnson administrations had actually succeeded in reducing poverty.[2] For these policy intellectuals, the "fact" of persistent or increasing poverty signified only that the progressive programs of the War on Poverty had been aborted by succeeding administrations. The issue has not been settled by the considerable body of empirical research carried out either by attackers and defenders of the War on Poverty or by researchers who have tried to steer a neutral course.[3] As of this writing, as the Clinton administration calls for new approaches to health care, welfare reform, and educational restructuring, and old poverty warriors renew their calls for progressive policies, the controversy seems likely to re-erupt.

In 1986, James Q. Wilson and Richard J. Herrnstein published a book in which they claim that crime is rooted in the genes because "bad families produce bad children."[4] The storm of debate provoked by their book reactivated a controversy that had been stimulated in 1969 by Jensen's assertion that "the lower average intelligence and scholastic performance of Negroes" could involve not only environmental but genetic factors.[5] The capacity of controversy to resist resolution by appeal to evidence is dramatically illustrated by a vitriolic exchange that unfolded, in 1986, in the pages of *The Scientific American,* following its publication of Leon Kamin's devastating review of *Crime and Human Nature.*[6]

Kamin, a psychologist, had written that the Wilson/Hernnstein book was Reaganite rhetoric dressed up as social science. Having read 150 of the more than 1000 articles cited by Wilson and Hernnstein, Kamin concludes that

> Tiny snippets of data are plucked from a stew of conflicting and often nonsensical experimental results. Those snippets are then strung together in an effort to tell a convincing story, rather in the manner of a clever lawyer building a case. The data do not determine the conclusions reached by the lawyer. Instead, the conclusions toward which the lawyer wants to steer the jury determine which bits of data he presents.[7]

In their letter of reply, Wilson and Herrnstein reassert their view that "individuals differ, in part for biological reasons, in their predispositions toward high rates of certain kinds of common crimes," and point out that the evidence on which they relied "comes chiefly from numerous studies of twins and of adopted children carried out here and abroad by many different scholars, presumably of many different political persuasions."[8] They challenge Kamin's attack on their argument, accusing him, along with "a handful of other professors sharing his radical perspective," of a willful refusal to attend to the conclusive evidence.

> Kamin dismisses this evidence with the airy phrase that criticisms of such work are "numbingly familiar" and make any findings about

the genetic contribution to any form of human behavior (such as intelligence) "wholly inconclusive." Quite the contrary. . . . The overwhelming majority of specialists in the various topics have long accepted the existence of genetic influences on intelligence, alcoholism, schizophrenia and some learning disabilities. Certain forms of aggressive and criminal behavior now seem liable to such influences as well. Kamin nowhere makes a serious argument against the evidence.[9]

In his response to the Wilson/Herrnstein letter, Kamin defends his criticisms on scientific grounds:

I documented in my review a number of instances in which Wilson and Herrnstein miscited, misrepresented and misunderstood the research literature they claim to be summarizing for their readers. They now assert that my specific examples were a "picking of nits drawn from fewer than a dozen of the more than 1,000 studies cited in our book." Alas, my review had to be of finite length, and I could cite only a few of the errors and misrepresentations with which the book swarms. To prepare the review, I read a few hundred of the studies cited by Wilson and Herrnstein. It is hard for me to believe Wilson and Herrnstein have actually read these papers. . . . Based on a sample of a few hundred cases, I soberly report my judgment that very few of Wilson and Herrnstein's citations are accurate, and that still fewer are adequate.[10]

Since these letters were published in 1986, the debate over the genetic basis for criminality has not gone away, nor has it proved any more amenable to resolution by appeal to facts. On January 31, 1992, the *New York Times* reported, in an article by Fox Butterfield entitled "Studies Find a Family Link to Criminality," a new set of statistics compiled by the U.S. Department of Justice showing that "more than half of all juvenile delinquents imprisoned in state institutions and more than a third of adult criminals in local jails and state prisons have immediate family members who have also been incarcerated." Butterfield's article cites Herrnstein's reaction to the new data: Herrnstein calls the statistics "stunning." He takes them to show that "the more chronic the criminal, the more likely it is to find criminality in his or her relatives," which seems to him to prove that whatever it is that determines criminality "is transmitted both genetically and environmentally [so that] kids brought up in criminal families get a double exposure . . . [that] accounts for this enormously dramatic statistic."

But Butterfield's article also includes a quotation from Marvin E.

Wolfgang, professor of criminology and law at the University of Pennsylvania, who gives the data a very different interpretation:

> I'm not denying the statistics, but you should remember that most of these people come from low socioeconomic backgrounds, disadvantaged neighborhoods, where a high proportion of people will be sent to jail whether they are related or not . . . so it may be that the neighborhood rather than the family is the important factor in fostering criminal behavior.

It is eminently clear that the controversy over the genetic basis of criminality will never yield to evidence alone. In controversies like this one, or the controversy stimulated by Murray's *Losing Ground,* the contestants can readily discount their opponents' evidence or patch their arguments to take account of it, and are fully capable of constructing conflicting interpretations of new evidence. Reason ends up taking sides rather than building bridges of rational persuasion from one side to another. Like clever lawyers or committed ideologues, social scientists allow their preferred conclusions to dictate the strategies by which they select and interpret data. In the world of policy controversies, as partisans employ their preferred consultants or set up their own vehicles for policy research, analysts and evaluators tend, willy-nilly, to be co-opted by one or another of the antagonistic parties. The old ideal of a neutral, rational, policy-analytic capability seems nowhere in evidence.

We do not mean to present a wholly negative picture of policy controversies in the public sphere. As contention escalates in the forums of the academy, the legislature, and the media, issues may be forced into public consciousness, and society may be driven to take action on long-deferred problems or inequities. The civil rights, feminist, environmental, and peace movements provide cases in point. Moreover, controversy is inevitable in a democratic society and may be productive when it leads to an airing and illumination of fundamental policy issues. Nevertheless, the intractability of policy controversies and the impotence of policy research to resolve them exact a twofold price.

First, sustained policy contention can undermine public learning, because any attempt to conduct public inquiry into policy issues requires a minimally coherent, more or less consensual framework within which the results of policy initiatives can be evaluated and the findings of investigations can be interpreted. When policy controversies are enduring and invulnerable to evidence, what tends to result is institutionalized political contention, leading either to stalemate or to pendulum swings from one extreme position to another, as one side or another comes to political power. This may not be so bad if the policy situation is one that benefits from neglect or inaction, or if many contending actors happen to interact in such a way as to produce a happy policy outcome. But inaction is as likely to be harmful as helpful, and happy accidents do not often result from contention.

Second, intractable policy controversies are a threat to liberal democracy. Society has a limited capacity to manage policy contention. We may be able to live with a certain number of policy disputes because we have institutions—the voting booth, the courts, the bargaining table—designed to enable us to get things done, or at any rate to keep the peace, in the face of our inability to achieve a reasoned consensus on matters of great public concern. But in present-day American society and in many other liberal democracies, these intermediary institutions are strained to the breaking point. One has only to consult the recent history of policies in the fields of environmental protection, welfare, health, education, and affordable housing. With increasing frequency, policy antagonists have taken their disputes to the courts. In some instances such recourse has forced reluctant public agencies to change direction. More often, it has brought public or private policy initiatives to a halt, producing a stalemate or a suboptimal policy compromise with which all sides declare themselves dissatisfied.

When we look at American society through this lens, we see what Lester Thurow calls a "zero-sum society": a contentious, litigious society characterized by the proliferation of special interest, one-issue groups, each of which defines winning in terms of its own particular policy commitments.[11] More and more of our energy and intelligence are expended in the pursuit of win-lose policy games. Professions, such as law, economics, public administration, and public policy analysis, that might become vehicles for the resolution of controversies are captured by them instead and made to reinforce and reproduce them. All of this leads to the multiplication of intransigent policy dilemmas that give rise either to stalemated policy or to pendulum swings.

Recognizing the price we pay as a society for the existence of intractable policy controversies, and for our inability to deal with them effectively, we have very good reasons for seeking to understand them more deeply. How can we make sense of their intractability? How can we better understand the policy-making processes in which they arise and stubbornly persist?

## VIEWS OF POLICY CONTROVERSIES
## AND POLICY RATIONALITY

Three main traditions of policy research have evolved from the 1950s to the present day. Each contains a more or less explicit view of how policy is made, how it ought to be made, how policy disputes arise, and how disputes can best be settled. Each is organized around a dominant conception of rationality in policy practice.

The first tradition to arise following World War II still remains, in all likelihood, the dominant approach to the theory and practice of policy making. It is the tradition of policy analysis or policy science, which treats policy choice as its central question and policy maker as rational actor as its preferred model. The second tradition, which we call politics, arose, in reaction to the first, in the late 1960s and early to mid-1970s. It embraces a pluralistic model of the policy-making process. From its perspective, policy making is a process of political contention in which multiple interest groups holding conflicting interests and perspectives vie for control over the definition of policy and the allocation of resources, and policy outcomes are products of a competitive political game. The third tradition, that of consensual dispute resolution, arose in the late 1970s and began to flourish in the 1980s. Starting with an acceptance of the "political" view of policy making as a game of conflicting interests and powers, it proposes a theory and practice of mediated negotiation, rooted in a model of economic rationality, for setting policy disputes in such a way as to achieve joint gains.

These three traditions have dominated approaches to policy problems and disputes in the postwar period. In spite of their differences, all rest on a common foundation of understanding, bear the marks of the historical process in which they have evolved through interaction with one another, and can be seen as a family of related ideas and practices. Though they differ in their views of policy making and their conceptions of the objects and objectives of rational policy practice, they share the central idea of instrumental rationality: that policy makers are rational actors who choose the means—policy positions, strategies of political action, or negotiating ploys—that they believe to be best suited to the achievement of their ends, which are rooted in their interests.

Each of the three traditions contains a framework for reflection on policy making, which may be used to describe the reflective practice of policy makers. But we see these frameworks as inadequate to the challenge of explaining or coping with policy controversies. Because the three traditions are all versions of instrumental rationality, and in their various ways take the interests of the actors in the policy-making process as objective and given, they neither explain the intractability of policy controversies nor offer a plausible approach to their resolution.

## THE POLICY-ANALYTIC MOVEMENT

In the mid-1950s, Harold Lasswell, who deserves as well as anyone the title of founder of the policy-analytic movement, offered the following definition of the policy sciences:

> A policy orientation . . . that cuts across the existing specializations . . . is directed toward the policy process and toward the intelligence needs of policy. The first task . . . is the development of a science of policy forming and execution. . . . The second task . . . is the improvement of the concrete content of the information and the interpretations available to policy makers.[12]

Aspects of policy science as Lasswell conceived it are now taught in all schools of public policy in the United States. Virtually every university features a program in public policy analysis and administration, and it is a rare government agency that does not have its own policy analysis department. In spite of the cutbacks introduced by the Reagan and Bush administrations, the number of policy-analytic consultants has continued to grow.

In the late 1980s, Richard Nathan reviewed the career of the policy analysis movement, whose central intellectual thrust he sees as deriving from the application to public policy and management of micro- and macroeconomic ideas.[13] Nathan distinguishes three such applications: (1) the development of the general theory of macroeconomics, especially Keynes's theory about how to produce steady, noninflationary economic growth; (2) the application of the microeconomic model of rationality to governmental practices, through the introduction of a comprehensive planning, programming, and budgeting system aimed at reforming the budgeting process; and (3) the introduction of the microeconomic model of cost-benefit analysis to the development of evaluation research. All of these applications rest on a conception of economic rationality according to which policy problems are seen as instrumental in nature, and policy makers are seen as rational to the extent that they do the best they can to satisfy the combined welfare functions of those affected by their policies.

Nathan, Peter deLeon, and many other critics of the policy sciences have given us an account of the limits of the microeconomic approach to policy rationality.[14] The Planning, Programming and Budgeting System (PPB), introduced by President Johnson in 1965, required that all federal agencies prepare planning documents and analyses in the spirit of the microeconomic model. Nathan reports that "the experience of PPB was, to say the least, disappointing":

The paper just did not flow or else it overflowed. Federal agencies used familiar bureaucratic strategems and continued to operate the budget process in the way that they were used to doing it. In some cases the agencies used the tactics of swamping the Budget Bureau with thick planning documents and elaborate issue papers that few, if any, of the high officials of the submitting agency had even seen. The end result was the death of the PPB system.[15]

Although the PPB departed from the scene, it left an important legacy in the form of the evaluation research branch of the policy analysis movement, which is still very much alive. It is an elaborate system that involves people working outside of government in universities, independent research centers, and consulting firms. According to Nathan, this army of external evaluators—marching, with economists in the vanguard, to the tune of PPB—has conducted the government's major demonstrations and evaluation studies.

But in spite of its continued vigor, the evaluation movement has never succeeded in resolving several of its central problems. The first of these is the problem of defining criteria for evaluation. By what standards should a program or project be evaluated? The conventional answer is that a program should be evaluated by its purposes. But most programs have multiple, conflicting, and evolving purposes that are discovered only in the course of carrying out the programs. In addition, not all of these varying purposes lend themselves to quantification, as the cost-benefit approach to evaluation would require. Often, in order to carry out the task of evaluation, evaluators must impose measurable purposes of their own devising.

A second difficulty of evaluation research is the "black box" problem: outputs tend to be evaluated without a clear understanding of the processes that generate them. Why, for example, in the well-known "negative income tax" experiments conducted in the 1970s, did income guarantees contribute to marital disillusionment for white families and not for black ones? Without understanding how income assurances threatened family viability, one could not have confidence in the policy implications of findings derived from the experiments. Nevertheless, the very existence of these findings threatened the political acceptability of income reforms.

Evaluation has acquired the reputation of being a "killer" because it shows, almost invariably, that programs fail to produce at least some of their intended consequences or produce undesirable side effects, while at the same time the evaluation treats the sources of such negative outcomes as a black box. Often, however, information about the processes that lead to observed outcomes—for example, information about who uses services, who drops out, and why—is simply unavailable. As deLeon has pointed out, most sophisticated program evaluations are "not able to address the pivotal policy questions: Are the programs 'working'? If not, why not, and what could be done?"[16]

Finally, many critics of program evaluations have noted that these evaluations tend to be biased toward providing knowledge for the function of legislative oversight rather than knowledge useful to citizens' groups, some of which are direct consumers of the program in question.[17]

Once we recognize that programs have uncertain, conflicting, or emergent purposes; that, although economics has been the main provider of inputs to policy analysis, other disciplines have contributions to make; that the interests of the user, and not only the legislative overseer, ought to shape evaluative inquiry; and that different methods of evaluation, qualitative as well as quantitative, are needed—then we are forced to confront unresolved questions central to the feasibility of program evaluation. These questions hinge on the existence of multiple and sometimes incommensurable evaluative perspectives.

With PPBs, cost-benefit analysis, and program evaluation, policy scientists tried to sidestep such questions by establishing objective, value-neutral standards for policy judgments. But this conception failed in an important number of areas—for example, in health, welfare, and social security, and in the highly touted negative income tax experiment.[18] In all of these areas, policy adversaries were unable to agree either on value-neutral standards for judgment or on an unambiguous reading of the meanings of experimental data. What followed was a widespread disillusionment with the whole policy-analytic movement.

## POLITICS

The policy researchers' main response to this disillusionment in the late 1960s and throughout the 1970s was an awakening to politics. If there were no value-neutral standards and no objective bases for making policy choices across the boundaries of adversarial positions, then what rose to attention was the political contest itself, the antagonistic games of institutions and interest groups that could be seen as producing policies as outcomes. Policy disputes became central and policy rationality became problematic.

In the early 1980s, when the political approach to policy had reached its zenith (as we can now see in retrospect), James Coleman described its position with characteristic clarity.[19] Against the "rational actor" of the policy scientists, he proposes a "pluralist model." Whereas the rational actor model "implicitly assumes that there are no fundamental conflicts

13

of interest, and that when research has clarified consequences of a policy, conflicts will vanish, or at least that there will be an 'objectively correct' policy,"[20] the pluralist model treats policy "as the resultant of a balance among conflicting values and interests . . . [and] assumes multiple rational actors, each with differing interests, each with legitimate partial control of policy, and each with needs for information in order to pursue its interests rationally."[21] Coleman's political pluralism challenges the assumption that policy judgments can be objectively and rationally made by disinterested spectators, and treats policy as shaped by the contests in which interest groups strive to achieve their conflicting purposes.

Recognition of the essentially political nature of policy making is also a salient feature of the stream of research on the implementation of policy, which began in the late 1960s and early 1970s with the work of Jeffrey Pressman and Aaron Wildavsky, Eugene Bardach, and others.[22] These researchers saw, as many practitioners had long since known, that policies are made not only in the legislative and regulatory deliberations of governmental bodies in Washington, D.C., but in local settings, like Oakland, California, where, in dense institutional and political fields, espoused policies are converted to practice. In the work of these researchers, policy making came to be seen as a game of autonomous institutions and pressure groups, each acting on the basis of its own freedoms, powers, and interests. Often, as Pressman and Wildavsky showed, the game resulted in a radical distortion of centrally formulated policy intentions.

In the 1980s, an observer of the urban policy scene, Douglas Yates, noted that in the complex and chaotic political fields characteristic of large American cities, the policy-making game resembled a pinball machine; he claimed, in consequence, that cities are virtually "ungovernable."[23] Michael Lipsky, a policy critic, proposed that we "turn policy on its head," seeing policy not in the formal utterances of legislators or government officials but in the patterns of behavior produced by street-level bureaucrats.[24]

In spite of their criticisms of the rational-actor model of policy choice, political pluralists like Coleman and proponents of the view of policy implementation as a political game tend to remain wedded to the assumptions of microeconomic thinking. They are disposed to attribute "political rationality" to each contestant in the political contest insofar as that player strives rationally to pursue its own values and interests. As James March and Johan Olsen have written, most contemporary theories of politics rest on microeconomic assumptions:

> Political phenomena as the aggregate consequences of individual
> behavior, action as the result of choices based on calculated self-

interest, history as efficient and reaching unique and appropriate outcomes, and decision-making as the allocation of resources, are [seen
as] the essential foci of political life.[25]

To the extent that political theorists see policy making as a political
game within which the moves of individuals and institutions result
from "choices based on calculated self-interest," they can account for
the existence of policy disputes. But they must find it difficult to
account for the intractability of policy controversies, for if players of the
political game are rational actors, why should some disputes prove
stubbornly resistant to settlement by means of bargaining and
exchange? To the extent that political pluralists also share the economists' view of interests as objective and given, they must find it difficult to think in new ways about resolving the disputes that prove
intractable.

Theorists of the political policy game have not found it easy to
address these questions or the companion question of policy rationality.
When each player in the game is conceived as a rational actor making
choices based on rational self-interest, what can be said about the rationality of the game as a whole? It is well known that games in which
each player acts on the basis of calculated self-interest may result in
outcomes that are suboptimal for all players.[26] Some political theorists
have drawn from their analyses the lesson that those who play the political game should learn to play it more astutely, with greater awareness
of the effects of their moves on the actions of other players and the larger dynamics of the game. But this type of recommendation, when it is
adopted by all the players, tends to promote the rise of an ever more
sophisticated process of political contention, along with the predictably
dysfunctional outcomes of such a process.

Other researchers, notably Charles Lindblom, have argued that
policy making should aim at accommodating competing interests
and claims through a disjointed process of incremental moves.[27]
They conclude, in view of the false promise of the policy sciences,
that this is the best for which we can hope. But disjointed incrementalism, for all its attractiveness as an account of actual policy making, seems to have little to say about the predicament posed by the
existence of intractable policy controversies. Moreover, it tends to
ignore the existence of groups that, in the incremental accommodation to conflicting interests, occupy a privileged position of disproportionate power.

Coleman does address the issue of disproportionate power as he
draws out implications of the pluralist model for the uses of policy
research:

> Policy research pluralistically formulated and openly published may strengthen the hand of those interests without administrative authority, by redressing the information imbalance between those in authority and those outside. The dangers of this pluralistic policy research, if any, are to weaken central authority vis a vis outside interests, not to strengthen it.[28]

Coleman's conclusion may prove to be right. Still, it is not clear to us how pluralistic policy research, considered in and of itself, could avoid falling into the trap of serving mainly to exacerbate policy contention.

## MEDIATED NEGOTIATION

By the late 1970s a new intellectual and institutional response began to make itself felt, focusing on public disputes and combining in its treatment of them both microeconomic and political perspectives. Consensual dispute resolution, or mediated negotiation, is a branch of the larger policy research movement. Its language, theory, and ideology are derived, on the one hand, from the legal practice of handling labor-management disputes and, on the other, from the microeconomic tradition of the policy sciences, which the tradition of consensual dispute resolution has converted to a theory of bargaining for joint gains.

One of the main sources of this submovement was an awareness of the inefficiency of governmental regulation in such fields as environmental protection. In the late 1960s, environmental impact statements were invented to control the harmful effects on the natural environment of power plant and factory smokestacks, industrial wastes, real estate development projects, and the like. Public and private agencies whose actions might plausibly injure the environment were required, under state and federal laws and regulations, to file assessments of the probable environmental impacts of their actions and to take steps designed to mitigate those impacts. On the basis of the impact statement and the comments of interested parties, a central government agency was to determine whether the proposed action met environmental standards.

By the early 1970s, it had become apparent that parties to the review process—environmental interest groups, developers, and industrial firms, among others—had learned how to use social protest, informal strategies of political influence, or resort to the courts in order to manipulate the review process for their special purposes. It became increasingly likely that an interest group opposed to a development, such as an industrial firm, halfway house, or waste disposal facility, could readily block it, even when there was broad public consensus that some such development was publicly desirable. As disputes proliferated, the courts found themselves overloaded with issues for which they were technically ill-prepared, and their judgments often proved less than satisfactory to the interested parties.

In the mid-1970s, in the wake of the widespread social learning that had produced this impasse, a new profession arose, devoted to the negotiated settlement of policy disputes. Like the political theorists, the new professionals saw policy disputes in terms of interests and powers, which they subjected to rational analysis in microeconomic terms, but *their* method was to get underneath the disputants' stated negotiating positions in order to discover and work with their underlying interests.

Practitioners of mediated negotiation try to get people to sit down together to explore their interests in the policy situation, seeking to combine an analysis of the field of interests at play in the situation with a variety of strategies for arriving at agreements. Mediators explore how the negotiating "pie" might be enlarged, and exploit the fact that the same outcome may have different meanings to stakeholders with different interests. In these and other ways they pursue what might be called "negotiating rationality," seeking to achieve joint gains for the participants by converting win-lose to win-win situations.

Because of its record of success and persuasive argument and its perceived promise for the settlement of troublesome public disputes, mediated negotiation has become a vigorous profession. But limitations in the original conception have become increasingly apparent, especially to its practitioners. The intellectual basis of these limitations is linked, interestingly enough, to a certain failure of attempts on the part of these practitioners to explain some of their own successes.

There are two interrelated sources of the limitation of consensual dispute settlement. The first has to do with the boundaries of disputes that lend themselves to settlement by joint gains, and the second, with the presumed constancy of interests.

It is widely recognized, especially by the proponents of consensual dispute settlement, that some policy disputes are resistant to mediated negotiation; in these cases, agreement is elusive or so fragile that it comes apart when participants leave the bargaining table. It is more difficult to define the boundaries of these disputes and assess their relative importance.

In *Breaking the Impasse* Lawrence Susskind and Jeffrey Cruikshank,[29] following what we take to be the conventional wisdom of the field, address this issue by distinguishing between two kinds of disputes— "distributional" and "constitutional":

> Distributional disputes focus on the allocation of funds, the setting of standards, or the siting of facilities (including how we use our land and water). Constitutional disputes, such as those surrounding school desegregation, abortion, prayer in the schools, homosexual rights, the teaching of creationism, affirmative action, and the right to die, hinge primarily on interpretations by the courts of constitutionally guaranteed rights. . . . We leave it to others to decide whether consensual approaches to dispute resolution can (or should) be used in resolving constitutional questions. However, when the focus is on the distribution of tangible gains and losses, and not on whether something is legal or illegal, we are firmly convinced that consensus-building strategies can help.[30]

Susskind and Cruikshank devote very little effort to the task of showing that the rights they have in mind are constitutional, in the strict sense of the term. Their more fundamental distinction seems to pivot on the difference between disputes over the distribution of costs and benefits and disputes over rights and duties, which resembles the Kantian distinction between teleology, which has to do with the ends of action, and deontology, which has to do with rights and duties. As Kant and many philosophers after him have argued, questions of rights and duties are not reducible to an analysis of the consequences of action.

In any case, later in their book Susskind and Cruikshank shift the grounds of their distinction, pointing out that it is "risky for negotiators to trade commitments on issues in which *basic values* are involved" [our emphasis]:

> In such cases, constituents may disavow the commitments made on their behalf or move to appoint new spokespeople. This can cause great instability. If public officials seek to settle policy disputes involving fundamental values (should public funds be used to pay for abortion? should additional nuclear power plants be built? should neo-Nazis have the right to march in public?), dissatisfied disputants will almost certainly pursue the matter in other forums until they are satisfied. If your dispute involves constitutional questions or revolves around the definition of basic rights, consensus may be unattainable. Unless there is room for inventing, packaging, trading and redefining issues, it may not be possible to reach agreement.[31]

Notice how the language shifts here from "constitutional" to "basic" rights, and from "rights" to "basic values." The upshot appears to be that when public disputes revolve around conflicts of basic values, it may not be possible, by mediated negotiation or other means, to reach agreement.

In this formulation, Susskind and Cruikshank's distinction between the two kinds of disputes bears at least a functional resemblance to our distinction between policy disagreements and policy controversies. The disputes about which these proponents of mediated negotiation are least sanguine are the ones we take to be of greatest importance.

In the tradition of mediated negotiation, the "basic values" of the parties to a dispute are closely linked to, or even identified with, their "interests." The tradition's main line of thought is that bargaining does not, and should not, affect the interests the participants bring to the bargaining table. Mediators may influence their clients' views of the range of options available to them, the consequences of their actions, the possible impacts of consequences on existing interests, and the scope of a settlement package. But conventional wisdom holds that the effectiveness of consensual dispute resolution depends on the *constancy* of participants' interests.

This view derives in part from the microeconomic origins of bargaining theory. It resembles economists' traditional assumptions about the constancy of consumer preferences. Although bargaining often begins with the mediator's attempt to get the parties to understand and describe their interests, and although mediators often help the participants to change their views of what serves their interests, the interests themselves must hold steady or else the win-win bargaining process would be confounded. How can one develop reliable approaches to the achievement of joint gains if the participants' views of gains become unstable?

It is true that theorists of mediated negotiation sometimes embrace the idea that participants should try to gain an intimate understanding of their adversaries' positions. For example, Susskind and Cruikshank prescribe role-playing exercises in which disputants are encouraged to switch positions in order to build their respect for and understanding of opposing points of view. But such exercises are usually intended not to change the participants' views of their interests but to aid them in inventing win-win options, especially because "the key to such packaging is that the opposing teams value the same things differently."[32] As David Laws, another student of mediation, points out, the exercise of "sitting in your opponent's chair" is usually understood by proponents of mediated negotiation as a merely strategic device:

> It is easier to sell people on the idea of integrative negotiation by telling them that it will help them get more of what is valuable to them, than by telling them that the process may change their view of their own interests or those of their adversaries, or even change the way in which they look at and understand the world.[33]

Yet some observers of mediated negotiation are beginning to notice that change in the way participants "look at and understand the world" may be one of the main results of their involvement in the mediation process. For example, a recent study of a negotiation over regional and local targets for the development of affordable housing in Connecticut, mediated by Susskind, includes the observation that in the course of negotiations participants began to see both the issue and their interests in a new light:

> Instead of seeing the housing issue as being simply one of homeless people on the streets of Hartford or Bridgeport, many began to understand that their communities needed to make sure that their own municipal workers have a place to live. . . . This kind of reframing or transformation is at the heart of much public dispute mediation. It is much more than merely assimilating technical data. Representatives who come grudgingly to the bargaining table, expecting at the most to make horsetrades with other interest groups, instead get caught up in group learning and civic discovery that may fundamentally alter their expectations, goals and even language.[34]

Laws sees such transformations as occurring "behind the curtain" in many negotiations, and wonders why they are discussed so infrequently. He observes that the proponents of mediated negotiation tend to be inattentive to the role that change in the formulation of interests sometimes plays in the achievement of agreements, and cannot deal in theory (though they sometimes do in practice) with stubborn disputes that might be resolvable only through the participants coming to change their views of what their interests are.

Yet change of interests becomes much less mysterious when we think of a group's interests in a situation as defined by the state of affairs it chooses to create in the light of its way of understanding and representing that situation to other groups and to itself. As Deborah Stone has observed:

> Interests must be understood as deriving from . . . two senses of representation, the artistic and the political. Groups . . . *portray* issues deliberately in certain ways so as to win the allegiance of large numbers of people who agree (tacitly) to let the portrait *speak for them.* In this way the definition of interests is inextricably linked with the definition of issues. . . . Representation in this dual sense is necessary to give life to interests.[35]

Hence, when participants in a negotiation come to change in fundamental ways how they represent the policy issue or situation with which they are dealing, they are likely also to change the definition of their interests.

## CONCLUSION

The past thirty-five years have witnessed the development of a broad-gauged policy research movement in which three main traditions have evolved in historical sequence. Each tradition has advanced a model of rationality, a framework for reflection on the policy-making process. The dominant tradition of policy choice, based on the rational actor model, hoped to treat policy disputes as instrumental problems that could be solved through the application of a value-neutral policy science. Disillusionment with the practical fruits of this tradition, such as PPB and evaluation research, coupled with scholarly criticism of its claims to objectivity and value-neutrality, contributed to the rise of a political perspective on the policy-making process—a pluralist model in which policy making is seen as a political game of multiple rational actors, each with its own interests, freedoms, and powers. One consequence of this development has been a revival of interest in policy disputes and in the problems of theory and practice posed by the existence of multiple values, interests, and perspectives.

Although the model of political rationality has not led directly to powerful new prescriptions for policy making, it has helped to fuel the development of a new tradition, consensual dispute resolution through joint gains, which has had a significant impact on both theory and practice for resolving policy disputes. This emerging profession has had notable successes but is beginning to become conscious of its limitations. A large and important class of policy disputes revolving around basic rights and values is held to be inherently resistant to resolution through mediated negotiation. The conceptual basis for this limitation is seen to lie in the assumption, central to both the practice of mediation and the microeconomic model on which it is based, that disputants' interests are objective, given, and constant.

So we are left with a predicament. We have briefly surveyed the three branches of the policy research movement that have dominated the study of policy making and policy disputes since World War II. We have found that each tradition contains a model of policy rationality that offers critically important potentials for insight and action. Yet we have also found that neither in isolation nor in aggregate do these traditions—all variants of a core microeconomic model of instrumental rationality—provide an adequate framework for reflection on policy controversy. They do not resolve the questions with which we began: How should we make sense of intractable policy controversies? How should we understand the policy-making processes in which such controversies arise and persist? How should we account for the processes by which they are, or might be, resolved through reasoned discourse and reflection in policy-making practice?

# CHAPTER 2

# Policy Controversies as Frame Conflicts

T his chapter presents the framework for reflection on intractable policy controversies that we propose as an alternative to the three we have discussed in the previous chapter. We see policy positions as resting on underlying structures of belief, perception, and appreciation,[1] which we call "frames." We see policy controversies as disputes in which the contending parties hold conflicting frames. Such disputes are resistant to resolution by appeal to facts or reasoned argumentation because the parties' conflicting frames determine what counts as a fact and what arguments are taken to be relevant and compelling. Moreover, the frames that shape policy positions and underlie controversy are usually tacit, which means that they are exempt from conscious attention and reasoning.

## FRAMES AND GENERATIVE METAPHORS: AN EXAMPLE FROM URBAN HOUSING

The issue domain of urban housing is a good one in which to explore policy frames. Over the last sixty years or so, people have held very different views about urban housing. The issue has provoked extensive controversy in both developed and developing countries, and there have been some very dramatic shifts in ideas in good currency about the problem.

The examples with which we begin are drawn from the rather distant past—the debates about urban renewal policy in the United States in the late 1950s and early 1960s.[2] Yet, as we shall see, the frames underlying these debates are still alive and well.

The first piece of writing we shall examine is drawn from Justice William Douglas's opinion, handed down in 1954, on the constitutionality of the Federal Urban Renewal Program in the District of Columbia.

> The experts concluded that if the community were to be healthy, if it were not to revert again to a blighted or slum area, as though possessed of a congenital disease, the area must be planned as a whole. It was not enough, they believed, to remove existing buildings that were unsanitary or unsightly. It was important to redesign the whole area so as to eliminate the conditions that cause slums—the overcrowding of dwellings, the lack of parks, the lack of adequate streets and alleys, the absence of recreational areas, the lack of light and air, the presence of outmoded street patterns. It was believed that the piecemeal approach, the removal of individual structures that were offensive, would be only a palliative. The entire area needed redesigning so that a balanced, integrated plan could be developed for the region including not only new homes but also schools, churches, parks, streets, and shopping centers. In this way it was hoped that the cycle of decay of the area could be controlled and the birth of future slums prevented.[3]

It is useful, in order to construct the frame underlying this paragraph, to consider it as a story—a story told about a troublesome situation—in this case, the presumed plight of older urban neighborhoods—in which the author describes what is wrong and what needs fixing. In this story, the community itself is one main character, and the planner, or expert, is another. The community, once healthy, has become blighted and diseased. The planner, beholding it in its decayed condition, conceives the image of the community become healthy once again, with "new homes . . . schools, churches, parks, streets and shopping centers." But this can be achieved only through redesign of the whole area, under a balanced and integrated plan. Otherwise the area will "revert again to a . . . slum area, as though possessed of a congenital disease."

According to a second story, however, the places called slums are not all the same. Some of them are, indeed, decadent and impoverished, the victims of cycles of decay exacerbated by federal policies of "immuring" and of "urban renewal." Others, such as the East Village in New York City, or Boston's West and North Ends (of which Jane Jacobs said, "If this is a slum, we need more like it!"), are true low-income communities that offer their residents the formal services and informal supports that evoke feelings of comfort and belonging. The task is not to redesign and rebuild these communities, much less to destroy buildings and dislocate residents, but to reinforce and rehabilitate them, drawing on the forces for "unslumming" that are already inherent in them.

This story can be made out in Peggy Gleicher and Mark Fried's summary of their study of West End residents.

> In summary, then, we observe that a number of factors contribute to the special importance that the West End seemed to bear for the large majority of its inhabitants. . . . Residence in the West End was highly stable, with relatively little movement from one dwelling unit to another and with minimal transience into and out of the area. Although residential stability is a fact of importance in itself, it does not wholly account for commitment to the area. . . . For the great majority of the people, the local area was a focus for strongly positive sentiments and was perceived, probably in its multiple meanings, as home. The critical significance of belonging in or to an area has been one of the most consistent findings in working-class communities both in the U.S. and in England. . . . [Patterns] of social interaction were of great importance in the West End. Certainly for a great number of people, local space . . . served as a locus for social relationships. . . . In this respect, the urban slum community also has much in common with the communities so frequently observed in folk cultures. . . . These observations lead us to question the extent to which through urban renewal we relieve a situation of stress or create further damage. If the local spatial area and orientation toward localism provide the core of social organization and integration for a large proportion of the working class and if, as current behavioral theories would suggest, social organization and integration are primary factors in providing a base for effective social functioning, what are the consequences of dislocating people from their local areas? Or, assuming that the potentialities of people for adaption to crisis are great, what deeper damage occurs in the process?[4]

These are powerful stories, powerful in the sense that they have shaped public consciousness about the issue of urban housing. Each in its time guided the writing of legislation, the formation of policy, the design of programs, the diligence of planners, the allocation of funds, the conduct of evaluation. Each, moreover, has had its period of dominance. The story of blight and renewal shaped public policy in the 1950s, when the idea of urban renewal was at its height. In the 1960s, the story of natural community and its dislocation expressed the negative reactions to urban renewal. In the later 1960s and 1970s, the further history of urban renewal in Boston bore the marks of both of these stories. Under the leadership of Edward Logue, the powerful director of the Boston Redevelopment Authority, the elimination of crowded and dilapidated buildings continued, justified in considerable measure by the need to preserve the city's housing stock from blight and decay, and new housing, schools, parks, and shopping centers were developed. But this later urban renewal proceeded with the addition of carefully orchestrated community-based participation, motivated in no small measure by the horrible example of the destruction of Boston's old West End.

Each story conveys a very different view of reality and represents a special way of seeing. From a problematic situation that is vague, ambiguous, and indeterminate (or rich and complex, depending on one's frame of mind), each story selects and names different features and relations that become the "things" of the story—what the story is about. In the first, for example, they are community, blight, health, renewal, cycle of decay, integrated plan; in the second, home, spatial identity, patterns of social interaction, informal networks, dislocation. Each story places the features it has selected within the frame of a particular context—for example, of blight and the removal of blight; of natural communities, their threatened dissolution, and their preservation.

Each story constructs its view of social reality through a complementary process of naming and framing. Things are selected for attention and named in such a way as to fit the frame constructed for the situation. Together, the two processes construct a problem out of the vague and indeterminate reality that John Dewey calls a "problematic situation." They carry out the essential problem-setting functions. They select for attention a few salient features and relations from what would otherwise be an overwhelmingly complex reality. They give these elements a coherent organization, and they describe what is wrong with the present situation in such a way as to set the direction for its future transformation. Through the processes of naming and framing, the stories make the "normative leap" from data to recommendations, from fact to values, from "is" to "ought." It is typical of diagnostic-prescriptive stories such as these that they execute the normative leap in such a way as to make it seem graceful, compelling, even obvious.

How are such functions carried out?

In our two stories, the naming and framing of the urban housing situation proceeds through generative metaphor—a process by which a familiar constellation of ideas is carried over (*meta-pherein,* in the Greek) to a new situation, with the result that both the familiar and the unfamiliar come to be seen in new ways. One thing is seen as another—A is seen as B—just as in the familiar drawings of the Gestalt psychologists a figure may be seen as a vase or the conjunction of two profiles, as a young woman or an old one, as a duck or a rabbit. When A is seen as B, the existing description of B is taken as a putative redescription of A.

In the first of our stories, the urban housing situation is seen as a disease that must be cured and, in the second, as the threatened disruption of a natural community that must be protected or restored. In both cases, the constellation of ideas associated with B is inherently normative. In our ideas about disease and about natural community, there is already an evaluation—a sense of the good to be sought and the evil to be avoided. When we see A as B, we carry over to A the evaluation implicit in B.

Once we are able to see a slum as a blighted area, we know that blight must be removed ("unsanitary" and "unsightly" buildings must be torn down), and the area must be returned to its former state ("redesigned" and "rebuilt"). The metaphor is one of disease and cure. Moreover, the cure must not be a "mere palliative"; a particular, holistic view of medicine is involved in this metaphor. It would not be enough, the experts said, to remove the offensive structures piecemeal. "The entire area needed redesigning so that a balanced, integrated plan could be developed for a region. . . . In this way it was hoped that the cycle of decay of the area could be controlled and the birth of future slums prevented." Effective prophylaxis requires an integrated and balanced plan. Just as in medicine one must treat the whole person, so in urban renewal one must treat the whole community.

Once we are able to see the slum as a "natural community" (Gleicher and Fried's "folk community" or Herbert Gans's "urban village"), then it is also clear what is wrong and what needs doing. What is wrong is that the natural community, with its homelike stability and informal networks of mutual support, is threatened with destruction—indeed, by the very prophylaxis undertaken in the name of "urban renewal." We should think twice, as Gleicher and Fried put it, about dislocating people from their local areas; natural communities should be preserved.

Each of these generative metaphors derives its normative force from certain purposes and values, certain normative images, that have long been powerful in our culture.[5] We abhor disease and strive for health. The disease metaphor is discernible not only in frames associated with urban blight but also in human service professionals' use of the term "problem families," which connotes a social pathology that calls for therapeutic intervention. It is equally discernible in the assertion of a genetic predisposition to criminal behavior, where it is the genetic stock itself that is seen as either "healthy" or "diseased." Indeed, popular culture seems often to identify the good life with the healthy life and to make progress synonymous with the eradication of disease.[6]

Just as we strive for health and abhor disease, we have a strong affinity for the "natural" and a deep distrust of the "artificial." The idea of the natural, with its Romantic origins in the writings of Rousseau and its deeper sources in pantheism, still works its magical appeal. One can also discern the workings of a powerful metaphor of wholeness, which may be associated with the healthy and the natural. When we define the problem of a social service system as fragmentation, for example, and prescribe the remedy of coordination, it is as though we thought of the service system as a shattered vase. The metaphor of wholeness and fragmentation also underlies the familiar call for an integration of medical services currently delivered by a wide range of medical specialists, no one of whom sees the whole patient, as the general practitioner of a bygone era is supposed to have done.

In such examples it is possible to see the workings of a metaphor, or myth, of a Golden Age, according to which present problems are understood as a falling away from a more ideal state attributed to the past. This image underlies both the metaphor of fragmented services, which are seen as having once been whole, and the metaphor of natural communities, which are seen as having been disturbed by such artificial interventions as urban renewal. It is plausible, we believe, although we shall not try to prove the point here, that the number of metacultural frames at work in a society and, even more, the number of generative metaphors underlying these frames are relatively small and constant over long periods of time.

A situation may begin by seeming complex, uncertain, and indeterminate. However, if we can once see it in terms of a normative dualism such as health/disease, nature/artifice, or wholeness/fragmentation, then we shall know in what direction to move. Indeed, the diagnosis and the prescription will seem obvious. This sense of the obviousness of what is wrong and what needs fixing is the hallmark of policy frames and of the generative metaphors that underlie them, and it is central to our account of the intractability of the frame conflicts implicit in policy controversies.

## FRAME CONFLICT AND POLICY CONTROVERSY

In a policy controversy such as the continuing controversy over urban renewal and the treatment of urban housing, two or more parties contend with one another over the definition of a problematic policy situation and vie for control of the policy-making process. Their struggles over the naming and framing of a policy situation are symbolic contests over the social meaning of an issue domain, where meaning implies not only what is at issue but what is to be done.

Typically, the contestants in a symbolic contest enter into it on the basis of their interests in the policy situation. For example, they may be representatives of existing communities threatened with dislocation, real estate developers attracted by an opportunity for profitable development, or representatives of an urban regime committed to promote the physical rehabilitation and economic revitalization of the inner city. There is a reciprocal, but nondeterministic, relationship between the actors' interests and their frames. Frames and interests are logically independent concepts; they are by no means identical. Nevertheless, interests are shaped by frames, and frames may be used to promote interests. One might say, for example, that real estate developers and urban planners favor the language of "blight" and "slum clearance" because these names are linked to a frame that prescribes actions favorable to increases in real estate profits and the urban tax base. One might say, with equal validity, that how actors understand their interests is shaped by their frames—that advocates for working class neighborhoods, for example, have an interest in neighborhood preservation because they see neighborhoods as natural communities, very much as Fried and Gleicher do.

The political interpretation of policy controversies, discussed in the previous chapter, treats controversies as disputes among actors who hold conflicting interests and use their respective powers to promote their interests, thereby initiating a win-lose political game. But it is the frames held by the actors that determine what they see as *being* in their interests and, therefore, what interests they perceive as conflicting. Their problem formulations and preferred solutions are grounded in different problem-setting stories rooted in different frames that may rest, in turn, on different generative metaphors.

Frames are not free-floating but are grounded in the institutions that sponsor them, and policy controversies are disputes among institutional actors who sponsor conflicting frames. The actors are in contention with one another; the frames they sponsor are in conflict, in the sense that they represent mutually incompatible ways of seeing the policy situation. Just as we cannot see the familiar Gestalt figure at one and the same time as both an old woman and a young one, so we cannot see the urban housing situation at one and the same time as both prophylactic slum clearance and the preservation of natural communities. One

29

person's blight is another's folk community. What one person sees as unsanitary and unsightly another may find comfortable, homelike, or even picturesque.

Evidence that one party regards as devastating to a second party's argument, the second may dismiss as irrelevant or innocuous. Or the second may easily patch his or her argument so as to incorporate the new evidence within it. So, for example, when Gleicher and Fried call attention to the rich networks of social interaction that filled the old West End, a partisan of urban renewal might point out that the new, high-rise, upper-middle-class development that replaced the old West End has its own networks of social interaction, or might point to the fact that the working-class people displaced by urban renewal in the West End were subsequently able to create new social bonds in the inner-city suburbs to which many of them moved (a possibility also recognized by Gleicher and Fried).

For all these reasons, there is no possibility of *falsifying* a frame; no data can be produced that would conclusively disconfirm it in the eyes of all qualified, objective observers. The reason for this is that if *objective* means frame-neutral, there *are* no objective observers. There is no way of perceiving and making sense of social reality except through a frame, for the very task of making sense of complex, information-rich situations requires an operation of selectivity and organization, which is what "framing" means.[7] As we have illustrated above, those who construct the social reality of a situation through one frame can always ignore or reinterpret the "facts" that holders of a second frame present as decisive counterevidence to the first.

When we attribute the stubbornness of policy controversies to conflicts of policy frames resistant to refutation by appeal to evidence, we come very close to the position Thomas Kuhn has advanced in the philosophy of science.[8] Kuhn distinguished periods of normal science, in which scientists operate within a shared paradigm and agree on the rules of the game for settling their disagreements, from periods of scientific revolution, in which disputes cut across scientific paradigms and there is no agreed-upon framework for reaching agreement. In periods of scientific revolution controversies are not resolved by reasoned appeal to evidence, although they may fade away because the holders of a competing paradigm suffer a conversion experience, or because those individuals simply die out and are not replaced.

In his *Philosophy and the Mirror of Nature,* Richard Rorty generalizes Kuhn's distinction, differentiating normal from abnormal discourse in science as well as in other fields of inquiry. By "normal" Rorty means discourse that proceeds under a shared set of rules, assumptions, conventions, criteria, and beliefs, all of which tell us how disagreements can be settled, in principle, over time. Here, even though a dispute may in fact persist, there is a belief—perhaps illusory—that it can be settled through reasoned discourse, a belief based on the assumption that the ordinary rules of discourse "embody agreed-upon criteria for reaching agreement."[9] This description would apply, in our terms, to policy disagreements. Abnormal discourse occurs, by contrast, when agreed-upon criteria for reaching agreement are not present as a basis for communication among the contending actors. Such situations are not defined by the participants in terms of an objective framework within which disagreements can be arbitrated or managed. This is, in our terms, the realm of discourse that revolves around conflicts of frames in policy controversies.

## KINDS, LEVELS, AND SOURCES OF FRAMES

Part II describes how frame conflicts arise in policy debate and practice and explores the prospects for their resolution through policy inquiry. In order to set the stage for these explorations, however, we must introduce certain terms and distinctions to be illustrated and discussed in greater detail: policy discourse and its several types; rhetorical and action frames; and the several levels of frames, which we call policy, institutional action, and metacultural frames.

### POLICY DISCOURSE

By *policy discourse* we mean verbal exchange, or dialogue, about policy issues. The root sense of this term probably lies in the experience of a literal conversation between individuals. When we speak of discourse within or across institutions, we metaphorically extend the meaning of the term.

Because there are no institutional vacuums, interpersonal discourse must have an institutional locus within some larger social system. Even a chat between close friends occurs in the institutional setting of someone's house or a walk around the park. This institutional embedding is important to the nature of discourse in several ways. The institutional context may carry its own characteristic perspectives and ways of framing issues, or it may offer particular roles, channels, and norms for discussion and debate.

When discourse is public, it takes on the special properties of the institutions reserved in our society for dialogue about issues of public concern. These are *policy forums* that serve as institutional vehicles for policy debate. They include legislative arenas, the courts, public commissions, councils of government and political parties, the editorial pages of magazines and newspapers, and radio and television programs, as well as the seminar rooms and lecture halls of academia. Policy forums have their own rules, and discourse tends to conform to the norms of the forum in which it occurs. In a court of law, for example, where people expect to engage in an adversarial process, they tend to keep to themselves whatever doubts they may feel about their own positions. At the bargaining table, each utterance tends to be construed as a move in the bargaining game. In all such forums, individual utterances are likely to have meanings and consequences that go beyond the interpersonal context in which they occur. For example, if there is a possibility that words uttered in a forum may be released to a larger public, who knows how that public may respond?

## RHETORICAL FRAMES AND ACTION FRAMES

There is a discourse of policy debate and a discourse of policy practice. In policy debate, policy stories and the frames they contain serve the rhetorical functions of persuasion, justification, and symbolic display—the functions to which Deborah Stone alludes when she asserts, in the passage quoted, that "groups . . . portray issues deliberately in certain ways so as to win the allegiance of large numbers of people who agree (tacitly) to let the portrait speak for them." In policy practice, on the other hand, policy stories influence the shaping of laws, regulations, allocation decisions, institutional mechanisms, sanctions, incentives, procedures, and patterns of behavior that determine what policies actually mean in action.

We distinguish between rhetorical and action frames. By the former we mean frames that underlie the persuasive use of story and argument in policy debate; by the latter, frames that inform policy practice. Sometimes the same frames serve both functions. More often, frames implicit in the language used to "win the allegiance of large groups of people" differ from the frames implicit in the agreements that determine the content of laws, regulations, and procedures. For example, in the field of welfare policy in the United States, the rhetoric of the "safety net," which figured prominently in speeches on welfare policy by officials of the Reagan and Bush administrations, was accompanied by changes in regulations that seemed mainly intended to crack down on "welfare cheaters."

## POLICY, INSTITUTIONAL ACTION, AND METACULTURAL FRAMES

Action frames operate at different levels of specificity, as the image of the policy ladder suggests. We distinguish three levels of action frames: policy, institutional action, and metacultural frames.

A policy frame is the frame an institutional actor uses to construct the problem of a specific policy situation. For example, in the mid-1970s the Boston Redevelopment Authority (BRA) framed the problem of low- and middle-income housing mainly in terms of the need to "preserve the city's healthy housing stock," which led the BRA to adopt policies that gave priority to the rehabilitation of existing stock and the clearer separation of "decayed" from "healthy" stock.[10] This policy frame did not lead to policies that emphasized either the income level of the occupants of rehabilitated housing or the shortfall between the need for affordable housing and the available supply.

An institutional action frame is the more generic action frame from which institutional actors derive the policy frames they use to structure a wide range of problematic policy situations. As agents of thought and action, institutions possess characteristic points of view, prevailing systems of beliefs, category schemes, images, routines, and styles of argument and action, all of which inform their action frames.[11] It is in this sense that, in a given policy environment, people learn what to expect from a development authority, a tenant advocacy group, a real estate firm, or a city government.

Institutional action frames tend to be complex and hybrid in nature. They do not usually consist in a single, coherent, overarching frame, but in families of related frames. For example, the same development authority that in one situation sponsors the preservation of healthy housing stock may, in a situation of a different sort, frame policy issues in terms of landlord neglect and tenant disaffection. Moreover, the action frames held by individuals may be only loosely coupled to the action frames of the institutions of which they are members. Individuals' frames may represent selections from or variations of the institution's larger store. For example, individuals closer to street-level operations tend to see problems and respond to them differently than individuals closer to the agency's top and center. Individuals, at whatever level, may differ in their ways of interpreting the action frames that prevail within the agency, or in the degree to which they conform to the agency's prevailing line of thought and action.

Institutional action frames are local expressions of broad, culturally shared systems of belief, which we call metacultural frames. The oppositional pairs disease and cure, natural and artificial, and wholeness and fragmentation belong to the realm of metacultural frames. Metacultural frames, organized around generative metaphors, are at the root of the policy stories that shape both rhetorical and action frames. For example, the debate between Wilson and Hernnstein and Leon Kamin, referred to in the previous chapter, is a contemporary version of the nature vs. nurture debate that flourished at the turn of the century, suggesting that in the policy domain of crime—or, more broadly, social pathology—cultural metaframes of nature and nurture remain powerful for thought and action in our society. The nature frame lends itself to prescriptions that favor restraint and segregation of criminals, swift and sure punishment, and (at worst) attempts to control the reproductive behavior of people who are believed to carry the wrong kinds of genetic material. The nurture frame suggests policies that remove or mitigate environmental factors presumed to be conducive to criminality or other forms of social pathology.

Traditionally, liberals in American society have tended to favor the nurture frame, which is consistent with the idea of a public responsibility for the improvement of environmental conditions judged to be conducive to social pathology. It is among conservatives (though not of all types) that the nature frame is held, in conjunction with a broad prescription of social control: rigorous law enforcement coupled with "more and better prisons."[12] While both liberalism and conservatism in our society are so complex and multilayered that one cannot uniquely attribute a pure metacultural frame to either view, versions of particular metacultural frames clearly tend to be associated with traditional political-economic perspectives.

## THE DIFFICULTIES OF FRAME CONSTRUCTION

The frames that shape policies are usually tacit, which means that we tend to argue *from* our tacit frames *to* our explicit policy positions.[13] Although frames exert a powerful influence on what we see and how we interpret what we see, they belong to the taken-for-granted world of policy making, and we are usually unaware of their role in organizing our actions, thoughts, and perceptions. In order to reflect on the conflicting frames that underlie policy controversies, we must become aware of our frames, which is to say that we must construct them, either from the texts of debates and speeches or from the decisions, laws, regulations, and routines that make up policy practice.[14] But frame construction is difficult, for both practical and theoretical reasons.

In terms of practical methodology, it may be difficult to tell, in an actual policy situation, what frame really underlies an institutional actor's policy position. First, the rhetorical frames that shape the public utterances of policy makers may be incongruent with the frames implicit in their patterns of action. In their public utterances, policy makers may hitch on to a dominant frame and its conventional metaphors (the free market, privatization, and "community empowerment, for example), hoping thereby to purchase legitimacy for a course of action actually inspired by different intentions. When policy antagonists challenge one another's legitimacy, they may begin gaming, seeking deliberately to obscure the action frames that underlie their stated positions.

Second, the same course of action may be consistent with quite different policy frames. In American welfare policy, for example, there was a marked continuity in the policy actions taken by the Ford and Carter administrations, even though the two administrations espoused very different views of welfare policy. Conversely, the same frame can lead to different courses of action. Liberals, who advocate the same welfare policies, when such policies are expressed at a high level of generality, tend to disagree among themselves about the proper treatment of ineligibles on the welfare rolls.

Third, as Pressman and Wildavsky showed, the meanings of policy made by a central governmental body in the early stages of policy formation may be transformed at local levels at the stage of policy implementation. Even at the local level, the frames implicit in the discretionary judgments made by street-level bureaucrats, such as housing managers or welfare officials, may differ from the policy frames espoused by state legislators.

Fourth, it may be difficult to distinguish between conflicts within a frame and conflicts that cut across frames. Our judgments on this score may differ depending on how we construct the more generic institutional action and metacultural frames that underlie conflicting policy positions.

Finally, it may be difficult to distinguish between real and potential shifts of frame. The introduction of a new piece of legislation may signal the potential for a reframing of national policy (as the introduction of supplementary security income, SSI, suggested a reframing of American policy toward the poor), but that potential may lie dormant because other reforms, essential to the activation of that potential, are not forthcoming. Conversely, even in the absence of formal deliberations and decision, policy may be reframed as a result of cumulative, incremental adaptations to a changing situation.

These practical difficulties in constructing policy frames may be overcome, at least in principle, by carefully nuanced observations and analyses of the processes by which policy utterances and actions evolve over time and at different levels of the policy-making process. Sophisticated frame construction must attend to the differences between central and local policies, potential and actual changes of frame, the rhetorical frames implicit in espoused policies and the action frames implicit in policy-in-use,[15] formal policies and the policies implicit in the practices of street-level bureaucrats, and visible shifts of policy and the cumulative effects of small changes of policy made in response to changing situations.

In contrast to practical difficulties of frame construction, there is a generic, theoretical difficulty that does not yield in any obvious way to careful methods of observation and analysis. Frames must be constructed by someone, and those who construct frames (the authors of this book, for example) do not do so from positions of unassailable frame-neutrality. They bring their own frames to the enterprise and, what is more, they may be unaware of doing so. For example, a policy analyst who shares the Wilson-Herrnstein position on criminality might go about the task of constructing the frames implicit in that debate very differently than would an analyst who shared Kamin's position.

If we are right in our approach to frame construction, then any given construction of a policy frame can be tested against relevant data—for example, the texts of policy debates or the artifacts and routines of the policy-making process. Frame-critical analysts can and should ask whether these constructs fit the data, exploring, for example, whether these constructs account adequately for the things and relations the frame sponsor singles out for attention or selectively ignores, or for the way in which the frame sponsor's policy story executes the normative leap from facts to recommendations. In spite of the availability of such tests, it is quite possible that frame-critical analysts who proceed from different frames of their own may disagree about the nature of a particular frame conflict, and may be unable to resolve that disagreement through reasoned evidence and argument alone. In such an eventuality, we glimpse an epistemological predicament, to which the following chapter turns.

# CHAPTER 3

# Rationality, Reframing, and Frame Reflection

The search for policy rationality is a quest for hope. The hope is that human reason may have a modest place in the reality of policy practice; that policy makers need not inevitably function only as partisan adversaries or as players who unilaterally seek their own advantage in the political game, or as swimmers whose feeble strivings toward reason are bound to be overwhelmed by a sea of chaos and complexity. The hope is that individuals may contribute to the pragmatic resolution of the controversies in which they are embroiled, if only they learn how better to conduct their inquiry.

But if we accept the fact that controversy is central to policy making, and if we analyze controversies as conflicts of action frames, then in what sense may policy practitioners hope to be rational? The prevailing models of policy rationality—choice, politics, and negotiation—can at best provide a radically incomplete framework for rational policy practice. Based as they are on a microeconomic core of instrumental rationality, they cannot explain or respond effectively to the intractability of policy controversy.

Starting with the analysis of controversy as frame conflict, we propose that human beings can reflect on and learn about the game of policy making even as they play it, and, more specifically, that they are capable of reflecting *in action* on the frame conflicts that underlie controversies and account for their intractability. In our view, human beings are capable of exploring how their own actions may exacerbate contention, contribute to stalemate, and trigger extreme pendulum swings, or, on the contrary, how their actions might help to resolve the frame conflicts that underlie stubborn policy disputes. We believe that hope for human reason in the chaotic, conflictual world of policy making lies in a view of policy rationality that gives a central place to this human capability for reflection "within the game."

This chapter explores three conceptual obstacles that lie in the path of such an approach:

> 1) The complexity and ambiguity of the relationships that may hold among reframing, frame reflection, and the resolution of policy controversies.
>
> 2) The relativist predicament that derives from the fact that there is no frame-neutral position from which to describe, judge, or reframe fundamentally discrepant world views.
>
> 3) The conceptual and practical problems associated with the idea of reciprocal reflection across conflicting frames.

Consideration of these issues will leave us sobered, but it will also suggest some guidelines for our further inquiry. We shall briefly discuss four authors whose work illuminates the path we intend to follow: Albert Hirschman, who has explicitly embraced a "bias for hope" in policy and development; Charles Lindblom, whose lifelong study of policy making is firmly grounded in the Deweyan tradition of policy inquiry; James March, whose theory of the garbage describes the chaos of institutional life, and whose recent analysis of "the new institutionalism" represents an important departure from the pure theory of the garbage can; and John Forester, who has suggested a promising direction of development for the fledgling profession of mediated negotiation.

These authors do not answer the quest for a kind of rationality appropriate to policy practice, nor do they provide a clear conceptual basis for a frame-reflective approach to policy controversy. Nevertheless, they offer useful points of departure. Their writings will help to inform the program for an empirical epistemology of reframing with which we shall bring this chapter to a close.

## REFRAMING WITH OR WITHOUT FRAME REFLECTION

We focus on frame reflection in the belief that it may contribute to a kind of reframing that resolves the controversies that arise in policy practice. But is it possible that frame reflection may not lead to reframing? Or that reframing may occur without frame reflection? Or that the resolution of policy controversies may be logically independent of both processes?

We observe, to begin with, that frame reflection may serve merely to reinforce stalemate or antagonism. In his practice of international realpolitik, for example, Henry Kissinger has made a great deal of the need to put oneself in the other party's shoes.[1] For Kissinger, however, reflection on the other person's way of looking at things mainly serves the purposes of image- or impression-management. Kissinger seems to believe that an image manager should try to understand how others think so as to discover the meanings they attach to the manager's actions, in order to manipulate them more effectively. This view suggests a considerable respect for the importance of learning in human affairs. It suggests that you should attend to the lessons that contestants may draw from their experiences of, say, combat or negotiation. In its more sophisticated form, it underlines the importance of "getting into their heads" in order to predict the lessons they are likely to draw from your actions, which may, in turn, enable you to design your actions so as to communicate the lessons you want them to draw. But if all parties in a dispute were to practice such reflection (having learned that, as well as other, modes of manipulation), the result may be mutual paralysis.

Second, we observe that, in spite of the extraordinary durability of metacultural frames and frame conflicts, policy issues and problems have been reframed, over periods that range from a few years to a few decades, in response to discontinuities that provoke radical change in world views. It is not difficult to find examples of reframing in the issue domains of disarmament, welfare policy, environmental protection, and poverty in the Third World. But when reframing occurs, it may serve not to resolve policy controversy but to provoke it. Moreover, reframing may not come about as a consequence of frame reflection but as a byproduct of actions undertaken for other purposes, setting the stage for *subsequent* frame reflection.

Recent political-economic developments in Eastern Europe are an interesting case in point. In the late 1980s, the groups that first sponsored political protests in Eastern Europe never believed they were trying to create a revolution that would fundamentally reframe their economic systems. This outcome was a wholly unintended effect, which occurred once the constraints against political protests were removed. As Albert Hirschman has observed, no social scientists, historians, or political observers foresaw the revolutions of 1989. Rather, he points out:

> All these developments unfolded in a remarkably short time and as a
> huge surprise to "experts" and ordinary television viewers alike. But

the lesson—that the utmost modesty is in order when it comes to pronouncements about the future of human societies—does not seem to have sunk in. . . . numerous voices were heard uttering self-assured opinions about the implications of these changes for this or that country. . . . It does not seem to have occurred to these people that if the events, which is the point of departure for the speculations, were so hard to predict, considerable caution is surely in order when it comes to appraising their impact.[2]

We agree with Hirschman that caution is in order when appraising the impact of reforms that come about without anyone's prior intention. One thing is reasonably clear, however. When Eastern European societies swing from the socialist state to some version of a market economy for which they are unprepared, they find themselves in economic chaos that calls for some degree of centralized economic control.[3] This is precisely what they have just rejected. Yet, in order to shift away from centralized control, they need a strong central government that can restrain expectations and manage the economic hardship that inevitably follows from the shift. The crisis in which they find themselves requires a rethinking of the frame as a whole. This does not mean, of course, that prior to the crisis produced by the first swing of the pendulum, thoughtful persons in Eastern Europe had not reflected on the weaknesses of their political-economic system. What they had not reflected on was its possible destruction, because such a thing was unthinkable.

When the policy pendulum swings from one unworkable extreme to another, what may be needed in the new situation is a mixture of an old frame that has been rejected and a new frame that does not altogether fit a new situation in which the previously unthinkable has become reality. In order to make such a reframing work, the policy makers must reflect on the old *and* new frames—accepting, in this process, elements of the old frame delegitimized by their recent reforms. They must import elements of the old frame that stand in direct conflict with the new one, producing emerging frames through the kind of dialectical policy discourse discussed in chapter 2.

We conclude, then, that the relationships among frame reflection, reframing, and the resolution of policy controversies are anything but straightforward. Frame reflection may occur but not give rise to reframing. Reframing may occur without the benefit of frame reflection, but it may actually generate a need for such reflection. Although frame reflection may at times contribute to a kind of reframing that resolves policy controversy, it is neither necessary nor sufficient for that purpose.

## FRAME REFLECTION AND THE RELATIVIST TRAP

Even this highly qualified linkage of frame reflection, reframing, and the resolution of policy controversies stirs up troublesome questions. On what basis do we assume that frame conflicts are resolvable, even in principle, through frame-reflective policy inquiry? In what sense can it be reasonable to reframe policy issues and problems? Is there an objective basis for choosing among frames, or reframing policy issues, in one way rather than another? How can we possibly resolve frame conflicts when frames themselves determine what counts as evidence and what interpretations of evidence are acceptable?

If we find no credible answers to these questions, we are caught in the predicament of epistemological relativism. We must then reluctantly concede that we have no reasonable basis for deciding among policy frames, all of which may be internally consistent and compelling in their own terms and, hence, equally worthy of choice.

The relativist predicament is by no means new. It has appeared, in many different forms, in the writings of philosophical skeptics throughout the ages. In the period following World War I, however, a particular form of epistemological relativism became critically important to the development of an intellectual movement, the sociology of knowledge, which has special relevance to our present inquiry.

In an essay called "The Sociology of Knowledge and Surrender-and-Catch," sociologist Kurt Wolff tells how the two founders of the sociology of knowledge, Karl Mannheim and Max Scheler, "confronted the problem of relativism . . . and suffered from the incapacity to overcome it."[4] The sociologists of knowledge or, as Wolff prefers to call them, the sociologists of intellectual life, recognize that to know is to interpret reality. They claim that all interpretations are necessarily conditioned by the particular society, historical period, and social status from which they originate. In other words, what you see and know depends on who you are, when you are, and where you sit. This doctrine Mannheim calls the "self-relativization of thought." At various times in his life, he asks himself whether it implies that validity itself is always relative.

In his final years, Mannheim appears to have given serious consideration to the possibility that his question might have to be answered in the affirmative. He writes that intellectual phenomena can be approached from many different angles, thereby giving rise to types of interpretations that "rise and change along with the historical development of consciousness and thus offer the possibility of an ever increasing and transforming penetration of the intellectual world,"[5] but he stops short of specifying just how many types of interpretation there are. Wolff suggests that the number of possible interpretations may be infinite. If so, he points out, then "the question is what is left of [a phenomenon] once it has been interpreted in an infinite number of ways. . . . To put it differently: What is the reality which is infinitely interpretable? What is there *objectively* which is appropriated subjectively in an infinite number of ways?"[6]

In the end, Mannheim admits that the problem of relativism eluded him. In what is probably his last statement on the issue, he writes that although he wanted to "break through the old epistemology radically," he has not succeeded. He concludes that this might not be one person's work but the work of a whole generation, for "nothing is more obvious than that we transcended in every field the idea that man's mind is equal to an absolute Ratio in favour of a theory that we think on the basis of changing frames of reference, the elaboration of which is one of the most exciting tasks of the near future."[7]

In Wolff's view, Mannheim "forgets that there *is* an external or objective world—in which we have to live." But he points out that what Mannheim forgets, Max Scheler, cofounder of the sociology of knowledge, remembers. Scheler proposed that the nature of "objective" reality might be found in the world's tendency to resist our interpretations:

> Being real itself is given originarily only in *the resistance with which some inner and outer configurations of things assert themselves against {our} impulses* [our emphasis]. . . . To be real is not to be an object. . . . It rather is to be resistance to the primordially flowing spontaneity which is one and the same in willing and noticing of whatever kind.[8]

Scheler seems not to have pursued this thought. Yet, even in its embryonic form, the idea opens up an interesting way of imagining a nonrelativistic approach to frame reflection. For if the world resists our acts of willing and interpreting, stubbornly presenting us with phenomena mismatched to our frames, then we may be able to discover the limitations of our frames, even though it is only through them that we can detect their mismatch to reality. True, we could not say that we ever perceive policy situations "as they are." Nevertheless, we could recognize a potential for becoming aware of patterns that resisted our frame-induced interpretations of reality, especially if we were to open ourselves to help from others in overcoming our frame-induced blindness.

In recent years, some writers have embraced epistemological relativism, among them postmodernist writers who seem often to glory in their discovery of multiple, conflicting, fundamentally irreconcilable interpretations of reality.[9] But for many philosophers and social theorists, especially those who write with practice in mind, epistemological relativism is a thoroughly uncomfortable and ultimately unacceptable trap. In their efforts to escape from relativism, such thinkers have generally taken one of three main routes.

The first strategy is very much in the spirit of Scheler's view of reality as resistance to interpretation. It is premised on the idea that individuals who hold conflicting views of *some* reality, about which they are locked in intractable controversy, nevertheless live in a *larger* reality, an everyday world about which they share many perceptions. For example, two policy practitioners who see the recent events in Eastern Europe in radically different ways may nevertheless agree on the existence of certain social facts in the political-economic situation of the region. They may agree, for instance, that unemployment has risen to a certain level and has remained there for a given length of time. They would apprehend this fact, as it were, *through* their frames; agreeing on an elementary description of it, they would very likely disagree about its proper interpretation. Nevertheless, both of them, seeing the stubbornly resistant fact through the lenses of their own frames, might recognize a need to restructure their framing of the situation in order to take account of it. Just possibly, they might coordinate their independent efforts at reframing in such a way as to enable them to converge on a new frame. But there is nothing in the strategy of truth-through-the-lens-of-a-frame that suggests how such a possibility might be realized.[10] For this purpose, it would seem, one of the two following strategies would be necessary.

The second strategy would resolve frame conflicts by appealing, not to a shared perception of fact, but to consensual, logically independent criteria for evaluating frames and choosing among them. For example, disputants might evaluate their respective frames by reference to a common criterion of utility.

The third strategy is that of "mapping," or translating from one frame to another. If such frame-mapping or -translation were reciprocal, policy antagonists might come to understand one another's conflicting views, which might enable them to make an informed choice among their conflicting frames or to synthesize elements of them in a new frame that they would jointly construct.

These three strategies raise further troublesome questions. How might the sponsors of conflicting frames ever get from a shared perception of "facts" to a coordinated restructuring of their frames? Are there consensual, logically independent criteria for choosing among conflicting frames, and if so, is it possible to apply them in an objective way?

Are there workable procedures for mapping, or translating, across conflicting frames, and, if so, how may they be used to enable policy antagonists to arrive at shared understandings? The first of these questions is discussed in chapter 7 in relation to the idea of "background learning." The second and third questions are considered in the following sections.

## FRAME CRITERIA

In order to pose the problem of choice among frames, we must already have stepped far enough outside our frame to see that our position is not self-evident and that other ways of framing the issue are possible. Once this happens (and we shall have more to say about how it may happen), we face the question of the basis for a reasoned choice among possible frames.

James March has suggested that "a speculation is good if it is true, beautiful, and just."[11] Truth, in March's view, has to do with the verifiability of the propositions implied by the premises contained in the argument of a frame. Beauty refers to the eloquence with which the argument is formulated, especially the parsimony of its chains of inference. Justice connotes an ethical evaluation of the judgements of right or wrong to which the frame leads us.

To March's list of criteria, we add two more. The first is coherence, which is associated with inclusiveness: to what extent does our framing of the policy situation integrate a large number of disparate values and beliefs in a single, self-consistent perspective that "makes sense"? The second additional criterion is utility, or fruitfulness: to what extent does our way of framing the situation suggest interventions that will plausibly achieve our purposes? To what extent, in other words, will we be able to solve the problems we have framed?

The difficulty with any model of frame choice based on allegedly superordinate criteria is that the sponsors of conflicting frames are likely to apply the "same" criteria—beauty or utility, for example—in different ways. As Thomas Kuhn points out in the analogous case of scientific theories, criteria for theory choice, such as accuracy, simplicity, and fruitfulness, "function as values"

> and can thus be differently applied, individually and collectively, by men who concur in honoring them. If two men disagree, for example, about the relative fruitfulness of their theories, or if they agree about that but disagree about the relative importance of fruitfulness

and, say, scope, in reaching a choice, neither can be convicted of a mistake. Nor is either being unscientific. *There is no neutral algorithm for theory choice* [our emphasis], no systematic decision procedure which, properly applied, must lead each individual in the group to the same decision.[12]

Similarly, the parties to a policy controversy may agree that frames should be judged by their coherence and beauty, but disagree about which frame more nearly exhibits these qualities. They may agree that frames should meet the criteria of truth and utility, but disagree about what facts merit explanation and what tests are worth performing, or what constitutes a useful outcome.

It is illusory to suppose that criteria for choosing among conflicting frames can be applied in a way that is free of interpretation through the frames themselves. Frame-evaluative criteria do not remove the specter of relativism or teach us, in Rorty's phrase, how to study abnormal discourse from the point of view of some normal discourse. This is not to say that they are useless. Even though they are not neutral algorithms, they may contribute to a search for reciprocal understanding. But such a search implies the feasibility of our third strategy, to which we now turn.

## DISCOURSE ACROSS CONFLICTING FRAMES

It is plausible that when scientists or policy makers are caught up in frame conflict, their ability to reach agreement depends on their learning to understand one another's point of view. In order to do this, however, each party would have to be able to put in terms of his or her own frame the meaning of the situation as seen by the other in terms of *the other's* frame. The antagonists might then create a reciprocal, frame-reflective discourse. Reflecting on the frames of their adversaries, as well as on their own frames, they would try to reason their way to conflict resolution—though "reason" is here extended well beyond the boundaries of instrumental rationality.

How do we imagine that the holders of conflicting frames could ever be gotten to sit down together to hold such a conversation? Even if they were willing to do so, how, in principle, could they communicate reliably across their conflicting frames? Proponents of consensual dispute resolution might answer the first question (if they were willing to extend the boundaries of their discipline to include frame conflicts) in terms of the disputants' "BATNA," or "best alternative to a negotiated agreement."[13] They might argue that the disputants would be willing to sit down together if they believed that by doing so they could achieve a better outcome than by continuing their dispute. As to the second question, both Thomas Kuhn and Jurgen Habermas have suggested possible, albeit idealized, answers.

## KUHN'S APPROACH TO RECIPROCAL TRANSLATION

In a passage of unusual precision, Kuhn takes up the communicative predicament posed by conflicts of scientific paradigms. His analysis strongly suggests an analogy to policy controversies.

Kuhn points out that the practice of normal science depends on the ability, shared by all members of a community of scientists, to group objects and situations into similarity sets. These groupings are primitive. Scientists acquire them as they become familiar with canonical problems, such as calculating the acceleration of a ball rolling down an inclined plane or the changing rates of speed in the motion of a point pendulum. Kuhn emphasizes that the members of a scientific community are able to group objects into similarity sets "without an answer to the question, 'Similar with respect to what?'"[14]

In scientific revolutions, some of the similarity relations change. Kuhn tells us that "objects that were grouped in the same set before are grouped in different ones afterward and vice versa":

> Think of the sun, moon, Mars and earth before and after Copernicus; of free fall, pendular and planetary motion before and after Galileo; or of salts, alloys and a sulphur-iron filing mix before and after Dalton. Since most objects within even the altered sets continue to be grouped together, the names of the new sets are usually preserved.
>
> Nevertheless, the transfer of a subset is ordinarily part of a critical change in the network of relations among them. Transferring the metals from the set of compounds to the set of elements played an essential role in the emergence of a new theory of combustion, of acidity, and of physical and chemical combination. In short order, those changes had spread through all of chemistry. Not surprisingly, therefore, when such redistributions occur, two men whose discourse had previously proceeded with apparently full understanding may suddenly find themselves responding to the same stimulus with incompatible descriptions and generalizations.[15]

Speaking from incommensurable viewpoints, as they now do, the two men experience a communications breakdown, which is especially troublesome when it pertains to the "phenomena upon which the choice of theory most centrally depends." Under these conditions, Kuhn asks, how can people even hope to talk together much less to be persuasive? Because the troublesome words have been learned in part from their direct application to exemplars, the disputants cannot resolve their disagreement simply by stipulating the definitions they will assign to these words. Nor can they resort to a "neutral language which both use in the same way" because "part of the difference is prior to the application of the languages in which it is nevertheless reflected."[16]

Kuhn's approach to such a communicative predicament is to suggest, in a highly speculative way, that scientists who hold conflicting paradigms might "see themselves as members of different linguistic communities and become translators."[17] But he immediately reflects on how difficult it would be to get these scientists to sit down together in the first place. Why, after all, should they do so? If, by some chance, they did sit together long enough to conduct an experiment in reciprocal translation across paradigms, how could reasoned persuasion ever result from their discourse? In spite of his misgivings, Kuhn goes on to explain how the process might work. In order to sort out their communication breakdown, the protagonists could draw on the everyday vocabularies they shared:

> Each may . . . try to discover what the other would see and say when presented with a stimulus to which his own verbal response would be different . . . each will have learned to translate the other's theory and its consequences into his own language and simultaneously to describe in his language the world to which that theory applies.[18]

Such a process (which seems, in Kuhn's description, to include a reciprocal version of the strategy we have labelled truth-through-the-lens-of-a-frame) would be foreign to discourse in normal science, and it would be threatening. Moreover, as Kuhn goes on to say,

> To translate a theory, or world view, into one's own language is not to make it one's own. For that, one must go native . . . not simply translating out of a language that was previously foreign. . . . [At] some point in the process of learning to translate, [one] finds that the transition has occurred, that he has slipped into the new language without a decision having been made.[19]

Kuhn suggests that one of the participants in the dialogue, going native in the other's language, might be converted to the point of view expressed in that language. In contrast to rational persuasion, conversion is essentially mysterious. Kuhn offers no practical suggestions for bringing it about. He seems to think that the exercise of reciprocal translation might prepare the way for conversion, but only as going out on a date might prepare a couple for the mystery of falling in love.

## HABERMAS'S EMANCIPATORY DISCOURSE

Jurgen Habermas has also described the broad outlines of an idealized discourse that might be enacted by participants who hold radically different points of view. But whereas Kuhn focuses on the possible structure of translation across conflicting paradigms, Habermas focuses on an ideal speech situation—a situation, essential to democratic society, where "public decisions are reached by autonomous citizens in a process of unconstrained exchange of opinion"[20] and conflicts of perspective are resolved through contests of argument that proceed under conditions of truth, freedom, and justice.

Habermas advocates a consensus theory of truth which tends to equate truth with the procedures for reaching it.[21] He argues that truth claims can be validated only through a contest of arguments in which good, rational, and defensible reasons for adopting or rejecting a normative position can be developed and communicated. Such a contest requires norms of freedom under which only the best arguments will prevail. Justice comes into play because the participants must enjoy, as autonomous citizens, a reciprocal and symmetrical distribution of rights, which means that each participant has an equal chance of initiating, questioning, or defending assertions, and an equal chance of having an argument accepted on its own merits.

Habermas states that such a discourse must be free from both domination and deception. The threat of domination creates uncertainty as to whether a decision will be reached through the force of the argument alone, or by factors extraneous to the argument. If a discourse is not open—if participants are less than truthful or cover up relevant information—then the contest of arguments is curtailed and the best arguments may not prevail.

## CRITIQUE OF IDEALIZED DISCOURSE

When Kuhn suggests how scientists committed to conflicting paradigms might see themselves as representatives of different linguistic communities and sit down together to become translators, he imagines a conversation. But the kind of conversation he imagines is remote from any particular issue that needs resolution. He does not reconstruct a particular controversy, such as the one that occurred in the 1950s and

1960s when the proponents of the new theories of plate-tectonic geology struggled with the defenders of the old geology. Nor does he examine the context in which such a dispute might actually arise. As a result, he isolates the imagined conversation from concrete scientific practice and, in doing so, divorces it from the circumstances of an actual conversation in which it might have a chance to succeed. In fairness, we must point out again that Kuhn goes to considerable pains to avoid claiming that real-world scientists would actually try out his suggested procedures or, if they did so, reach agreement by means of them.

Habermas also presents an idealized discourse defined in terms of the abstract procedures that would govern it. In his case, these are principles of freedom, openness, and justice—principles that seem impossibly remote from the conditions under which issues like international relations, state security, or fiscal policy, might actually be discussed in the public sphere. Philosopher Seyla Benhabib points out that the political realists among Habermas's critics have taken him to task on these grounds, accusing him of "complete utopianism in the domain of politics."[22] But, in her view, the Habermasian ideal is not a proposal for action but a feat of political imagination that "projects institutions, practices and ways of life which promote nonviolent conflict resolution strategies and associative problem solving methods." She believes that such practices have their approximate counterparts in everyday life, as when we ask a child, "But what if other kids pushed you into the sand, how would you feel then?" or say to a partner, "But let me see if I understand your point correctly."[23] Such interventions depend, in Benhabib's view, on a pivotal cognitive competence that bears more than a passing similarity to Kuhn's imagined capability for reciprocal translation across linguistic communities:

> What I have suggested . . . is that if we view discourses as a procedural model of conversations in which we exercise *reversibility of perspectives* [our emphasis] either by actually listening to all involved or by representing to ourselves imaginatively the many perspectives of those involved, then this procedure is also an aspect of the skills of moral imagination and moral narrative which good judgment involves.[24]

In the chapter from which we have drawn these passages, Benhabib does not go on to suggest how the skills required for "reversibility of perspectives" might be cultivated, much less introduced into practical discourse on matters of fiscal policy. Habermas, for his part, has never, to our knowledge, found or invented an actual practice corresponding to his idealized speech situation, although he has declared his intention to search for one and has, to that end, considered and apparently abandoned a number of candidates.[25]

The different approaches to idealized discourse suggested by Kuhn, and proposed by Habermas, share a predicament common to many such ideals: they are formulated at a high level of abstraction, and in a way that seems impossibly remote from actual practice. Yet, as later chapters show, they illuminate some of the conditions under which a practice of frame-reflective inquiry might actually proceed.

## APPROACHES TO REAL-WORLD POLICY MAKING

Part II presents our view of such a practice, its potential for the pragmatic resolution of situated policy controversies, and its place in our proposed model of policy rationality. This section considers the work of four authors who have strongly influenced our development of these ideas. Like Kuhn and Habermas, these authors venture into the sea of theoretical issues surrounding the nature and limits of policy rationality; but, unlike Kuhn and Habermas, they keep the mainland of practice in sight.

Our four authors share a good many things. They reject microeconomic models of policy choice based upon a "bedrock" view of objective interests, and they reject, with equal firmness, such related ideals as comprehensive planning and models of progress based upon instrumental rationality. They refuse to give a privileged place to the expertise of the professions and the social sciences. Nevertheless, as advocates of limited reason they continue to display what one of them, Charles Lindblom, has called "the tattered flag of the enlightenment." Their several perspectives will help to clarify both the starting points and the approximate boundaries of the path we intend to follow.

### JOHN FORESTER AND THE PROSPECTS
### FOR THE FUTURE OF MEDIATED NEGOTIATION

Kuhn and Habermas have imagined an idealized, cross-frame discourse remote from situated controversy. In contrast to them, practitioners of mediated negotiation seek out real-world policy disputes, but refrain from probing the intellectual and appreciative sources of conflicting interests. Sometimes, as we have noted earlier, mediation does create a group climate in which disputants come to rethink their interests. But, because mediators tend to regard the constancy of interests as essential to their strategy of bargaining for joint gains, their practice theories tend to treat interests as fixed and given. The mediators advocate reflection on policy options, action consequences, and the range of issues that disputants might agree to put on the table, but not on the conflicts of basic values and associated understandings that underlie policy disputes. It is just at the point where such conflicts arise, however, that mediators have begun to discern the limitations of their methodology.

Kuhnian or Habermasian versions of ideal discourse, which are frame-reflective in our terms, cannot affect the fate of real-world policy controversy unless they find counterparts in actual policy practice. The mediators' effective practice cannot extend to policy controversy unless it moves toward frame reflection. If it were to develop in this direction, however, it might become a practical embodiment of ideal discourse.

A recent essay by planning theorist John Forester contains just such a proposal.[26] Forester's critique of consensual dispute resolution begins, like ours, by pointing out the limitations of a bargaining theory based on microeconomics. What such a conception misses, according to Forester, is that the public managers, planners, and policy makers who play intermediate roles in policy inquiry actually, or at least potentially, shape public discourse. They alter the political future by molding the public's understanding of the stakes in a dispute, the distribution of power, and the subjects that merit public concern.

Rejecting the "view from nowhere"[27] that treats mediators as neutral parties, Forester seeks an alternative account that would place public dispute resolution in the context of a "modern republican conception of political conflict, political participation and political life."[28] Following the theories of Hannah Pitkin,[29] Forester argues for an account that would articulate "a broader conception of political life [and] the public interest [through] . . . deliberation and debate, mutual recognition and discussion, learning and civic discovery." Within such a framework, Forester suggests, mediators in public disputes will be "less like experts, judges or implausibly neutral bureaucrats" and more like "new friends who can create a space for speaking and listening, for difference and respect, for the joint search for new possibilities, and ultimately for newly fashioned agreements about how we shall live together."[30] He adds, "Just how must be the subject of another essay."

Our exploration of frame-reflective inquiry into policy controversies will propose answers to the "how" that Forester leaves as a question at the end of his essay. But his description of public discourse in a democratic republic, and his educative conception of mediation in public disputes, suggests critically important conditions for the kind of policy inquiry we have in mind—especially the condition of "civitas," discussed in later chapters.

## Lindblom's Reprise of Deweyan Inquiry

Throughout his remarkable scholarly career, Charles Lindblom has steered a steady course that is essentially Deweyan in spirit. In the 1960s, contrary to the then-conventional wisdom of comprehensive planners and policy scientists, he proposed the notion of disjointed incrementalism.[31] Policy, he argued, begins with concrete situations and choices. It makes progress by small departures from the status quo and by continually adapting its strategies to small changes in politics. Policy analysis is incremental, exploratory, serial, marked by adjustment of ends to available means, and socially fragmented.

In his advocacy of disjointed incrementalism in policy analysis and muddling through in policy practice, Lindblom expressed appreciation for the wisdom of experienced practitioners and skepticism toward the technical-rational aspirations of social and policy scientists. In the 1970s, his *Usable Knowledge,* coauthored with David Cohen, extended this line of thought to the whole field of social problem solving. Cohen and Lindblom celebrate the everyday knowledge of ordinary people. They point out that all expertise rests on a veritable iceberg of tacit, taken-for-granted knowledge, largely unacknowledged, and that in any given instance of choice the claims of professional social inquiry deserve no special privilege.[32]

Lindblom's *Inquiry and Change,* written in 1990, takes this argument further still, in a way that more fully reveals its Deweyan origins.

The theory that John Dewey developed more than half a century ago takes *inquiry,* in a sense far broader than its colloquial meaning of *investigation,* to signify a generic interplay of thought and action.[33] For Dewey, inquiry arises in response to an obstruction in the flow of action, when the inquirer encounters a problematic situation that is inherently doubtful or indeterminate. Thought serves mainly to convert a problematic situation to a solvable problem. In the field of public policy, what Dewey stresses is how to get public deliberation moving again when the policy discourse of democratic institutions becomes ensnared in intransigent controversy—as in the abortion controversy, which has become a polarized debate about absolutes, the rights of the mother and the life of the fetus. Dewey believes that the pressure to unblock the flow of inquiry can create a readiness to rethink the conflicting imperatives that led to the blockage of inquiry in the first instance.

Lindblom is thoroughly Deweyan in his pragmatic conception of inquiry and his insistence on linking that conception to the theory of democracy. He writes:

I want to call attention to thinking that is engaged in real-world problem solving, to the relation, consequently, between thinker and the world thought about, and to the open-ended and exploratory quality of thought. I also want to call attention to interplay between thought and action as part of the process of probing or inquiry itself. And, not least, I want to play up aspects of systematic and productive thinking about real-world problems that depart from conventional scientific methods.[34]

Lindblom argues that society "cannot do more or better than inquiring or probing" which proceeds "in a broad, diffuse, open-ended, mistake-making social or interactive process, both cognitive and political."[35] But this exercise of limited reason crucially depends upon the free competition of ideas, which links it to democracy (and to Habermas's conception of the ideal speech situation). Probing is "impaired" by any restriction of the free play of ideas, whether by unreflective reliance on convergent views that result from a common experience of socialization, or by the domination of business or government leaders, professionals, planners, social scientists, or others from the ranks of the elite and advantaged.

Lindblom believes that probing can be extended to social conflicts, including policy controversies. The "volitions" that enter into social conflicts (preferences, wants, interests, values, and needs) are not the unmovable foundations of inquiry but are shaped and corrected *within* inquiry. Hence,

At any point at which conflict exists, more inquiry and mutual persuasion continue to be a possibility. . . . The principal conflict-resolution mechanism of most (all?) societies is not governmental or state imposition but various social interchanges that move people toward agreed volitions.[36]

Like Lindblom, we treat policy inquiry as an interplay of thought and action, undertaken in the midst of action, and we explore the varied, open-ended ways in which inquiry may unblock seemingly intractable controversies. But our approach differs from Lindblom's in two main respects. First, our unit of analysis is not the broad, societal process through which issues are probed, but the narrower careers of policy issues situated within particular arenas and forums. Second, and perhaps as a consequence of the first difference, we give less attention than Lindblom does to the role of lay citizens. Ordinary people enter into our stories as their views and interests are seen and represented (more or less well) by elected officials, bureaucrats, interest groups, and advocates. We focus on the nature of the rationality that is feasible for, and appropriate to, those who have the standing that enables them to sit at the policy table. We devote less attention than Lindblom does to the question of those who do not sit at the table and the process by which they may acquire standing. In this sense, Lindblom's view represents an important extension of our own.

## MARCH'S REDISCOVERY OF INSTITUTIONS

In his 1989 book with Johan Olsen, James March has ventured ambivalently beyond the pure theory of the garbage can. According to the pure form of that theory, "problems, solutions, decision makers, and choice opportunities" flow through a system like independent and exogenous streams, and "neither the processes nor the outcomes appear to be closely related to the explicit intentions of the actors."[37] Early in their most recent book, *Institutions Rediscovered*, March and Olsen make clear that the garbage can is a condition that may be more or less in evidence. When it is less so, there may be institutional space for deliberate intervention and a limited exercise of human reason.

March and Olsen name a variety of strategies for deliberate institutional change, ranging from "mundane adaptation" to "comprehensive shocks," but they emphasize two main approaches to change: aggregative and integrative. The aggregative tradition embraces a "logic of exchange" (related to our negotiating rationality). It emphasizes bargaining relations among relatively autonomous, self-interested parties. The integrative tradition embraces a "logic of unity" (related to the frame-reflective approach we shall explore). It treats conflicts of interest as a basis for deliberation and decision, aims at mutual understanding and trust, and seeks out "synthesis and conversions rather than antithesis and concessions."[38] March and Olsen suggest that we move cyclically from one logic to the other. We may believe for a time that the complications of institutional life do not present a bar to reform, "while at the same time recognizing that within a few decades, we will redisover the evils of integration and will once again embrace exchange in the name of self-interest."[39]

March and Olsen believe that institutions not only adapt to environmental forces, but actively create their own environments "by the way they act in a confusing world." They believe that institutions change in ways that are characteristically complex, uncertain, and discontinuous:

> For the most part, institutions evolve through a relatively mundane
> set of procedures sensitive to relatively diffuse mechanisms of control.
> Ideas about appropriate behavior ordinarily change gradually

through the development of experience and the elaboration of world-views. Such processes tend to result in significant lags in the adjustment of institutions to their environments. The lags, in turn, make institutional history somewhat jerky and sensitive to major shocks that lead not only to occasional periods of rapid change but also to considerable indeterminacy in the direction of change.[40]

All such phenomena raise serious complications for standard ideas of rationality. March and Olsen point out that it is difficult to "describe a decision, problem solution or innovation with precision, to say when it was adopted, and to treat the process as having an ending." Moreover, they claim, interests, objectives, and interpretations cannot be understood as pre-existing foundations for deliberate change, because "change develops meaning through the process by which it occurs."[41]

*Institutions Rediscovered* is a transitional book. On the one hand, the authors present a garbage can view of the life of institutions, according to which belief in intentional choice through politics can only be considered a "well-elaborated and reinforced myth" designed to maintain a semblance of social order. On the other hand, they recognize a distinct though limited institutional space within which individuals may reason their way toward conflict resolution, reform, and collective learning. March and Olsen do not attempt to provide a coherent view of how that space may be occupied, but, by calling attention to critically important phenomena of institutional life, they do set the stage for such an attempt.

## ALBERT HIRSCHMAN'S BIAS TOWARD HOPE

The reader will have already noticed how often we have referred to Hirschman's work. His position in a range of fields—economic development, theory of organizations, political economy, intellectual history—is unique and uniquely important for the enterprise in which we are engaged.

From his earliest book on economic development,[42] Hirschman recognized the peculiarly uneven, complex, and often counterintuitive ways in which institutions, countries, and policies evolve. At the same time, he has consistently championed the view that societal development and institutional reform may be deliberately pursued through the exercise of human reason. His theory of development is a theory of imbalanced growth in which difficulties of all kinds—shortages, excesses, tensions, and mistakes—may function as stimuli for individual and collective learning. His belief in the human capability for learning, invention, and recuperation from error underlies the "bias toward hope" that he has sustained throughout his working life.[43]

Hirschman's writings richly illustrate the operation of the world views, paradigms, and perspectives that we have labelled frames, and the intractable controversies to which frames often give rise.[44] At the same time, he is a practitioner who emphasizes the importance of producing knowledge usable by practitioners—the public officials who seek to promote national development, the administrators who try to improve organizational performance, and the managers who try to run effective projects.

More than this, Hirschman is an intellectual who has steadfastly maintained a skeptical stance toward formal theories that claim universal applicability, while at the same time he has turned an appreciative eye toward the habits of action of individuals "on the ground," whose local, often tacit knowledge and wisdom through practice he has sought to articulate. Therefore, he has given highly useful descriptions of the marketlike strategies of "exit" and the political strategies of "voice" through which better-performing organizations have managed to resist the prevailing trend toward deterioration in organizational performance. He has described "linkages" and "pacing mechanisms" through which policy makers can create institutional structures that elicit or compel the kinds of learning essential to development. He has formulated and, in his own practice, illustrated the coaching strategies through which an advisor may help local practitioners to build on what they already know in order to pursue more effectively a distinctive, local path toward development.

Hirschman's seemingly paradoxical attitude toward development—his treatment of tension, imbalance, and conflict not as evils to be avoided but as sources of creativity and learning—is mirrored in his own intellectual journeys, in which he seeks out and embraces apparently contradictory truths, finding, in the process, both reasons for skepticism and sources of insight. We find this feature of Hirschman's thought most appealing, and our approach to policy controversy has been influenced by it. At the same time, we suspect that our attempt to sketch a broadly applicable theory of design rationality may very well strike Hirschman as intellectual hubris.

## AN EMPIRICAL EPISTEMOLOGY OF REFRAMING

Intractable policy controversies exist and are fundamental to the policy-making process. Controversies are not well explained by prevailing accounts of policy making, nor do prevailing models of policy rationality offer promising strategies for their resolution. Frame analysis helps us to account for their origin and stubborn survival, but also leads to an awareness of the relativist trap, which makes their resolution seem all the more difficult. The potentials for frame reflection, which grow out of frame awareness, are evident only in two unsatisfactory forms: idealized models of discourse for which no practical application is at hand, and a practice of mediated negotiation, some parts of which may have outdistanced its own espoused theory.

Yet we know that people do sometimes change their minds, even in fundamental ways, and we know of not-so-rare events in actual policy disputes where positions have been reframed in such a way as to open up to accommodation controversies that had at first seemed hopelessly intractable. These observations constitute the point of departure for our interest in an empirical epistemology of reframing. We want to explore how such processes actually work. Therefore, we shall ask: How do policy controversies emerge in policy-making practice? How, on occasion, are policy positions reframed? In what relation to frame reflection, and with what consequences for the resolution of controversies, is this accomplished? How do policy practitioners reason, when they reason well, and what view of policy rationality accounts for their reasoning?

When we pose these questions, we have two related purposes in mind. We want, first of all, to articulate a frame-critical approach that challenges the prevailing, objectivist view of policy analysis. We shall argue for an approach that recognizes the discrepant frames from which conflicting policy positions arise, that seeks to bring them to consciousness, and that subjects them to critical reflection. Second, we advocate a frame-reflective approach to policy practice, which would recognize the ability of practitioners to reflect on the frames that shape their conflicting positions and thereby foster a normative approach to public discourse within which policy controversies are more likely to be resolved through reflective inquiry.

In the empirical study of policy controversies, these two purposes call, as we shall see, for somewhat different emphases. Nevertheless, they converge on a common task: constructing the frame conflicts involved in situated policy controversies, exploring their trajectories, and describing the practices through which they are managed. As we approach this task, we shall draw liberally on the insights of the four authors we have discussed in the preceding section.

## THE CASE STUDIES

Our essay in the empirical epistemology of reframing consists of three case studies of policy practice, presented in the following chapters. The first deals with a policy-making process of some forty years' duration that has led to a nationwide phenomenon of early retirement in Germany. The second is about the development of policy for the role of computers in higher education at MIT between the late 1970s and the early 1990s. The third has to do with the development of a program for the homeless in Massachusetts during the 1980s.

We have chosen these cases for several reasons. First, we know them well and, therefore, have access to a great deal of information about them. Second, they represent very different kinds of policy issues, settings, types of institutions, and periods of time. The lessons we draw from them may be less subject to the restrictions that would be inherent in a narrower selection of policy domains and contexts. Finally, we have chosen these cases because the policy controversies involved in them have not remained stuck on dead center. The controversies that surface in all the cases give rise not to paralysis or stalemate, but to adjustment or accommodation—and in some instances, as we shall argue, to reframing.

We take up the three cases in a sequence that begins with a relatively distant overview of the structure of policy making and then zooms in to permit a relatively close inspection of policy practice. In the first case, early retirement in Germany, we take a position of considerable distance from the thoughts and actions of individual policy makers. This case will serve mainly to introduce our view of the "policy dialectic" and our particular conception of policy making as designing. In the cases of Project Athena and homelessness, individual actors come into view; we observe their actions and gain access to their thoughts. These cases illustrate the communicative dimension of policy design, and provide material for the analysis of design rationality.

# PART II

# The Cases

# CHAPTER 4

# Early Retirement in Germany

This chapter describes the long-term evolution of a national social policy: the development of early retirement in post–World War II Germany. We tell the story of this development in outline and analyze it as an example of processes essential to our proposed epistemology of reframing—policy dialectic, policy design, and design rationality.

The phenomenon of retirement might be considered in several ways. If it were defined simply as the receipt of a public pension, then its history might be confined to such matters as eligibility criteria, funding levels, and demographic shifts. Or it might be considered, in the American tradition of microeconomic analysis, in terms of an individual worker's decision to retire and the structure of incentives within which that decision is made. We believe, however, that the first appearance of the phenomenon of early retirement from work in Germany cannot be exclusively understood in either of these ways. An adequate explanation must include the role of institutional actors, such as the firm and the state, which, at least in the German case, played such important roles in setting the stage for individual retirement decisions. This institutional story cannot be told in isolation from a broad policy environment that includes the interactions of social, cultural, labor market, and public policy trends in the postwar period.

Early retirement is an abrupt and permanent exit from employment by men less than sixty-five years of age, a nonreversible transition from active work to disengagement from paid employment. The magnitude of the trend toward early retirement in contemporary Germany can be inferred from a few salient facts: between 1970 and 1989, the employment activity rate dropped from 70 to 34 percent for men aged 60–64 and from 88 to 79 percent for men aged 50–55, with the result that by 1989 about 30 percent of all Germans over the age of fifty-five received a public pension. These facts represent a striking change in the demarcation of prime from older workers.

The trend to early retirement takes on additional significance when it is combined with two other trends in the behavior of the labor market. For the sake of comparison, we note these trends in both Germany and the United States. First, the proportion of persons sixty-five years or older in the total population is rising dramatically. Between 1990 and 2030 this proportion will increase in Germany from 16 to 26 percent and in the United States from 2 to 20 percent. This shift results from "double aging": an increase in longevity combined with a decrease in fertility. Between 1950 and 1980, life expectancy increased from 66.4 to 73.3 years in Germany and from 68.4 to 73.5 years in the United States, whereas in the same period the fertility rate fell from 2.1 to 1.4 children per family in Germany and from 2.2 to 1.8 children per family in the United States—rates below those necessary to maintain a stable population. Second, there has been a startling decline in the rate of labor force participation on the part of those who are sixty-five and older. Between 1965 and 1985 this rate declined in Germany from 24 to .2 percent and in the United States from 27 to 10 percent. Taken together, these two trends mean that by the year 2030 in Germany the 15-to-64 age group, no greater than it was in 1990, will have to support almost twice the number of elderly persons.

Industrial economies such as Germany are work-oriented societies where employment provides the primary source of social meaning. The rise of early retirement, combined with double aging and declining labor force participation on the part of those sixty-five and older, challenges traditional assumptions about the organization of the life course. Shifts in the traditional age boundaries of work and exit from work are likely to have significant effects on the organization not only of work but of social life as a whole. Although these effects are only gradually coming to light, it is already clear that they will include greatly increasing demands on the nation's system of social protection—that is, the governmental, private, and family systems that protect against such social risks as old age, illness, disability, and unemployment. Hence, a brief history of Germany's social protection system is in order.

German's social protection program originated in the Bismarckian social insurance system of the late nineteenth century, a system in which benefits varied with contributions based on prior earnings, as well as on industrial sector and social class. Immediately after World War II, Britain's Beveridge Plan exerted a powerful influence on all European models of social protection. Beveridge proposed a system, based on common citizenship, that would be universally available to everyone in retirement, with everyone contributing the same amount and receiving the same flat-rate benefit. The British tried to impose such a plan on Germany's Bismarckian tradition of social insurance but the Germans resisted, maintaining their prewar plans and administrative structures for a full decade after World War II.

In 1957, however, Germany revamped its social security system. It preserved the essential features of earnings-related social insurance but weakened many of the class-related dimensions of that system. Although white- and blue-collar workers, miners, and other industrial groups continued to have special plans and separate administrative structures, benefit levels were much more uniform. In practice, class and occupational distinctions lost much of their earlier meaning. Of course, as in most countries, the civil servants (*Beamten*) were still treated as a special class with a much more generous system of social protection.

By the 1970s, the Beveridge model had collapsed in almost all the countries that had accepted it. What emerged to replace it in Britain, Sweden, and the United States was based on its opposite principle: private earnings–related insurance benefits that varied with the industrial sector and the size of the firm in which protection was provided. In contrast to these abrupt and fundamental changes, the German experience has been one of continual marginal adjustment. What is most striking about the system of social security that emerged in Germany after World War II is that it maintained continuity of structure while adapting resiliently to a shifting policy context. This pattern also holds true of the story of the rise of early retirement, to which we now turn.

## ELEMENTS OF THE STORY

Early retirement emerged in Germany over a period of about forty years, during which time some elements of the policy-making process changed: the patterns of interaction between the two main institutional actors, the firms and the state; the views these actors held toward the social security system; the priorities they attached to different policy issues; and the conditions of the policy context to which they adapted. But we can speak of one policy-making process rather than many disconnected processes, because of elements that stayed more or less constant: the set of institutional actors in the policy arena, the family of interrelated policy issues, and the social security system itself, around which much of the story revolved.

As the early retirement story unfolded, the number of actors expanded. The firms divided into management and unions, and the unions into chemical and mechanical. The state divided into the ministries of social security and labor, the courts, and the local employment offices. These different actors confronted a family of interrelated policy issues and imperatives for action that, in light of their different interests and purposes, they tended to perceive and interpret in different ways at different times.

At times, for example, the state gave precedence to the imperative of managing the labor market, striving to keep unemployment within bounds and meet industry's changing demands for labor. At other times, the state focused on protecting the financial integrity of the social security system. The unions generally sought to preserve jobs and maintain income security for older workers. The firms strove mainly to adapt efficiently to the changing contexts of international competition and the domestic labor market. These different priorities, stemming from the various institutions' action frames, held a potential for conflict. But when frame conflicts occurred, they were expressed not as absolute disjunctions of values but as differences of emphasis on values and interests that were shared, for the most part, by all of the actors.

The policy discourse of the key institutional actors, which unfolded in a variety of policy forums—the federal legislature, the courts, federal and local bureaucracies, political parties, academia, and the media—was one of antagonistic cooperation. At times, the actors disputed over the definition of policy issues and the use, or modification, of particular policies. At other times, they shared a more or less consensual view of issues and policies. But their contention took place within a framework of cooperation because they stood in interdependent relationships to one another within a larger cooperative system. When they cooperated, it was within a framework of potentially conflicting imperatives for action.

We divide the early retirement story into four main stages that correspond to moments of antagonistic or cooperative policy discourse:

| | |
|---|---|
| **STAGE 1** | State and federal courts make Social Security system more adequate, humane and flexible.     (1966–73) |
| **STAGE 2** | Firms use this infrastructure to create early exit and pass on costs to the state. (This is also the period of "twilight discourse.")     (1979–present) |
| **STAGE 3** | State tries, ambivalently, to shift costs back to the firms.     (1981–present) |
| **STAGE 4** | The state tries again: Raising the age of retirement.     (1989 reform) |

## STAGE 1: THE STATE ACTS

Following World War II, Germany as a whole perceived an urgent need to bring returning veterans into the work force. There was a broad societal consensus that jobs must be provided for the veterans, not only as a just reward for their service to the state but also as a protection against the social disorder they might create if they returned to find no jobs awaiting them. There was an equally broad consensus that older workers displaced by the younger veterans should be provided with an adequate pension. Finally, there was a broadly shared perception that the state had an obligation to support the firms, relatively weak in the immediate postwar period, as they tried to manage the adjustment of their work forces. The policy discourse of this period was marked by consensual use of the phrase, "The old must make way for the young," which became the election slogan of the Conservative party.

In the later postwar period, in 1957 and again in 1973, coalition governments, the first led by the Conservatives and the second by the Social Democrats, initiated reforms of the pension system with the primary intention of making the structure of benefits more humane and responsive to people's needs. We discuss only two of the many changes included in these reforms.

The 1957 reform package contained Germany's first early-retirement measure: it enabled long-term unemployed older workers to retire at age sixty instead of sixty-five. This program came to be known as "the 59ers," because at age fifty-nine an unemployed worker could effectively retire. Because the German government assumed that these workers had suffered during the war and would not be able to find work once they became unemployed, it argued that the humane thing to do would be to make it possible for older workers to get a public pension after a year of unemployment. Of course, the Conservative government's willingness to push for this measure also had a great deal to do with its wish to prove the viability of market capitalism in Germany during the early stages of the Cold War. Whether or not the new rule was driven by this motive or by a genuine sense of social reform, many German workers opted to take advantage of it. They collected unemployment compensation for one year and then became eligible for a public old-age pension at age sixty.

In 1973, the Great Coalition (the first and only government formed as a coalition of Conservatives and Social Democrats) introduced a flexible retirement scheme that allowed workers to retire at sixty-three or, if they were severely handicapped, at sixty-two. The program's main assumption was that people with different preferences and needs should be treated flexibly rather than in a uniform way.

In 1969 and again in 1976, the Federal Social Security Court discovered that the pension law neglected the partially disabled. Under German pension law, a person who was not totally disabled was expected to be able to get part-time employment. However, the first economic recession of the mid-1960s proved that in many local labor markets no part-time jobs were available. Lawsuits were filed, and the courts responded to them by arguing that if no part-time jobs were available in a local labor market, a partially disabled person should be eligible for full disability benefits. In 1976, when this "concrete method of interpretation" for determining job availability turned out to be hard to implement in practice, the court sought a simplifying rule. It developed the general principle that a partially disabled person, unemployed for one year, would be automatically entitled to full disability benefits.

When it interpreted long-term unemployment as an index of job availability, the court stretched the law, combining unemployment and disability claims as potential justifications for early retirement. After 1976, a worker could seek early retirement at age sixty following long-term unemployment, or following a shorter period of unemployment if he could prove partial disability without having access to a part-time job, or if he were severely handicapped. Many workers took a middle road. Since 1976, about 20 percent of new male entries into the pension system received a pension based on some combination of labor market and medical reasons.

The new rules governing workers' access to old-age pensions provided a social infrastructure that could be used for purposes very different from those intended by the framers of the original postwar social security legislation. The state, the political parties, and the courts had been key actors in initiating a stream of consecutive, adaptive reforms as well as in engineering creative extensions of existing regulations. They had invented the 59er rule combining the firms' pension payments with the use of the state social security system as a way of smoothing the transition of older workers out of the work force. Once the policy invention had been made, however, it became an object in the policy environment, capable of taking on different meanings for different actors as the policy context shifted. With the new script, the old actors (state, courts, and political parties) could modify and extend their positions and domains, while new actors (such as firms and unions) could enter the social policy arena. Thus, the explicit reforms of 1957 and 1976 set the stage for more dramatic changes that would no longer require explicit changes in the rules.

In retrospect, the most striking characteristic of the first stage of the early-retirement story was a blurring of the lines between social protection and labor market policies. The long-term unemployed older worker gained privileged entry to the public pension system, and disability benefits were based not only on medical judgments but on the availability of part-time work. In partial recognition of this erosion of the boundaries, the state continued to subsidize the public pension system, although its contribution of about 15 percent of the total cost remained unchanged. At the same time, as a recent Organization for Economic Cooperation and Development (OECD) report has noted, "the deterioration of the labor market itself played an important role in increasing the importance of the 'alien' claims upon the pension system."

These events foreshadowed later developments that would foster conflict between the state and the firms. The legislature and the courts had made the instruments of the welfare state more responsive to the needs of special groups in the labor market, but they had provided no new state funding to offset the increased financial burden. One way out of this dilemma would have been to create a separately funded labor market policy that stressed the retention of older workers, but the politicians were unwilling to finance such a policy. They were also reluctant to press the firms to retain older workers, just as they resisted compelling the firms to create part-time work for the disabled. When unemployment rose in the 1970s, therefore, it was the state administrators of the unemployment and pension funds who felt the financial pressure. By the end of the 1970s, they began to squabble over the distribution of increasing costs.

## STAGE 2: ENTER THE FIRMS

In the second stage of the evolution of Germany's early-retirement policy, the firms moved to center stage using the social policy instruments created in the postwar period to rationalize their internal labor market and shed most of their older workers.

The firms were responding to a shifting policy context that can be usefully, though not precisely, divided into local and global components. At the local level, the firms followed the new script that had resulted from the events described. At the global level, they were influenced by the changing state of the national economy, especially by periods of unemployment and economic growth, changes in Germany's geopolitical situation in the Cold War period, the changing cultural givens of German society, and the development of the international industrial marketplace in which Germany sought to compete.

As the crisis of the returning veterans subsided in the 1960s, the demands of international competition rose. The firms faced the challenge of adapting their work forces to competitive pressures driven, in large part, by technological innovation. In response to these pressures, Germany developed a new technical training system, and the firms tried to slough off older workers and draw in the younger, technically trained workers who would be better suited to their technologically advanced production systems. They used the 59er rule for this purpose, drawing on the social security system to secure state subsidies for the restructuring of their work forces.

In the 1970s, in the wake of recessions triggered by the oil crisis, and in view of a perceived need to accommodate labor supply to slack demand, the firms initiated a far-reaching program of early retirement. Based on a broad consensus among individual workers, unions, the federal government, and the local labor market offices, the German firms created a social policy that shifted the costs of early retirement to the state by making proactive use of the social infrastructure created in the 1950s and early 1970s.

The firms adopted an approach that required no fundamentally new laws or policies but relied on the invention of new pathways to early exit, ingeniously combining a variety of social programs and funding sources. Perhaps the most important such pathway was created by encouraging older workers to use the firms' unemployment benefits to "top up" the value of the unemployment and social security benefits provided, under the 59er program, by the state. An OECD report described this common practice as follows:

> [In German firms] employees aged 59 or above are selected, or are encouraged to apply for dismissal. . . . The enterprise tops up the

unemployment compensation, sometimes to a level that is as high as previous net wages and sometimes compensates for the reduction in the public pension to the level which would have been obtained had the employee stayed until 63.

Of course, this pathway was at best quasi-legal. In principle, an unemployed person was supposed to be looking for work, which meant that he could not legally arrange with his employer to become unemployed in exchange for a public-private benefit package. Nevertheless, because of its concern with the overcrowded labor market, the state changed its regulations to make this practice effectively legal. In 1986, it permitted workers fifty-eight or older to receive unemployment benefits without registering for work; by the mid-1980s, even though the formal rules permitted retirement only at sixty-five or (in the case of flexible retirement, sixty-three), recipients of social security benefits had an average age of 58.8.

Social contracts of this kind were bound to be very appealing to both individual workers and unions, since they permitted retirement without significant financial sacrifice. Indeed, by shifting the costs of early retirement to the state, the firms had been able to make it so attractive to individuals that the boundary between personal choice and involuntary expulsion from work was no longer clear. The new pattern of early exit from the labor force took hold, and, as it did so, brought about changes not only in the meanings of social protection programs but in the larger society's cultural values and attitudes.

In programmatic terms, unemployment insurance, originally designed to cushion the impact of a temporary loss of work, came to function as a buffer for the transition between permanent exit from the labor force and eligibility for a public pension. In cultural terms, the de facto policy of early retirement contributed to a sense of national solidarity, and a worker's dignity began to seem compatible with the condition of early retirement. Workers began to feel entitled to early exit from work. The changes in the social security system initiated by the state had been put to unanticipated uses by the firms, with the result that the cultural givens of German society shifted so as to alter the ground rules of social policy. One consequence was that the public pension system ceased to operate as a self-financing scheme based on the principles of social insurance. The state had helped to create a new policy environment to which it would have to respond.

By 1987, early-exit pathways were no longer limited to industries that were troubled, declining, or undergoing rapid technological change. Even growing and profitable firms made use of them, and by the early 1990s almost 80 percent of all male wage and salary workers aged sixty to sixty-four had left employment. The extraordinary growth of the practice of early exit, and the resulting massive decline in the employment activity rates of older men, would not have been possible without the workers' and unions' agreement, the state's knowing collaboration, and a broad societal consensus. At first, however, politicians and public servants appear to have overlooked the enormity of the changes taking place.

## TWILIGHT DISCOURSE

The state turned a blind eye to its informal subsidy of the firms. In an economic climate of high unemployment, from the late 1970s forward, it joined the firms in a policy discourse that was characterized by ambiguity, ambivalence, and collusion. We call this a "twilight" discourse because it was only partly visible and only partly legal. This discourse led to a weaker state and a stronger firm, a change that might portend cultural changes of a deeper kind. It is always dangerous to infer intentions from consequences. What we do know is that once the state became fully aware of the effects of the discourse in which it had participated, it launched a strong, though ambivalent, counter-reaction.

In order to explore the shifting patterns of the twilight discourse, we discuss some of the background of the institutional and financial structure of the German welfare state. We hereby adopt a more complex notion of the state that we have treated until now as a monolithic actor. To present the point of view of this more complex cast of characters, we will also need to revisit some of the events already described.

The Federal Ministry of Labor and Social Order has within it an independent labor office, with responsibility for supervising the semi-autonomous local unemployment offices. The same ministry also supervises pension funds. At the central level, then, personnel services and social security cash transfers are the responsibility of the same federal office. Below the federal level, the structure is more complex:

> 1) The federal labor office is responsible for the unemployment and pension benefits of white-collar workers only; blue-collar workers are dealt with at the local level.
>
> 2) Both unemployment and pension funds are financed by equal contributions from employers and employees, plus a subsidy of about 15 percent from general revenues to cover the costs of "alien" claims.

3) Active personnel policies are conducted by the federal and local labor offices, which have few resources independent of those raised by the insurance funds.

4) These local and federal personnel offices carry out labor promotion activities independently from insurance and pension funds. They act only as gatekeepers, but their decisions affect the size and cost of the funds' activities.

Although local labor offices are responsible for dealing with high unemployment levels, they have few resources with which to do so. The substantial insurance funds are largely controlled by semiautonomous, bipartite insurance institutions. Rising unemployment, therefore, becomes a political embarrassment at both local and federal levels, giving rise to an urgent feeling that something must be done.

As the firms encountered economic hardship, the 59er rule became the personnel policy of choice since it allowed the firms to reduce their personnel without labor conflicts or an overaging of the work force. In order to make use of the 59er rule, however, the firms had to get approval from the local labor office, since this office was responsible for paying the unemployment benefits for a year. Both the firms and the local labor offices acted contrary to the letter of the law, for the law required recipients of unemployment benefits to be genuinely unemployed, that is, dismissed from employment, rather than having entered the ranks of the unemployed as part of a covert agreement with employers.

Why did the local labor office agree to this quasi-legal practice? One account holds that many firms threatened to start a massive layoff of workers forty-five to fifty years of age—a group not protected from firing, like those over fifty. These workers would then have had virtually no chance of finding work. Since it was clear that such a move would be very disruptive to the local economy, the local labor offices chose the lesser evil. They collaborated with the firms in the use of the 59er rule, which offered a "bloodless," if quasi-legal, solution. Charged with the mission of labor promotion but lacking the financial resources to create an active personnel policy of their own, the local labor offices chose to cooperate with the firms to divert unemployment to its most acceptable form: making room for the young by displacing the old.

The firms, for their part, needed to find a socially legitimate way of retrenching workers in a period of economic downturn. Mass layoffs could lead to protest and confrontation. The use of the unemployment insurance and public pension system to externalize costs easily became the central premise of the firms' social policy.

The workers were willing to enter into a social contract with firms since, with topping up, they were as well off financially in retirement as they were at work. Moreover, with the social stigma of early retirement decreasing over time, resistance to early retirement gradually disappeared. Even those unions that had initially favored shorter working hours at the same pay came to adopt a favorable attitude toward early retirement.

For more than a decade the federal labor office did not officially acknowledge the local practice. In fact, the labor office agreed not to see what it surely must have known. It feigned ignorance and thereby participated in the general collusion of the twilight discourse.

As long as relatively small amounts of money in the pension and unemployment insurance fund were used on alien claims, or the number of 59ers in the program remained small enough to be hidden in "normal practice," all of this presented no special problem. Moreover, some important industries, such as steel and coal, were especially well protected from detection, since their programs were financed by the European Community; in these industries the 59er rule became virtually official policy.

Reflecting back on the conditions that created the twilight discourse, we are still puzzled as to how such massive policy shifts could have occurred without undermining the public credibility of the institutions involved. Perhaps the twilight politics of Germany's early retirement policies, by keeping actions partly hidden, slowed down the learning process through which the disparity between intention and action might have become visible. Perhaps, when some of the actors later discovered what had been hidden, they could forget their collusion in the earlier fogging of events because, in the new context, these events seemed less relevant. If these speculations are correct, we can say that the twilight discourse permitted both slow learning and speedy forgetting.

## STAGE 3: AN AMBIVALENT COST SHIFT TO THE FIRM

In 1980, the federal labor office changed its policy of "not seeing" to one that focused on the "abuses" of local labor office practice. In the election campaign of 1982, these abuses became a major policy issue, and the Conservatives adopted the slogan, "Your pensions are not safe!"

In contrast to the consensual policy discourse of the first stage and the twilight discourse of the second, there was now an antagonistic discourse of conflicting imperatives. While tension between the firms and the state became stronger, a new tension arose within the state between the social security and the federal labor ministries. In some respects, these agencies contended with each other and, in other respects, with the local employment offices. Controversy surfaced within a now more complex policy arena, and actors who sat in different sectors of the economy and at different levels of government now advocated competing views of the policy issues.

All parties argued their positions on the basis of the public interest, but they gave different priorities to different elements of that interest. The state now described early retirement as a time bomb that could bankrupt the national social security system. It presented the informal use of the 59er rule to subsidize the firms as a distortion of the true function of the social security program. Accordingly, it sought to make the firms "pay their fair share," arguing that the firms had a social responsibility to ease the exit of surplus workers, which they had initiated in their own interest, just as the state had a primary obligation to protect the integrity of the social security system.

The firms, in turn, sought to justify their continued use of the social security system to subsidize their work force adjustments. They claimed that, in order to compete effectively in the international marketplace, they must be granted autonomy.

The ideas of autonomy and social responsibility, central to the action frames of the firms on the one hand and the state on the other, are essential to an understanding of the policy controversy that now arose.

## THE INSTITUTIONAL ACTION FRAMES OF FIRMS AND STATE

The firms' autonomy frame held that in order to respond effectively to the pressures of competition, the firms needed to be able to differentiate their production systems and modify levels and types of personnel. Hence, the firms claimed that their viability depended on their freedom to act in their own interests, tolerating little or no outside interference with their efforts to respond to changes in their competitive environments.

The firms wanted autonomy, but they also wanted to exploit the social infrastructure created by the state to assist them in the exercise of their autonomous judgments. A weak version of autonomy means that the firms are free to act with few constraints. A stronger version, advocated by the German firms, means that the firms should participate in reallocating collective resources for their own ends. Of course, strong autonomy can be exercised only where collective resources are plentiful, as in societies with elaborate welfare state structures. But countries vary dramatically in the level of resources available for specific social policies. In the United States, for example, unemployment insurance lasts for only twenty-six weeks, whereas it lasts for three years in Germany, five years in France, and for an unlimited time in the Netherlands. Hence, the degree to which firms can exercise strong autonomy varies not only among nations but also among specific policy domains.

The social responsibility frame holds that the firms can exercise autonomy only within a set of ever-changing social norms and in accordance with certain abiding principles. Every economy is embedded in a society, its performance socially constrained by that society's norms and values. A fully autonomous economy, subject only to its own laws, would threaten the viability of the larger society. In other words, firms must respond in a socially responsible way to economic and social changes—changes, for example, in the age structure and the labor market. Firms are expected to make profits, but within limits.

The social responsibility frame held by the German state has historical precedents. Modern capitalism is a very different phenomenon from the unfettered capitalism of the turn of the century. In 1905, for example, the U.S Supreme Court invalidated collective efforts to promote the general welfare by redressing imbalances in economic bargaining power. But in 1930, at the beginning of the Great Depression, the court reversed its position, permitting the federal government to restrict the firms' autonomy—for example, by limiting working hours, requiring the payment of a minimum wage, and imposing a minimum working age.

In Germany, too, the state tried to restrict the autonomy of the firms in the name of certain conventions of social responsibility, but in doing so it sought to preserve not only an individual right but a whole social policy system. With its "can't afford" arguments, the state attempted to protect the financial integrity of that system against the inroads of an expanding labor market policy disguised as social security.

Yet there was more at stake. The state and the courts held that the firms' use of the 59er rule distorted the proper allocation of responsibility for the protection of older workers. The German constitutional court was to argue explicitly, in its settlement of the repayment issue (to be discussed), that the firms, not the state, had the responsibility of caring for these workers:

> Since the practice of early retirement is neither economically nor socially desirable and erodes the fiscal viability of the unemployment and pension systems, it is . . . just and fair that the financial burden of these policies be carried by the employers who are primarily responsible for older workers. Moreover, it is to the common good

that the legislature emphasize the protection of older and long
tenured workers.

Of course, this ruling conflicted with the firms' desire for strong
autonomy and rejected the argument that economic growth depended
on the unconstrained, creative action of autonomous firms. The court
held, on the contrary, that in times of economic downturn the firms are
socially responsible for the welfare of their older workers.

## THE STATE'S CHALLENGES TO THE FIRMS

With the weakening of the social consensus on early retirement, the
state launched two challenges against the firms. In 1980, the social
security ministry sought to require employers who dismissed older
workers with at least ten years of tenure to reimburse the Federal Labor
Office for the cost of unemployment benefits paid in connection with
early retirement (Section 128 of the Labor Promotion Act of 1980).
The ministry argued that since workers age fifty or older were protected from firing (through paragraph 62 of the Industrial Relationship
Act of 1972), the firms were obliged to retain them until they were eligible for an old-age pension.

In 1984, the social security ministry demanded that the firms provide additional reimbursement to the pension fund in order to account
for the years between ages sixty and sixty-three during which, under
the 59er rule, retirees had received pensions prematurely. The ministry
wanted to replace the 59er rule with legislation that was less financially
generous to employees, and the firms contested their action. They took
the issue to the federal constitutional court, where they argued that
unemployed workers had received their 59er pensions under then-
prevailing law. The issue remained tied up in the legal system until
1990, at which time the court ruled in favor of the state. About one hundred thousand cases requiring reimbursement were then outstanding.

Along with the second measure of 1984, the German government
also passed a new temporary early-retirement program called the "preretirement rule." Designed to replace the 59er rule, this rule was
intended to make the firms pay for unemployment benefits if they did
not hire younger unemployed workers to replace older workers who
retired. The new rule stipulated that an individual who stopped working at fifty-eight or older would receive an allowance of 65 percent of
his or her last earning from the firm and would be required to continue
paying contributions to the social security system until he or she
became eligible for an old-age pension. However, if the firm recruited

an unemployed person to fill the position vacated by an older worker who retired in this way, the state would subsidize up to 35 percent of the firm's 65 percent allowance.

With the preretirement rule, the state officially acknowledged the use of early retirement as employment policy, thereby coming down on the side of the more conservative chemical unions and in opposition to the metal workers union, which supported a shorter work week. But as the state acknowledged early retirement, it sought to pass the costs of that practice back to the firms, hoping to reduce excessive pension claims by making early retirement too expensive for the firms to use. In addition, the state's preretirement law included a paragraph that addressed the unions' complaints about the firms' abuses of the 59er rule by giving individual workers exclusive control over the decision to take early retirement.

By 1988, four years after it was introduced, the preretirement program was judged to be an overall failure. Since there were many exceptions to the 59er practice, the new program had done little to halt the firms' raid on the insurance funds. Moreover, the firms had never supported the program, since it kept them from shifting costs to the state and reduced their power over the retirement decision. Because of its perceived unworkability, and because of the firms' protests, the German government terminated the program simply by failing to renew the temporary legislation. In the end, the message the state intended to send was different from the one the firms received. The state wanted the firms to reduce their use of the 59er rule, but the firms continued, as before, to shift the brunt of the costs of early retirement to the state.

Although the German state persisted in its demands for reimbursement, its challenges to the early-exit pathway remained ambivalent. In 1987, for example, it permitted older workers to get almost three years of unemployment benefits before retiring at age sixty with a public pension, and it extended unemployment benefits from twelve to thirty-two months for workers over age fifty-five. These two measures came to be called the "57er rule." At the same time, the state limited access to the pension system. It made recent work attachment a prerequisite for receiving disability benefits, a measure that mainly affected women who lacked recent work experience and could therefore no longer use disability as a pathway to exit from work.

By the end of the 1980s, therefore, the state's social policy had taken two divergent directions: It had limited access to the pension system by eliminating or making more difficult certain exit pathways, while at the same time, it had effectively lowered the retirement age by changing the 59er rule to a 57er rule.

# STAGE 4: THE STATE TRIES AGAIN—RAISING
# THE RETIREMENT AGE

The state's stance toward the firms remained ambivalent. A new set of mixed messages was contained in two new events: passage of the 1989 pension reform act, and the 1991 settlement of the reimbursement issue.

## Pension Reform

In 1989 the state passed a pension reform act, scheduled for implementation in 1992, that signaled its intention to slow down the pattern of early retirement through a fundamental redefinition of the pension rules. With this act the state reversed in some ways a position it had voiced in the course of the earlier debates: that early retirement contributed to the viability of the social security system by creating employment for younger workers.

The new act contains many far-reaching changes, of which the most important and controversial, in the context of our present discussion, is a gradual raising of the age limit for most types of public pensions. With the exception of the severely handicapped, women, and older unemployed workers, all of whom will be eligible for a public pension at age sixty, the normal pension age will be raised to sixty-five and the minimal eligibility age to sixty-three. Retirement before age sixty-five will be penalized by a 3.6 percent reduction in the pension benefit level. Finally, the act specifies that the normal pension age will eventually be raised to sixty-seven. Under the flexible retirement provisions of the new rule, an unemployed worker aged fifty-seven who receives benefits for three years will have to wait three more years before entering the public pension system at age sixty-three. Over time, this gap will increase to five years.

The 1989 reform reflects a desire not only to reverse the trend toward mass early retirement but to buttress the public pension fund's claim for financial stability against the demands of labor market policy. It is an attempt to decide the conflict between the firms and the state in favor of the latter, and to decide the conflict between the Social Security Ministry and the Federal Labor Office in favor of the former.

The new legislation is scheduled for implementation in 1992. At this time the firms and their workers will face the reality of increased limits on the pension age, and open conflict between the firms and the state may erupt again. This conflict might be avoided if firms back away from their policy of shedding older workers, or if they use their own resources to create new forms of social protection similar to the private early-retirement programs that exist in the United States and the Netherlands. Instead of raiding the state's social infrastructure for their own purposes, the firms would then pursue an active social policy of their own. However, most analysts agree that the firms are unlikely to take this route—partly because of their already high contributions to the existing public pension system, but largely because they still seem to be effective in tapping the state's social policy infrastructure for their own purposes.

### SETTLING THE REIMBURSEMENT ISSUE

As we have mentioned earlier, the firms refused to accept the legitimacy of the state's reimbursement rule and took the issue to the federal social security court. In 1991 that court ruled in favor of the firms. The court argued that since Section 128 forced employers to pay back the benefits they had received without taking account of special situations in which they may have been entitled to benefits from other social programs, it was unconstitutional. For example, state-supported sick pay was available to workers with a repeated history of absence from work due to illness. However, in order to find out which workers were entitled to these benefits, a search of past records would have been required—at an estimated cost of some ten thousand hours of work. Since the firms and the state had a mutual interest in avoiding this costly procedure, they reached a settlement. The social security ministry, representing the pension and unemployment funds, entered into an agreement with the employers' association according to which the firms were required to pay an amount that was, considering the cost of the programs at stake, no more than a token: 500 million German marks, or about 350 million U.S. dollars. This settlement of the issue was distinctly favorable to the firms. In effect, it extended the use of the new 57er rule without any further need to rely on a twilight practice.

We conclude, then, that in the struggle between the sponsors of conflicting action frames of autonomy and social responsibility, strong firms seeking strong autonomy won out against the efforts of a weak state to compel them to bear the burden of social responsibility. With this negotiated settlement, the policy controversy, which surfaced in the second stage of our story, was pragmatically resolved in a way that enabled the firms to continue to use the social security system to adjust the age structure of the work force in a "bloodless" way.

Yet, as already pointed out, the state's passage of the 1989 Pension Reform Act was a move that could produce an opposite effect by 1992, depriving the firms of the benefits of the de facto policy of early retirement. Taken together, pension reform and the settlement of the reimbursement issue reveal the state's internally conflicted attitude toward the firms, the social security system, and the complementary issues of social and labor market policy. How are we to make sense of this ambivalence? The German state emphasized the need to protect the integrity of its social security system by compelling the firms to behave in a socially responsible way. But it was also sensitive to other imperatives: managing unemployment, cushioning labor dislocations, treating older workers humanely, and avoiding interference with German industry's efforts to succeed in the international marketplace. The action frame of the state, as represented by federal ministries, courts, and local offices, was not the pure frame of social responsibility but a mixed, hybrid action frame that encompassed all of these imperatives.

## THE STORY BROUGHT UP TO DATE

With the Pension Reform Act of 1989, the state seized the high ground of "can't afford" morality and tried again to reverse the trend to early retirement. Will it succeed? Perhaps not. The world in which the reform was passed has changed dramatically.

The Pension Reform Act was approved on the same day that the East German government took down the Berlin Wall, setting in motion a process that has led to German reunification. The effects of reunification on the pension debate are still unfolding. For example, the former East Germany has lowered the male retirement age from sixty to fifty-five in an effort to deal with industrial restructuring and the threat of high unemployment. Thus, the former East and the former West Germany appear to be moving in different directions. Given these developments, it is uncertain what will be the final outcome of the state's effort to challenge the cost-shifting strategy of the firms and redefine the rules that permit early retirement.

As far as we can judge, there is little evidence for fundamental change. While the state has continued to be ambiguous in its policy practices, the firms and the employer associations have continued to fight for state funds for early retirement. Thus, when the government presented its policy guidelines for implementation of the 1991 reform, which required the firm rather than the unemployment fund to pay for the two years of benefits between age fifty-eight and sixty (the age at which an older employed person can enter the public system), it also provided for a host of exemptions. For example, neither small firms nor firms with economic problems (interpreted as situations where the repayment would threaten the health of the firm and cause loss of jobs) are required to abide by the rules of the reform law. The employer associations, in turn, have interpreted the state's willingness to grant exemptions as a sign of weakness and have started a massive campaign in favor of even more lenient regulations. If the exemptions are abused, we can expect yet another round of court battles between the state and the employer associations.[1]

Fundamental change in the practice of early retirement can be expected only if there is change in the domain of ideas about the firms' responses to competitive pressures. In Germany, the firms have pursued the strategy of early exit because it gives them flexibility in an otherwise rigid and regulated labor market, enabling them to adjust to technological innovation in a relatively painless way. More recently, however, several scholars have expressed skepticism about whether, in their pursuit of early retirement, the firms may have gone too far. These scholars believe that the modern firm needs mature, older workers with experience and judgment who are better able to learn on the job. It remains to be seen whether this new image of the older worker as learner and planner will supersede the earlier image of the need for young, technically trained workers and thereby produce yet another shift in the firms' policies toward the age structure of its work force.

## POLICY DIALECTIC AND DESIGN RATIONALITY

Here we take a second look at the early-retirement story to see what light it may throw on several questions central to our empirical epistemology of reframing: how controversies arise in actual policy making; how they are dealt with and perhaps resolved; and what implications they have for rationality and reflection in policy practice. We treat the early-retirement story as a "policy dialectic" within which policy makers function as "designers," and we begin a normative account of "design rationality."

### POLICY DIALECTIC

The Hegelian schema of thesis, antithesis, and synthesis is only a special case of the historical, transformative, and conflictual policy-making process that we call "dialectic." A policy dialectic, as we use the term, is a drama in which contention among institutional actors in a policy arena combines with the actors' adaptation to shifts in a larger policy environment so as to effect, over time, the transformation of a policy object.

Anthropologist Victor Turner has vividly described such a process. He writes of a policy arena as a "political bull ring . . . [a] cockpit of confrontation, encounter, and contention . . . a framework—whether institutionalized or not—which manifestly functions as a setting for antagonistic interaction aimed at arriving at a publicly recognized decision."[2] Policy arenas are, as Turner sees them,

> concrete settings in which paradigms ["frames," in our terms] become transformed into metaphors and symbols with reference to which political power is mobilized and in which there is a trial of strength between influential paradigm-bearers. "Social dramas" represent the phased process of their contestation.[3]

The policy dialectic, in short, is a symbolic contest that revolves around a policy object-in-the-making. The contestants are actors in the arena who represent different powers and interests rooted in conflicting action frames. They struggle to gain control of the policy object and cooperate, at times, to shape that object, as a consequence of which the object evolves, in form and meaning, and in ways intended and unintended, as a resultant of their actions. But the object also changes in form and meaning as a result of shifts in the policy context—both the global context subject to forces beyond the actors' control, and the proximal, or immediate, policy context with which they are in transaction as they act on their immediate policy situation and are acted upon by it.

Context shifts, changes in the meaning of the policy object, and actions taken by the actors combine to bring about new stages of the policy dialectic. At these moments the actors face new problematic situations and must try to set and solve new problems. At some of these moments, situated controversies arise as the new situation triggers conflicts of interests, powers, and action frames. The actors attempt to deal with their conflicts and solve the problems they set. But the policy dialectic is inherently open-ended. New solutions tend to generate new problems. The pragmatic resolution of existing controversies tends to set the stage for new controversies. Throughout this open-ended policy drama, the policy object is both the focus of the contestants' struggle and the product of their cooperative-antagonistic interaction.

Our story of early retirement is the story of a policy dialectic in which the German state and the firms create, through their cooperative antagonism, a new artifact of social and labor market policy. In its first stage, a global context characterized by national solidarity, and a threat of mass unemployment caused by the return of the World War II veterans, led the state to press the firms to create a new pathway through which older workers would make way for the young. The federal government and the courts encouraged the firms to use the social security system to subsidize their displacement of older workers. Legislative and regulatory actions by the federal government, legal rulings and precedents set by the courts, and informal responses by the firms combined to create a pattern of early exit from the work force.

Once the policy object—the social security system with its new periphery of rules and practices—was "out there" in the larger environment, it became vulnerable to being seen and used by other actors and, in a changing context, in ways the state had not anticipated. In the late 1960s, as the firms struggled to compete in the international marketplace, and in the recessions produced by the oil shock of the early 1970s, as federal and local labor offices attempted to cope with rising unemployment and slack demand for labor, the firms used the social security system to continue the pattern of early retirement, now as a means of pruning and restructuring their work forces. Local labor offices colluded with the firms in this quasi-legal practice, and the federal labor office informally adopted a policy of "not seeing."

After years of this twilight discourse, the social security ministry realized that its informal subsidy of the firms threatened the long-term financial viability of the social security system. A struggle over cost-shifting now arose that took the form of a symbolic contest of action frames. The firms claimed "autonomy"—the freedom to take actions necessary to secure their competitive position and assure continuing economic growth—and the state demanded that they take "social responsibility" for the older workers displaced by their restructuring of their work forces. In its role as guardian of the integrity of the social security system, the state tried to roll back the firms' proactive social policy, but it did so ambivalently. In the forums of the federal legislature, political parties, federal agencies, courts, employers' association, unions, and local employment offices, policy controversies multiplied. Some of the controversies related to the state's demands for reimbursement by the firms, and some to regulation of pathways to early exit by different groups of workers. In the late 1980s court decisions, negotiated settlements, and legislative reforms combined to produce a pragmatic resolution of these controversies in a way that distinctly favored the firms and increased the level of state welfare spending.

The policy dialectic of early retirement, a complex, long-term policy-making process, can be more clearly understood by contrast with what it is *not*. It is not a process of policy choice, as conceived by the policy scientists, nor is it policy choice followed by "implementation." Neither of these models describes how policy artifacts are shaped through the interplay of institutional actors in a policy drama that is at once a frame contest and a political struggle. Neither model tells how new problematic situations come into being and how policy objects take on new meanings as the policy drama combines with shifts in the proximal and global context. Moreover, although policy choices do sometimes arise in a policy dialectic, there may be long stretches in which no discrete event can be clearly identified as a "choice."

Neither is the policy dialectic adequately described as a process of political contention among interest groups—a political game of interests and powers that occasionally results in negotiated settlement. This model does capture the politics of the policy drama, but it ignores the interpretive frames that underlie interests and the conflicts of frames that underlie political conflicts. It does not focus on the more-or-less constant presence in the arena of a policy object that is shaped by the actions of the contending actors nor does it attend to the development of new states of the policy situation that result from the interaction of the unfolding policy drama with shifts in the policy context.

Finally, the policy dialectic is not reducible to a more-or-less chaotic interplay of meanings, ideas, interests, rules, and routines—problems looking for solutions and solutions looking for problems—along the lines of the pure garbage can model described by Cohen and March. This model does capture the organized anarchy that often characterizes stretches of a policy dialectic. But policy dialectics combine, in varying degrees depending on the case, the features of antagonism, anarchy, and coherence. The model of the garbage can ignores the relative coherence of a long-term dialectic, such as the one described by our story of early retirement, in which a relatively constant policy object is shaped over time through the intentional actions and communicative interactions of actors in the arena, and through their successive attempts to interpret and adapt to shifts of context.

## POLICY DESIGN AND DESIGN RATIONALITY

The models of rational choice, political contention, and the garbage can capture only limited dimensions or restricted zones of the policy dialectic. In contrast to these models, we propose a view of policy making as "designing," subject to "design rationality."

The design metaphor, we argue, allows us to explain how a policy dialectic may be relatively coherent in spite of its politics of contention and its garbage can quality. Although the dialectic is always conflictual and often disjointed and chaotic, it centers on a relatively constant policy object, such as the social security system in the German story. This constant object serves as an external "memory" of the actors' cumulative moves and anchors the sometimes divergent cycles of policy-making activity. The design metaphor enables us to understand how actors engaging in a symbolic contest that is also a political struggle may nevertheless display policy inquiry characterized by intentionality and intelligence. The limited rationality of policy inquirers is not well described by the instrumental rationality of the policy sciences, nor by Lindblom's rather pejorative phrase, "muddling through." Rather, as we try to show, the rationality of skillful policy makers is like the rationality of skillful designers.

Policy design is certainly not an unfamiliar idea. Indeed, some writers, like policy analyst Peter deLeon, refer to the existence of a "policy design movement." According to deLeon, the proponents of this movement have sought to address "the entire policy stream."[4] Reacting against the policy sciences, they have attempted to re-embed policy making in the social and political environments from which earlier researchers had abstracted it, compensate for earlier writers' neglect of implementation, and restore problem setting to its rightful place alongside problem solving. With these objectives of the policy design movement we certainly agree. We seek to go beyond them, however.

Although policies are not material objects and policy makers are not architects or engineers, designing in the narrow sense of "design professions," such as architecture or engineering, is an illuminating metaphor for policy inquiry. What this metaphor tells us depends, of course, on how we conceive of the design of material objects. Herbert Simon, one of the most influential theorists of design, describes designing as "heuristic search": search for optimal or satisficing (that is, "good enough") solutions within a search-space bounded by constraints and guided by heuristics.[5] He has boldly applied this view of designing to the entire field of professional practice, arguing that the professions rest on a yet-to-be-articulated science of design, a "science of the artificial." Our view of designing is very different from Simon's, although the scope we claim for it is similar to (and influenced by) his.

In the simplest material design situation, there is a designer, an object to be designed, and an environment in which that object is to be used. The designer makes a representation of the object—a drawing, model, or symbolic description—which will later be embodied in materials and put out into the larger environment. Such a representation is made under conditions of complexity and uncertainty.[6] It is made within a virtual world (the architect's sketchpad or computer screen, for example) that stands for the actual world in which the object will function, and within which the designer can make and test moves cheaply, at his own pace, and at relatively low risk.

The designer makes his representation of the object within a field of constraints, acting from intentions implicit in his values and purposes. However, the designer's intentions, constraints, and objectives are not fully given at the outset, and they are not fixed. They emerge in the course of making the object, through a process of seeing, making design moves, and seeing again. Working in some graphic or plastic medium, such as drawing, the designer sees what is "there" in a representation of a site or object, draws in relation to it, and sees what has been drawn, thereby informing further designing.[7] As the representation of the object takes shape and new qualities are recognized in it, new meanings are apprehended and new intentions are formed.

Detecting the intended and unintended consequences of his moves, the designer becomes aware of an evolving field of values, criteria, and constraints, which are always, to some extent, mutually incompatible. In this process, he sets new problems, constructs new possibilities for action, or formulates new dilemmas. For example, an architect may discover that her attempt to make the shapes of a building fit the complex contours of a site has produced an incoherent form. An engineer's attempt to make a razor blade sharper may also make it more vulnerable to corrosion.

Given the framing of a new problem, opportunity, or dilemma, the designer makes an invention aimed at solving the problem, realizing the opportunity, or resolving the dilemma. For example, the architect may invent a way of imposing a geometry onto the contours of the screwy site. The engineer may invent a way of double-honing the razor blade and coating it with silicone to retard its corrosion. Such inventions must be embodied in the artifact through further design moves. Not infrequently, such moves raise new problems that require a second invention no less important than the first.

Designing is also a process of discovery and learning. In the course of seeing/moving/seeing, the designer discovers unanticipated patterns, relationships, and possibilities, which may inform further designing. As she plays out webs of moves and discovered consequences, for example, an architect may learn about the nature of the problem implicit in a particular configuration of the features of the site, program, and constraints. An entire episode of designing may function, then, as a source of learning that enables the designer to readdress the project at hand or tackle a new project more intelligently.

Projecting this relatively simple view of designing onto the field of policy making, we see a policy designer who constructs, in some relatively protected forum, a representation of a policy or program that will be sent out, upon its completion, into an actual policy environment. As the representation of the policy object takes shape, the policy designer's seeing/moving/seeing reveals new meanings, goals, and criteria, some of which are found to be mutually incompatible, requiring the framing of new problems, opportunities, or dilemmas.

When a policy-making story like our German case is seen in terms of this simple view of designing, certain themes of designing and design rationality become clear. We mention them briefly here, leaving their more detailed discussion to later chapters:

- As the policy object takes shape, a designer notices how new meanings, constraints, and criteria emerge and, on the basis of these discoveries, successively resets the problem of the developing policy situation.
- Problem setting must be adequate to "facts" of the problematic situation that may be discovered as the unanticipated consequences of earlier moves are detected, and it must also take account of the multiple, partly incompatible requirements of which the designer becomes aware by designing.
- Policy designers invent modifications of the policy object in order to solve problems, exploit opportunities, or resolve dilemmas and these inventions may be more or less adequate to the problems they are intended to solve or the dilemmas they are intended to resolve. Moreover, these inventions may yield unintended consequences that the designer finds more or less desirable.
- The policy designer may learn from webs of moves, detected consequences, and appreciations derived from previous episodes of policy inquiry.

However, this simple picture of designing and design rationality leaves out critically important kinds of complexity, discontinuity, and uncertainty that are as important to policy design as they are to the design of material objects.

## MULTIPLE DESIGNERS

One critical source of complexity is hidden in the deceptively simple phrase, "the designer." Contrary to the picture described above, designing is a social process, and the designer is characteristically a collection of actors, each with its own interests and intentions, its own slant on the object, its own image of a desirable future state, and its own names for the things and relations it takes to be important. The design of a moderately complex building, for example, usually involves a collectivity that includes architects, clients, interior designers, mechanical engineers, developers, regulators, planners, and neighborhood groups. These actors may be free-standing individuals, or they may be organizations or interest groups within which are nested smaller groups or individuals, whose roles in the design process usually require them to work out more or less integrated positions and strategies of action.

Given the divergent interests and powers of the actors involved in it, the social process of designing is inevitably political. Sometimes the actors are antagonists who contend with one another over the form the object will take and vie for control of the design process. Sometimes the actors form a coalition; working in concert, they constitute what we call a "designing system." At other times, they exert their influence on the evolving object in relatively disjointed ways. Not infrequently—as in our German story—they combine several modes of interaction or shift from one mode to another, moving through periods of cooperative inquiry, ambivalent contention, fragmentation, or outright antagonism.

The policy-making story we described in the German case can now be seen as a drama of policy design in which the main institutional actors—the state and the firms—moved, as described above, through shifting modes of interaction. Initially, the state functioned as a unified designing system, crafting modifications of the public pension system, including the 59er rule, in order to make that system more humane and responsive to people's different needs. The firms responded informally to the policy object the state had designed. In later stages, the state and the firms fragmented into courts, federal ministries, local labor offices, employer associations, and unions, all of which acted, disjointly and sequentially, as policy designers. In order to use the social security system to subsidize the restructuring of their work force, for example, the firms invented their topping up strategy. At a still later stage, as the state came to see the financial implications of the de facto policy it had helped to create, and controversy erupted between the state and the firms, the now-differentiated actors become antagonists, vying with each other to modify the policy object and gain control over its design. At this stage, in order to shift the costs of early retirement back to the firms, the state invented the reimbursement scheme and the preretirement plan. Thus, the policy object was reshaped in form and meaning as a resultant, on the one hand, of the design moves invented by the various actors as they became aware of new problems and tried to solve them, and, on the other hand, of the other actors' responses to those moves.

The shifting interactional patterns of the policy design drama were reflected in shifting patterns of policy discourse. Speaking from their various action frames, often in different professional, political, or cultural languages, the actors sought to explain, persuade, debate, bargain, inquire, or mobilize the support of the larger public that acted as gallery to the policy arena. The consensual policy discourse of the first stage gave way to the twilight discourse of the second, and then to the antagonistic discourse of policy controversy in the third. Finally, with the negotiated settlement of the reimbursement issue, the passage of the 1989 Pension Reform Law and the firms' persistence in shifting the costs of early retirement back to the state, a pragmatic resolution of the controversy between state and firms was at least temporarily achieved—though, as we have noted, it appears likely that a new version of that controversy will soon arise again.

It is in large part through policy discourse among institutional actors that the tasks of policy design are carried out: New problems are set, and policy inventions are made to solve those problems; situated controversies arise, and means are sometimes negotiated and/or invented to resolve those controversies. On the quality of that discourse—its communicative reliability, for example, its openness to inquiry—depend, in considerable measure, the adequacy of problem setting, the effectiveness of policy inventions, and the likelihood that controversy will eventuate not in stalemate or pendulum swings but in some form of pragmatic resolution. Hence, the quality of policy discourse, disciplined by both design requirements and the political requirement of creating or maintaining a designing system, is critically important to design rationality.

## From the Representation of the Object to the Object in Use

While material objects usually start out as representations of things to be built, designing carries over into the processes by which they are constructed, used, and managed. A building, for example, is redesigned when working drawings are converted to a physical structure on a site and again whenever owners or users appropriate it and adapt it to their needs. Competent designers, attentive to the life of the object in its environment, learn to expect and prepare for the possibility that, over time, new meanings will attach themselves to the object they have designed and that modifications will be made.

In the virtual world of policy design, as in an architect's studio, the representation of a policy object is initially under the control of a designing system. But when that representation becomes an object that moves out into the larger environment, it is acted upon and controlled by its users in ways the initial designers could not fully anticipate—as, in the story of early retirement, the firms, with their proactive social policy, used the 59er rule to smooth the shedding of older workers.

Sometimes it is not only users in the narrow sense of the term but managers and regulators who are involved in redesigning a policy object. Formal policies espoused by public officials or bureaucrats may be transformed, through the interactions of agencies with private citizens and service-providing organizations, into policies-in-use.[8] Michael Lipsky shows, for example, how street corner bureaucrats in local welfare, housing, or health organizations can transform the meanings of public regulations through judgments that reflect their own interests or conceptions of good policy.[9] In our early-retirement story, we have seen how, *after* the initial design of the 59er rule, the courts' "concrete method of interpretation" stretched the law so as to combine unemployment and disability claims as potential justifications for early exit from the work force, and how local employment offices that wanted to soften the effects of high unemployment colluded with the firms to allow laid-off workers to collect unemployment benefits for a year even though they were not actively looking for work.

When the policy object takes on new meanings in use unanticipated by its designers, contention may rise to the surface. Seeing what users, managers, or regulators have made of the object they have designed, the initial designers may discover "flaws" in their design, which they seek actively to correct. But other actors, now operating as secondary designers, may take exception to such efforts at correction, as the German firms took exception to the state's attempts to reassert its control over early-retirement policy. Then a full-fledged controversy may erupt as would-be designers struggle to gain control of the object's form, meaning, and use.

## SHIFTING CONTEXTS

Just as old buildings may be put to new uses when new circumstances arise, so when the policy context shifts (and as the garbage can model predicts), actors may discover new meanings in policy objects left over from earlier rounds of policy making and invent new ways to use them. In the case of early retirement, the firms, the courts, and the bureaucrats developed different uses of the 59er rule as the global context changed—first, at the time of the crisis of the returning veterans after World War II, then in response to the demands of international competition in the 1960s, and again in the wake of recessions triggered by the oil shocks of the 1970s.

Shifts in the policy context may trigger controversy but may also help to create conditions favorable to its pragmatic resolution—for example, by promoting a change in the identity or power relationships of actors in the arena, or by fostering new alliances, changing the availability of resources, or creating a sense of crisis that overrides preexisting disputes. In the German case, new patterns of industrial competition may lead the firms to give greater importance to the learning capability of older workers than to the superior technical training of younger ones. When such conditions are created, a policy window opens[10] and a new round of design inquiry becomes possible.

## CONCLUSION

The case of early retirement illustrates the idea of a policy dialectic in which conflicting imperatives are expressed in the evolution of a policy drama that is at once a drama of political contention among institutional actors in an arena and a symbolic contest of action frames. The unfolding of the policy drama combines with the actors' adaptation to shifts in a larger policy environment so as to effect, over time, the transformation of a policy object—an object whose relative constancy helps to anchor the policy-making process.

The early-retirement case also suggests how the metaphor of architectural design may be developed—with emphasis on the interaction of multiple designers, redesign in use, and shifting contexts—in such a way as to reveal a special fit with the structure of policy dialectics and the mixture of anarchy, antagonism, and coherence that is characteristic of them. In this conception, the changing patterns of policy discourse among actors in the arena are critical to the performance of design tasks, including the surfacing and, on occasion, the pragmatic resolution of situated policy controversies.

We can also discern in this example the outlines of the kind of limited reason, design rationality, that is accessible to policy designers. However, the viewpoint we have taken in the case of early retirement is too distant to allow us to see how individuals play their roles in a process of policy design and how their practice as designers may reveal the norms and practices of design rationality. For a closer look, we must turn to the next two cases.

# CHAPTER 5

# Project Athena
at MIT

MIT gave the name "Project Athena" to a large-scale experiment in educational computing that it began in 1983, an attempt by the world's premier school of engineering to regain its sense of lost leadership in institutional, especially academic, information-processing systems. Understanding Athena requires a close look at the specifics of MIT history and culture, but the story of the project's development also has much in common with other policy stories discussed in this book. Not surprisingly, the Athena case embodies many features of a classic policy dialectic: institutional designers (in this case MIT engineers and sponsoring computer companies) create a policy object, the Athena system, which they put out into a larger arena (MIT as a whole). There, other actors respond to the object, guided by their own interests and frames. As they compete to control the object, it evolves in ways that differ from the intentions of any one of them.

The case of Athena is made more dramatic by the fact that its institutional actors, its architects and its challengers, held conflicting views of the project that corresponded to pre-existing political and cultural divisions within MIT and, more generally, to pre-existing notions about the relationship between technology and social progress.

Since the Athena project was a new stage on which to replay familiar patterns of controversy within MIT, it is not surprising that unlike the case of German early retirement, the main actors never enjoyed a Golden Age of consensus. In this case, the early debates on Athena's design foreshadowed conflicts that were to surface even more sharply during Athena's implementation.

---

This chapter is co-authored by Donald Schön and Sherry Turkle.

Those who were skeptical and resistant to Athena "talked back" to her designers, who had a hard time facing the disjuncture between their intentions and the meanings Athena had for her intended users. A fundamental frame conflict persisted: the skeptics and resisters remained, for the most part, skeptical and resistant. The advocates and defenders continued to advocate and defend, seemingly undeterred by what the skeptics took as compelling evidence of Athena's failure to produce its intended educational effects.

Yet a pragmatic resolution of the controversy was achieved through a series of "policy adjustments" that accommodated the real political threat posed by Athena's skeptics and resisters. This accommodation, together with the cooling effect produced by the disappearance of most of the external funding for the project, led to a "reframing" of Athena and to the more-or-less stable outcome which is Athena at MIT today.

Before we explore the details of our story, it is important to note that we, its authors, have the ambiguous status of insider-outsiders to the events that we recount. Both of us are professors at MIT who have been present throughout Athena's evolution. Both of us were members of MIT's Division for Study and Research in Education (DSRE), a short-lived program of educational research that MIT shut down just as it began Athena. DSRE was home to several of Athena's principal challengers, a group that included ourselves. We codirected a study of Athena that figured in the debates about the project that took place in the late 1980s.[1]

In addition, Sherry Turkle, a sociologist, was active in early discussions about the form Athena should take, and Donald Schon was from 1990 to 1992 head of the Department of Urban Studies and Planning, a department committed to the future educational use of the computer through its Computer Resource Laboratory, whose creation Athena made possible.

Thus, there is no question that we are interested parties, and, as such, we see this chapter as part of a continuing dialogue about educational computing within MIT. However, we shall try to distance ourselves from our insider roles, making use of our special access to the events and ideas of the Athena story in order to illuminate the issues around educational computing at MIT and the nature of the policy dialectic that unfolded around it.

## ORIGINS (1978–82)

The Athena story begins in the late 1970s, when a series of commissioned task forces produced reports that anticipated much of Athena's design and set out its underlying rationale. The main architects of Athena were in fact the individuals who commissioned these reports, chaired the committees that produced them, and approved of their recommendations, most notably Gerald Wilson, then dean of the School of Engineering, Michael Dertouzos, then and now director of the Laboratory for Computer Science (LCS), and Joel Moses, then chair of the Department of Electrical Engineering and Computer Science (EECS), and now dean of the School of Engineering. All of these individuals were past or present members of EECS, a department that by the late 1970s claimed a third of MIT's undergraduate majors.

Sensing the loss of MIT's leadership in institutional computing, excited by the educational potential of distributed computer systems, and keenly aware of a window of opportunity created by workstation vendors willing to give MIT large numbers of computers at no cost, these three men conceived of Project Athena. At the core of their conception was the image of a distributed computing system that would be "coherent"—a system of "common interfaces reflecting the language of science and engineering [that] would enable MIT people to share and build upon each other's programs, data, and knowledge."[2] This system was to represent the leading edge of the advancing field of institutional computing. The Athena architects saw the project as the successor to Project MAC, the MIT computer laboratory that had pioneered the development of time-sharing systems in the 1960s and became the Laboratory for Computer Science in 1975. Unique in their day, the time-sharing systems developed at MAC had enabled multiple users to gain simultaneous access to mainframe computing. In the years that followed, MIT played a major role in developing the next generation of institutional computing: free-standing workstations that functioned as "intelligent" computers in their own right. This trend, coupled with the rise of powerful minicomputers (whose performance began to resemble that of mainframe computers and whose cost was a great deal less), made time-sharing systems obsolete. Departments were now able to have their own computers. Athena would balance these centrifugal forces.

In the report of his 1979 Ad Hoc Committee on Future Computational Needs, Professor Dertouzos asserted that the force driving educational computing at MIT was, in the first instance, technological.[3] The institute faced certain indisputable technical facts: there would be an enormous increase in the number of computers at MIT, they would cost progressively less and less, and they would incorporate a range of important technological advances that could be turned toward educational uses. In his 1982 report on computers and education for the School of Engineering, Professor Moses, too, asserted that "by simply implementing the ideas various people are working on, and by providing reasonable access to our students, we will need a massive infusion of new computing equipment."[4] Moses also claimed there was "a pent-up demand for more traditional uses [of the computer] that would necessitate a major expansion of our computing resources devoted to education."[5] He seemed to believe that it was inevitable that education, along with other fields of human activity, would be transformed by the computer.

Both Dertouzos and Moses argued from the inevitable to the imperative: in their view, MIT must regain its lost leadership in academic computing. "In light of the excellence MIT expects of itself," Dertouzos concluded,

> We should not be simply satisfied with adequacy but should strive to achieve and maintain leadership in the use of information processing. . . . [This] is now and promises to continue being a major component of world-wide technological progress. . . . MIT [should] exert a pioneering influence in the development and judicious use of this technology for the educational, research, and other purposes of a major university.[6]

Dertouzos was convinced, as he has put it more recently, that "the technological growth of computers would go on relentlessly to the end of the century, making computing as ubiquitous and pervasive a factor as money! It was therefore inevitable that computing would touch education, along with everything else."[7] For him, it was unthinkable that the world's leading technological institute, with education at its core, should not experiment with the educational uses of the dominant emerging technology.

From this position followed three important consequences. First, because the essence of Athena was an effort to regain technological leadership, it would have to use state-of-the-art information-processing technology. Second, because the state-of-the-art is always a moving target, Athena would have to be continually changing. Athena would be a technological experiment for which MIT would be the "laboratory," just as with Project MAC, MIT had been the laboratory for the development of time-sharing. Third, Athena was to be a distributed, networked system that would be a world leader not only in the sophistication of its workstations and the terminals at its periphery, but in the software and operating system at its heart.[8] Athena's architects decided that UNIX, the computer operating system developed by Bell Laboratories and widely considered the wave of the future for "distributed computing," should be the network's standard.[9] The system also would have to be uniformly coherent, not only in its hardware and software, but in the computer languages it supported.

Indeed, the image of coherence became Athena's technological and aesthetic leitmotif. For its architects, Athena's beauty would lie in coherence, efficiency, flexibility, and universality. The accumulating riches of Athena (libraries of software and dynamic databases) would be continually growing and changing as a result of work done at its periphery. Moreover, Athena would not only provide access to central stores of information but would function as a communications network through which individuals would be able to exchange information with one another and with sources external to MIT. Its power would depend on the excellence of the "complex of pipes"[10] that would make up its infrastructure, designed to be extended eventually to include all of the institute's information processing functions—those related to research, libraries, and administration as well as to education. This view of Athena reflects a faith that, from the right technology, good things will come. Specifically, it defines an "MIT way" of proceeding with research on technology and education: build the ultimate in technically sophisticated information systems, and they will yield the most powerful educational results.

Athena's founders were bemoaning MIT's lost leadership in institutional computing at a time of dramatic change in the computing industry. By the early 1980s, distributed networks of advanced microcomputers were becoming the leading edge of the computer field as a whole, threatening to displace systems based on mainframes and minicomputers. The Athena architects saw Athena not only in reference to the network services of other great research universities such as Stanford, Berkeley, and Carnegie-Mellon, but in relation to the great telecommunications companies, the stock exchanges, and large service organizations. MIT's plans for Athena were thus of considerable interest to leading-edge computer companies that hoped to sell to these markets.

For the Digital Equipment Corporation (DEC), MIT looked like an excellent site in which to develop and test technology that it saw as the basis for its future business. Indeed, the design for Athena crystallized just as DEC lost out to IBM in its bid to provide computers for Carnegie-Mellon's new computing system. From the point of view of Athena's designers, DEC's prospective gift of numerous high-technology workstations precisely matched the specifications of Athena's emerging design and presented a window of opportunity that MIT could not afford to pass by.

Although Athena had been originally conceived as a project to serve the School of Engineering, then-provost Francis Low insisted that it be extended to the institute as a whole.[11] He believed that in an undertaking of this scale there simply could not be "haves" and "have-nots." Seeking to comply with Low's policy decision, Wilson and Dertouzos met with Lewis Branscomb, then IBM's chief scientist, and obtained, with help from him and others at IBM, a second large donation of computers. They decided to divide MIT into two computational worlds: DEC would supply technology for the School of Engineering and IBM would be used for all the rest.[12] Seeking this second gift was to have important consequences. Among other things, we shall see that it created roadblocks to the goal of achieving system coherency.

The original design for a project in the School of Engineering, now expanded to include the whole institute, rested on several sets of assumptions, some stated, some unstated. For example, the network and the sophisticated terminals attached to it were expected to be available and working with reasonable reliability during most of the period 1983–85, the time-frame of what was declared the original Athena experiment. This turned out to be a false assumption. The technology was late in arriving, and the suppliers often changed their plans for the number and types of machines they could deliver. Large numbers of students and faculty were expected to be willing to pay the price of learning to use UNIX, Athena hardware, and the set of languages that Athena approved for the project: C, Fortran, Forth, and LISP. This turned out to be a false assumption. The designers believed that the standards of the coherent system would not seriously constrain the imaginations or excessively challenge the competencies of the faculty members who were expected to develop new "courseware" for the Athena system. This too, turned out to be a false assumption. Finally, it was decided that to create an educational good in the domain of undergraduate teaching, one should exclude graduate students and the use of computers for research purposes. This turned out to be disruptive because profoundly countercultural: MIT routinely integrates graduate students and research into the undergraduate program.

In addition to highly problematic starting assumptions, there were others that spoke directly to the relationship of the network to the educational purposes that were its declared reason for being. These included a model of the "instrumental computer" as an educational tool, a "thousand flowers" view of software development, and a "federal" model of project management. It is to these that we now turn.

## EDUCATION: THE INSTRUMENTAL COMPUTER

Athena's designers conceived of the project as a quest for lost technological leadership in institutional computing and as a large-scale experiment in undergraduate education. But there was a lack of symmetry: the technological goals were concrete and understood in terms of specifics, while the educational goals were somewhat vague and communicated mixed messages. For example, there would often be some talk of doing exciting new things with computers followed by other talk about computers helping us do the old things, just more efficiently.

These mixed messages are apparent in the earliest documents relevant to Athena. For example, in his 1982 report Moses noted that he was "on the whole . . . excited by the range and number of ideas" for educational uses of computers that had been discussed in meetings he had held with interested faculty, although "no revolutionary ways of teaching traditional material were uncovered." Nevertheless, he had faith that once the network was in place and computers more widely available, we would discover revolutionary ways of teaching traditional material, even though he could not say just what these would be. In any case, he said, "If we do not create a relatively uniform environment in which computing is readily available to our faculty and students, no such revolution will likely take place."[13] In other words, the vagueness of Athena's initial educational intentions was justified in principle: given the right tools, MIT faculty and students would invent the educational uses of the computer.

It is significant that Moses wrote here of revolutionary ways of teaching traditional material. Athena's founders did not, for the most part, intend to change MIT's traditional subject matter or central pedagogical assumptions. For example, they thought that MIT students would still learn thermodynamics in the usual ways. But they did expect that the computer would make traditional instructional processes incomparably more efficient. Wilson would later say that the Athena educational experiment consisted of testing whether the computer could be used "to make the teaching of science and engineering more effective and efficient."[14] The computer would be used to shorten the time required for the performance of cumbersome numerical calculations. Students would solve problem sets and submit them to their instructors for correction, all by computer. Computers would facilitate the analysis of complex systems, present graphic displays of systems otherwise hard to visualize, and provide access to large databases.

In sum, Athena's founders thought, for the most part, in terms of the instrumental computer, by which we mean a computer that would be a more efficient educational medium without requiring any change in educational objectives, pedagogies, or ways of understanding subject matter. The computer would be a "useful tool," a phrase that became a universal refrain in the justifications of Athena.

Some of the writings that prepared for Athena's birth presented a somewhat different image of educational computing. The Task Force on Education and Computers, established in 1979 and chaired by Professor Dertouzos, suggested the image of a ladder that would lead from mundane to sophisticated applications of the computer. Text processing and calculation would be at the bottom of the ladder. Graphic models and simulations that would allow students to conduct "what if" experiments were to be in the middle. At the top would be such things as "intelligent tutors" and "higher level languages and programming environments where students can program and experiment with new situations."[15] The applications at the top of the ladder would lead to "paradigms for building a deeper and greater student experience." So it was not surprising that the report concluded that "perhaps the biggest asset of computers for education lies in helping the student gain a *deeper* understanding to traditional modes. . . . The main areas for future use of computers in education involve qualitative changes rather than efficiency improvements."[16]

These suggestions seem to have been overwhelmed by what turned out to be the main and more instrumental thrust of Athena's vision of computers in education. In any case, for some faculty members involved in the early discussions of Athena, even the highest rung of the committee's ladder of applications implied little real change in traditional education. For example, Professor Robert Logcher of the Department of Civil Engineering, who championed the idea of an intelligent tutor, saw it as a knowledge-based system that would relieve overworked faculty of the chore of grading and commenting on the problem sets around which much of MIT's traditional education was based. It was a time saver, not a paradigm changer.

Most often, in the pattern of the early Moses report, hoped-for radical educational changes were simply expected to follow from technical ones. For example, a paper coauthored in 1985 by Steven Lerman, a civil engineering faculty member who was Athena's first director,[17] stated that Athena would "provide students with a deeper understanding of fundamental principles" and "better prepare them to utilize the techniques and methods of the practicing scientist and engineer of the future," going beyond "mere calculation" to "discover along the way many more innovative ways to employ computers effectively in the educational process." But once the authors had boldly announced their vision of computer-based education, they did not go on to say how the required changes might actually be brought about. At the conclusion of their article they turned instead to a detailed technical description of the Athena system. Alternative educational ideas, evoked as possibilities in a few early documents, became minor themes in a story line dominated by the idea of the computer that helps you to do the old things more efficiently.

## SOFTWARE DEVELOPMENT: A THOUSAND FLOWERS

Even in the report of the 1979 ad hoc committee, Dertouzos recommended the support of experiments in educational computing, and Athena's eventual design, as described in Lerman's 1984 "Introduction to Project Athena," included some $12 million over the five years of the project to support educational experiments.[18] Athena had a clear model of the form of such experiments: the MIT faculty would develop instructional software to be used in teaching traditional MIT subject matter. Professor Logcher, looking back on the early days of Athena in a later, October 1987, interview, noted that the idea was that "there are a lot of bright people around here and if you give them some resources, they're going to do interesting things. That's MIT's attitude towards a lot of things."

In this way, Athena's design rested on the belief that, once the network was in place and discretionary resources were made available, a thousand flowers would bloom. It rested on the belief that substantial numbers of MIT faculty would want to invest their time in the development of educational software, and that they would be able to develop it without detracting substantially from their main research pursuits. They would do it, so to speak, "with their left hands." Finally, it rested on the assumption that their imaginations would not be constrained nor their competencies excessively stretched by the challenge of developing new courseware within the parameters of the coherent system. All of these assumptions would be sharply challenged, as we shall see, in the later phases of Athena's development. At the beginning, however, they seemed obviously true to Athena's engineer-architects.

## ATHENA'S ADMINISTRATION: THE FEDERAL MODEL

The development and maintenance of the network, the development and enforcement of standards for coherence, and the conduct of experiments in educational computing all would require an administrative structure. In his 1979 report, Dertouzos had argued for a mix of decentralization and centralization, stressing that the maintenance of common standards of hardware and software would require central administrative control, whereas a network-based laboratory for experiments in educational computing would require flexible administration and local ownership and control of computers. Moses, in his 1984 "Report on the Computing Environment at MIT in 1990," recommended creating a central organizational unit to oversee certain campuswide information services that are "near natural monopolies," and for which there are important economies of scale.

In the administrative structure eventually adopted by Project Athena, an Athena executive committee, under Dean Wilson, became the principal vehicle for oversight of Project Athena, and a central Athena office was created, under Lerman, to fulfill a variety of functions. It would provide hardware and software, develop software tools for system users, modify the operating system, install and maintain approved software languages, develop software network interfaces, and so on. For all of these purposes, Athena's central office grew to include some fifteen to twenty technical staff members, in addition to technical staff supplied by DEC and IBM.

In order to manage allocation of the funds it expected to raise for support of faculty development of educational software, Athena adopted a model reminiscent of federal research and development programs. Two faculty resource allocation committees were to put out requests for proposals, select projects for funding, and monitor project performance. Athena hoped that its "thousand flowers" would be elicited and selected through a centrally administered peer-review system—interestingly, one that bypassed the departments as centers of institutional initiative and decision making. Again, there were critical tacit assumptions: faculty would not be put off by a selection process staffed by members of other disciplines than their own and would willingly accept a central administrative structure that bypassed their own departments.

## ATHENA'S CHALLENGERS

From the earliest days, Athena had challengers as well as advocates. One group consisted of MIT faculty who were strong advocates of educational computing but highly critical of Athena's style of pursuing it. They did not see the future in terms of a unified computer environment, as all of Athena's founders did, and they did not see the computer primarily in terms of the more efficient teaching of traditional subject matters, a view held by at least some of Athena's founders and emphasized in Athena's actual development. Rather, this first group of challengers saw the computer as a highly personalized conversational partner, an incubator of microworlds for the conduct of thought experiments, and, in Professor Seymour Papert's words, a new repertoire of "things to think with." Rather than focus on the ways in which computers could make traditional teaching more efficient, these faculty members thought that Athena should emphasize the creation of computer environments where students and faculty might come to see and do things in new ways.

Additionally, there were some who challenged Athena's starting assumptions about technology and education. Professor Joseph Weizenbaum, a computer scientist, and Professor Kenneth Keniston, a psychologist, stressed the opportunity cost of the Athena initiative and argued that one must not confuse technical and educational sophistication. It should not be assumed, they said, that a leading-edge distributed computer network would also be leading-edge in its educational consequences. One of us, Turkle, questioned whether the emphasis on a coherent system would conflict with the richness and diversity of the computer cultures that were spontaneously arising within MIT. She stressed the computer's ability to contribute to, rather than constrain, the natural pluralism of the MIT community. She believed that computers could facilitate a range of learning styles among MIT students and faculty, and argued that the advantages of a uniform and centrally imposed computer environment needed to be carefully weighed against its costs.

Finally, Professor Harold Abelson, a computer scientist, was a forceful and persistent critic of what he saw as Athena's overriding technological emphasis. He believed, as he wrote in a 1985 memorandum to the Project Athena Study Group, that

> the major thing we need to keep in focus is a view of Athena as an educational experiment. This needs to be emphasized because the great majority of current Athena activity is concerned, not with education, but with building the technological infrastructure to support "the Athena experiment." My guess is that if we went out at present to interview people working with Athena, we would mostly get reactions to the current state of the implementation, the current prob-

lems of building the system, and so on. So we need to put priority on framing the issues in such a way that Athena activities continue to be viewed in an educational context.

Abelson believed that the main significance of educational computing would lie not in relieving the drudgery of number crunching or the burden of correcting students' problem sets, but in the transformation of subject matter. Therefore, he thought, Athena's educational impact should be mainly judged by the "curricular shifts [that] have come about as a consequence of Athena, both within specific subjects as well as across departments and programs."[19]

Although they came to their criticisms of Athena from different starting points, all of Athena's challengers shared Abelson's skepticism about what they saw as the technocentrism of the Athena design. They believed that educational considerations should drive the design of Athena's technological and institutional arrangements, not the other way around, and that Athena's experiments should be designed, at least initially, with an eye to the *educational* questions raised by the computer. These included: How do computers enter into the process of thinking, learning, and teaching? Specifically, how might computers change how faculty and students think about their subject matter?

For Turkle, especially, the computer was more than an instrumental machine. She saw it as having powerful subjective effects, changing, for example, how people saw themselves as learners. She thought there should be an attempt not only to chart Athena's educational effectiveness in teaching the old things in a new way, but to study if and how the system afforded new learning experiences. For this, it would be necessary to study the experiences of faculty and students as they used the new system.

This last point, the idea of educational research and evaluation, became a lightning rod for controversy. Neither Athena's designers nor the two MIT provosts who approved Athena were enthusiastic about a specifically educational evaluation. Indeed, when serious evaluation of student experience with Athena was proposed—by Professor Keniston, in faculty discussions held during Athena's design phase, or by Schon and Turkle during the discussions of their early reports on Athena—the idea was actively resisted.

Although the word "hypothesis" was widely used in conjunction with the idea of Athena as an educational experiment, there was little or no discussion of hypothesis testing. Athena's founders did not propose to study how students actually used educational software. Rather, they took the educational effectiveness of their proposed innovations for granted. "We just wanted to get something in place," Professor Logcher said in an interview conducted in 1989. "We were convinced that the group hypothesis would be so *obvious* [our emphasis] that no one would question it. . . . That's typical around here. . . . These are engineers as opposed to social scientists. . . . There was no concern that I saw of actually going through a formal activity of an evaluation process." In his preamble to the Report on the Computing Environment at MIT in 1984, Professor Moses wrote simply, "We assume that Project Athena will be successful."

Behind the reticence about evaluation was the belief, widespread among the engineers involved in the design of Athena, that there were no educational first principles and no methods of educational research capable of providing valid information about the effectiveness of educational computing. So it was not surprising that John Deutch, who succeeded Francis Low as provost, saw no reason to fund an evaluation of Athena. He thought it would be unlikely to yield useful knowledge and might actually undermine the enthusiasm essential to Athena's success. Common sense was a better alternative, he thought, because the effectiveness or ineffectiveness of educational software should be easy to detect. As Professor Moses exclaimed in a 1989 interview, "If [the software's] effects are not dramatically obvious, don't do it!"

## THE EARLY DEBATES

Very little real communication took place between Athena's champions and their challengers. The two groups thought and argued from different frames, and because the design for Athena was of a piece with MIT's traditional view of itself and what Weizenbaum and others critical of MIT had called its "religion," the early debates over Athena were conducted as though between an orthodox and a heretical community, between partisans and critics of "the MIT way."

For the champions, the imperative of technological leadership in computing systems and the attractions of "coherence" were axiomatic. For the challengers, these tenets were at best open to debate and at worst a cover for a technically inspired engineering adventure that some thought had little educational focus or little to do with the computer's real educational potential. For Athena's champions, educational evaluation was irrelevant and an intellectual charade; for Athena's challengers, traditional educational evaluation might not be the right idea, but some attempt to understand the impact of this new, intensified computer presence was essential.

Moreover, the challengers and engineer-architects each tended to see the other as a self-appointed elite that threatened to usurp control. For the challengers, the threat came from engineers driven by technological rather than educational vision. For the engineer-architects, it was the humanists, social scientists, and what they called "educationists" who were threatening progress in the name of a nonexistent educational theory. Professor Dertouzos lumped these categories together and called them "humano-romantics," good humoredly contrasting them with "techno-romantics" like himself. In a later elaboration of these terms,[20] Dertouzos pointed out that when "confronted with impossible questions," both groups surrender to their beliefs—"the first, in the omniscience of the human spirit; the second . . . in the truth of science and the miracles of technology." "Devoid of any relevant facts," he went on to say, "either sect is a prisoner of their belief systems, equally encumbered or liberated, depending on the observer's religious affiliation!"

In addition to the champions and challengers, there was a third group among the MIT faculty that might best be called "reticents." This group included some individuals who saw the computer as irrelevant to the real work of education, and others who saw themselves as users rather than developers of existing software. Some reticents had already created computer environments in their departments or laboratories, which were scheduled to be cleared away to make room for Athena. Many of them resented—in silence, for the most part—Athena's intent to root out these settings as though they were slums.

As it turned out, the challengers were easily defeated by Athena's designers, who had the support of the central MIT administration and who represented MIT's most powerful school and department. Athena's design bore few if any signs of influence by the challengers, most of whom either dropped out or were relegated to the sidelines. Later on, however, the challengers' voices would be heard again, and MIT's central administration, whose role until now had been relatively minor, would re-enter the process to negotiate among conflicting views of Athena.

## IMPLEMENTATION (1983–86)

Project Athena began operation in 1983 with Steven Lerman as director. Because shipments of advanced workstations were delayed, the project first relied on IBM PCs and older time-sharing systems. By 1985–86, however, Athena had introduced individual workstations, interconnected and supported by numerous machines dedicated to management and file service. By fall 1986, what Lerman called "the first true workstation cluster" had opened for public use; and by 1987 no fewer than four hundred workstations were distributed across twenty clusters, a few faculty and staff offices, and selected student living groups.

By fall 1986, student utilization of Athena was high and steadily increasing. By fall 1989, over 80 percent of undergraduates and about 50 percent of graduate students had Project Athena accounts.[21] Although Dean Wilson had been able to raise only about $12 million of the $20 million for educational projects that he had originally projected—an outcome he found profoundly frustrating—new computer-based curricula were being developed in about fifty subjects, including foreign languages, chemistry, civil engineering, aeronautics and astronautics, mechanical engineering, materials sciences, and architectural design. Eleven of these had been designated by the Athena office as "flagship projects."

In spite of these tangible accomplishments, Athena's implementation ran into a series of unexpected troubles from the point of view of her engineer architects. These ranged from technical delays and difficulties and an unexpected and disappointing pattern of student use, to outright hostility from the School of Science.

## TECHNICAL DELAYS AND DIFFICULTIES

The advanced computers expected from DEC and IBM were two years late. The temporary systems were pieced together, programs were bug-ridden, and computers were constantly crashing. The flavor of this period is eloquently conveyed in a letter written in 1987 by a programmer in one of Athena's software development projects. "Basically," she wrote,

> the worst part has been that in trying to use the computer with students, almost nothing has been even reasonably reliable, ever. Students regularly encountered problems with the system: the computers were down, the terminals were not functioning properly, or something had been changed without any notification. Lecture demos would be planned only to find that the system driving them had been modified and wouldn't work. The programs we wrote were based on graphics and systems libraries which either changed themselves or performed differently as the hardware was changed. Thus we would find that previously developed programs would no longer work properly in the current environment. We not only couldn't rely on maintaining what we had done, but we were given almost no concrete information in order to make future plans. Everything was

always in flux, contradictory rumors abounded and little could be counted on.

These conditions were in part due to delays in the delivery of equipment, changing expectations about equipment, and technical problems with equipment once it arrived. They were also due to Athena's decision to make improving and updating the technical infrastructure an overriding priority even when it meant throwing curriculum developers and users into confusion.

Students were the most conspicuous victims of Athena's instability, suffering most immediately from its frequent crashes, bugs, and unannounced changes. Sometimes whole classes would groan audibly at the very mention of the word "Athena." Given the love-hate relationship that MIT's undergraduates have traditionally maintained with the institute (MIT is commonly referred to as "this place"), Athena came to be seen as one more unnecessarily inflicted evil.

Some faculty members also began to grumble openly. They, too, resented Athena's unreliability and the inconvenience caused by its recurrent changes. As one faculty member put it, "My computer knowledge is about to become obsolete for the sixth time!" In an environment where time is the most precious commodity, many faculty members simply chose not to use the Athena system.

## Faculty Disappointment with Students' Use of Athena

While students complained about what happened to them when they tried to use Athena, many of MIT's engineering faculty were shocked at *how* students used it. By 1985 it was apparent that approximately 70 percent of the student use of Athena was for things that the Athena planners had pretty much written out of the project as too "mundane"—things like word processing, electronic mail, and computer games. Reactions to this state of affairs among the engineering faculty ranged from amusement to horror. Had MIT procured $50 million dollars worth of equipment and engineered the most sophisticated online time-sharing network of its kind in order to support uses that could have been served as well or better by Macintosh computers or IBM PCs at a small fraction of Athena's cost?

## Disappointing Faculty Response

When Athena asked faculty for proposals to develop new courseware, the response was disappointing. Although some 111 proposals were funded in Athena's first five years, their quality fell well below the expectations of Athena's architects. With few exceptions a small number of devoted computer champions, together with their younger faculty protégés, made the serious investments in developing new courseware. In the metaphor of the Athena architects, fewer "bright people" had come forward to do "interesting things" than had been expected. The thousand flowers metaphor began to seem hollow.

## Lack of Enthusiasm for Educational Computing

Our case study work in the MIT departments of physics, civil engineering, chemistry, and architecture revealed that some reactions to Athena were really general reactions to the idea of educational computing. For example, some faculty members feared that students who came to rely on the computer's virtuosity in performing complex calculations would lose contact with the reasoning that underlay those calculations, and that the faculty would then become unable to detect and correct the students' misunderstandings. Some faculty members and students saw the computer as a threat to cherished activities that they saw as being at the heart of their disciplines. Architects, for example, feared the computer's infringement on the work of drawing. Some chemistry professors resented the idea that computers might enter the lecture hall and interfere with their presentation of chemical theory. Professors of civil and mechanical engineering saw computers as subverting the delicate work of structural analysis. Wherever such sacred space existed in a discipline, some of its practitioners feared the intrusions of the computer.

## Restrictions Inherent in "Coherence"

On a more general level, faculty bristled at the constraints imposed by the demands of the "coherent" system. For example, there was a widespread belief that they could receive Athena funding only if they used Athena-approved machines, computer languages, and the UNIX operating system that often seemed cumbersome and hard to learn. Many faculty members continued to favor Macintosh computers or IBM PCs, and wished to work in languages such as Logo or BASIC rather than, for example, the Athena-approved C. A number chose to bypass Athena and develop computer-based curricula on their own. In fact, Athena did fund some projects that did not play by the rules, but a significant portion of faculty found that the hassle of pleading for an exception was simply too great.

## TWO CLASSES OF PEOPLE

Because of its technical emphasis, it was inevitable that Athena tended to see MIT as a two-class system. The "higher" class, which it favored, was composed of the computer sophisticates, who liked to use UNIX and UNIX-based features such as the X Window System, which permits flexible textual and graphic interaction with many simultaneous tasks. The "lower" class consisted of computer novices, who found UNIX unmanageable, or other faculty members, who considered Athena's advanced features unnecessary to their preferred applications. In the Athena culture, the second group felt devalued. Among humanities professors, for example, Athena reinforced a long-held belief that they were the institute's poor relations.

Resentment over Athena's two-class system was not limited to the humanities and social sciences. It was evident, too, in the School of Science and extended even to some parts of the School of Engineering. Early in Athena's history, when Dean Wilson urged his engineering faculty to come up with more exciting proposals for new courseware, a professor of chemical engineering explained in a widely disseminated memorandum that the Athena community contained two very different subgroups—the "computer community" and the rest of the engineers who wanted only to "teach non-computer engineering with the aid of computers." The latter had little interest in Athena's technical niceties, he thought; they only wanted workable software and had no interest in developing it for themselves. This memorandum reflected a feeling, shared by many silent faculty members who resisted or were indifferent to Athena, that Athena had been undertaken by a small, elite group, without the participation or approval of the larger MIT community.

## MIT's INCENTIVE SYSTEM

Even the long-term champions of computers and education were dissatisfied with Athena, which they came to see as a trap for their younger faculty protégés. The history of Athena dramatized that software development, far from being an "exercise for the left hand," was an extremely demanding task. MIT's promotion and tenure process focuses single-mindedly on front-running research in a discipline, and the development of educational software did not count in this system. Faculty members who chose to devote themselves to educational software ran a great professional risk and would find it almost impossible to qualify for advancement.

Moreover, even if software development were to be accepted as relevant disciplinary research, where were the senior faculty who could help their younger colleagues turn that activity into acceptable research papers? Who could read and criticize such papers? It was clear that younger faculty hoping for tenure would invest in Athena at their peril.

## THE SPECIAL CASE OF THE SCHOOL OF SCIENCE

Most of MIT's scientists responded with indifference to Athena's blandishments. As Joel Moses ruefully expressed it in an interview in 1989, "We failed to win the hearts and minds of our colleagues in the School of Science." Indeed, Athena made some science faculty members angry. The Department of Physics, in particular, was a center of resistance to Athena. Some physicists had no use at all for computers in education, finding them a threat to "real physics." Professor Victor Weisskopf, a distinguished member of the physics faculty, was famous for saying, "When you show me this result, the computer understands the answer, but I don't think *you* understand the answer." Other physicists who did want to use the computer in education, to connect personal computers to laboratory instruments in order to speed up data processing and analysis or to write a computer-based physics text, found their initiatives stymied by Athena's policies, in particular those that restricted choice of machine, operating system, and computer language.

In looking at faculty reticence toward Athena, a distinction between "announced policy" and "policy in practice" is useful. For example, the Committee on Resource Allocation that oversaw Athena grants to the School of Science refused to provide support for faculty salaries during the academic year—apparently because Professor Deutch, then dean of the School of Science, worried that some faculty members might use Athena monies to avoid their obligation to support part of their salaries through externally funded research.

Athena's refusal to support the salary of Professor Robert Hulsizer, a highly respected member of the physics faculty who had proposed to devote his final years at the institute to an in-depth reworking of the physics curriculum using computers, became an issue that angered that department as a whole. The physicists took it as a sign of Athena's arrogance and insensitivity to their needs. Their reaction puzzled Dean Wilson, who was unaware of the Resource Allocation Committee's action within the School of Science. Wilson protested that the Athena Executive Committee, which he headed, had an explicit policy of supporting the faculty's academic-year salary. What else, after all, would curriculum development funds support? Yet the physicists' belief that

Athena would not support faculty salaries persisted long after the School of Science's Committee on Resource Allocation had reversed its position. The combination of the technical restrictions (the sense that in order to get things done one had to "fight" with Athena) and the sense that Athena had been unreasonable, shortsighted, and bureaucratic in the Hulsizer case, caused a few physicists who were actually computer enthusiasts to turn sour about Athena. They came to feel that Athena was preventing, not helping, them from making advances in educational computing.

The persistence of the physicists' belief that Athena did not fund faculty salaries may have reflected what was by then an entrenched hostility toward Athena. Many of the physicists saw Athena's regulations as a form of censorship jeopardizing their academic independence. Additionally, they bitterly resented the very idea of engineers trying to tell scientists what to do.

## "ATHENA IS NOT ABOUT EDUCATION"

As Athena matured, in the period 1984–87, both faculty members and students increasingly voiced the opinion that Athena was not about education but about technology. In chemistry and mechanical engineering, for example, the faculty was astonished that, although computer graphics had been identified from the outset as a major educational opportunity, Athena had failed to develop a usable graphics package. Some faculty bitterly noted that Athena meetings were wholly taken up with technical matters rather than with questions of education. More and more faculty members began to pick up Professor Abelson's original concern that Athena had never addressed the fundamental questions posed by the educational uses of the computer. Why, they asked, was the project being presented to the world as an experiment in education?

## ANALYZING THE CONFLICTS OF ATHENA'S SECOND STAGE

Athena provoked conflict for two main reasons. First, once Athena moved out into the larger MIT environment, the various MIT audiences saw it in the light of their own interests and frames. Indeed, the conflicts that followed Athena's early implementation reflected quite precisely the internal divisions of the MIT social world—for example, divisions among the schools and departments, between graduate and undergraduate students, between computer enthusiasts and computer skeptics. Athena's presence simply made these divisions more visible.

Second, Athena provoked conflict because of contradictions inherent in its original design—contradictions that were masked, in part, by untested assumptions about how Athena would be seen and used.

To begin with, Athena had committed itself to its technology (including hardware, operating systems, and languages) before its educational programs evolved. As a matter of principle, it had justified its commitment to "technology first" by its assumption that innovative educational developments would arise only after the technologically sophisticated network had been put in place, and because it had been put in place.

However, relatively few faculty members were tempted to develop new computer-based curricula; many preferred machines, operating systems, or languages that Athena prohibited in the name of coherence, and those who tried to use the growing commercial stock of educational programs found they could not do so on Athena's UNIX-based network. Hence, many faculty members felt their intellectual creativity was constrained by the very system that was supposed to liberate it.

As a large-scale intervention in classrooms and laboratories, Athena's success was bound to depend on its reliability and stability. But as an enterprise committed to technological development, necessarily reliant on continuing experimentation, Athena was bound to produce, at least in its early years, an environment of unreliability and instability. For many faculty members and students, the promise of future benefits was simply not worth the trouble of dealing with Athena's present difficulties.

Finally, in spite of its espoused commitment to educational innovation, Athena emphasized computer applications that exploited the technically sophisticated features of its machines, treating as mundane and second class the educational purposes for which most students and faculty actually wanted to use it.

How can we best understand these contradictions? One interpretation, frequently voiced at MIT in the late 1980s, was that Athena gave lip service to educational objectives but was really, from start to finish, a technological adventure shaped by MIT's close alliance with the computer industry. For some, this interpretation implied a certain cynicism in the insistent and continuing statements by Athena's engineer-architects that they were committed to the educational purposes of their experiment.

A more plausible interpretation is that its founders' strong belief in and commitment to technology blinded them to the contradictions inherent in Athena's design. It kept them, too, from listening to negative messages from the field that would have alerted them to these contradictions. Athena's engineer-architects shared a faith that educational benefits would inevitably flow from the world's most advanced institutional computing system. Their faith caused them to misread the needs of their student market and their faculty colleagues, and the degree to which continual upgrading of the Athena network would interfere with its educational purposes. Finally, their belief in cutting-edge technology caused them to resist the idea that competing (and, for them, "lesser") technologies such as the Macintosh computer and the DOS operating system would flourish, adapt to competition, and become the basis for new educational software.

Similarly, the founders' belief in the technical beauty of the coherent Athena system blinded them to the multiplicity and diversity of computer cultures that both existed and were growing up at MIT and, therefore, to the desirability of decentralized policies for the choice of hardware, software, and operating systems. As a result of their belief that MIT faculty would find courseware development "an exercise for the left hand," they did not appreciate the resistance many faculty members actually felt toward developing new computer programs. Their mistaken belief grew out of a confidence in the natural superiority of MIT citizens in all things technical, a confidence that the normal rules would not apply to this population. Their tendency to equate technical with educational sophistication also prevented them from considering the possibility that sophisticated technology might yield results that were educationally mundane. Indeed, they were not able to consider the possibility that mundane technology might produce significant educational results. More fundamentally, their overriding faith in the socially beneficial consequences of advancing information technology blinded them to the possibility that the most advanced distributed computing system might not stimulate educational innovation at all.

The fact that these misreadings persisted for a number of years, in the face of mounting counterevidence from the field, testifies to the power of the founders' faith. That faith had been challenged directly, by Professor Abelson, in the debates about Athena held at MIT in the early 1980s. However, for Athena's engineer-architects, it was the challengers, skeptics, and resisters who were blind to the beauty, power, and benefit of the coherent system. As Professor Moses was still saying nearly ten years later, "They just didn't see the beauty of the idea!"

## POLICY ADJUSTMENT (1987–89)

By January 1987, as the voices of disaffection grew louder, MIT's administration began to face up to Athena's long-term financial implications. Originally, Athena was to have run for five years as a separately funded project and was then to be incorporated into MIT's normal budget. In its first phase, supported mainly by gifts from DEC and IBM and curriculum development grants from other firms, Athena had placed only a modest demand on MIT's general funds. Now, however, Dean Wilson estimated that Athena's regular future operation would cost MIT between $2 million and $5 million per year, the equivalent of earnings on some $100 million of endowment. The replacement costs for equipment, turning over every five years, would come to an additional $1 million to $2 million per year. It had become clear that MIT would have to support whatever additional curriculum development it chose to undertake out of its own funds; industry resources for this purpose had been hard to get to begin with and now seemed to have dried up. In the light of these hard facts, Provost Deutch asked Wilson to come up with alternative programs and financing strategies for Athena's future.

By 1987, doubts about Athena's future and the fallout from the disappointments of Athena's early days had taken their toll on the morale of Athena's technical staff. Some had already quit; others were threatening to do so. So both budgetary and human resource concerns weighed heavily on Wilson and the Athena Executive Committee as they became increasingly aware of the conflicts Athena had stirred up within MIT.

### THE PASG STUDY OF ATHENA

In 1986, Provost Low had appointed a faculty evaluation committee, chaired by Dean John DeMonchaux of the School of Architecture and Planning, but when Professor Deutch replaced Low as provost, he feared that an evaluation of Athena might undermine the enthusiasm of the founders, which he saw as essential to Athena's success. Only at the insistence of Margaret MacVicar, the dean for undergraduate education, did Deutch reluctantly agree to make available a nonrenewable grant of $100 thousand for Athena's evaluation.

Dean MacVicar, who was to play an increasingly important role in Athena's development, was a physicist best known for having conceived and built up the Undergraduate Research Opportunities Program (UROP), perhaps the most durable and significant of the educational innovations MIT had undertaken in the 1960s. She had a deep understanding of how MIT worked as an institution and a long-standing commitment to undergraduate education. To her it would seem natural that Athena should be assessed as an educational experiment.

Several members of Dean DeMonchaux's group had participated in the early Athena debates, and some had also been associated with MIT's Division for Study and Research in Education, a home for educational research within MIT that ironically had been abolished just as Athena started up. With strictly limited funding and ambivalent administration support, the group was reluctant to attempt a full-scale evaluation of Athena. Preferring to undertake studies of Athena, they chose to call themselves the Project Athena Study Group (PASG). However, they had a hard time agreeing on just what to study. After about a year, Dean MacVicar called on the committee either to define its studies or dissolve itself, and PASG proposed three studies: an archival history of Athena's early years, a study of Project Athena in MIT student living groups, and a series of case studies of Athena-supported projects in four MIT departments. This last was led by Professors Schon and Turkle.

By January 1987, the case study team presented a first working paper to its steering committee. It contained a preliminary sketch of its findings, including a report on the contradictions in Athena's design already described. The steering committee included Professors Dertouzos and MacVicar, and the working paper was promptly transmitted to Dean Wilson. It immediately provoked stormy reactions.

Dertouzos told Schon and Turkle, "The bugs you have detected are of the *essence* of MIT." The working paper referred to Athena's treatment of the thousand flowers as a "Darwinian" strategy. This, Dertouzos said, was a criticism that assumed a competing, coherent theory of education that did not exist. "The MIT way," on the contrary, was to "throw things at people and wait to see who can swim upstream, trusting that the brightest people will produce . . . the crazy ideas that make MIT great!" As against a coherent theory of education, Dertouzos believed in the beauty of a coherent technical system that would enable a thousand educational flowers to bloom.

Dean Wilson, for his part, was incredulous that he could be seen as failing to promote Athena's educational purposes. Had he not struggled to raise the funds for curriculum development? Had he not made it clear, in word and deed, that he stood fully behind Athena's educational purposes? Moreover, he resented criticism from the nonengineering schools about Athena's design. In many ways, Wilson felt a victim of his colleagues' short historical memory. His design concept for Athena had been built around the needs of the engineering school. He had never sought to serve other constitutencies. When Provost Low had insisted, the project had accommodated the *administration's* demands that it serve all of MIT. It was unfair to criticize Athena for not adequately serving these other communities.

Dean MacVicar felt that Athena had polarized the institute. Francis Low had insisted that Wilson broaden Athena to include all of MIT in order to avoid haves and have-nots. Yet in practice Athena had created a two-class system, roughly corresponding to enfranchised engineers and disenfranchised others, thereby producing what MacVicar called a "positively explosive climate of anger." She thought that Athena's designers misread what they had created because they saw it only from the perspective of the enfranchised. "They thought they had an elephant," she said, "and it turned out to be a giraffe!"[22]

The PASG study was only one of several channels for negative reactions to Athena that were reaching Athena's decision makers in January and early spring 1987. There were, as well, the student press, the informal comments of students and faculty, and Dean MacVicar's independent sounding of MIT opinion. Through such channels Athena's designers learned that they had alienated large segments of their market, and that if they persisted in their policies they would probably stir up enough political opposition to cause Athena's demise.

Despite anger and hurt feelings, Dean Wilson and his colleagues heard and responded to these messages. Findings of the PASG study that had seemed incendiary when they were first presented—such as the need for greater decentralization of Athena's management, permission for students and faculty to use the technology for technically mundane uses (word processing, electronic mail), and relaxation of the constraints of the coherent system—became accepted in the Athena Executive Committee's discussions as obvious changes to be implemented. The committee developed a new strategy of accommodation, softening the policies that seemed to have provoked the greatest resistance to Athena while taking steps to insure the survival of what it saw as most central to the Athena program. This strategy of "sacrifice the periphery, salvage the core" was pursued in stages.

First, the executive committee decided to extend Athena for a second three-year term, arguing, as Dean Wilson put it, that the extension would be necessary in order to "complete the educational experiment." Crucial to this decision was the fact that Athena was still far from having achieved its announced technical objectives. Only a small fraction of the originally intended workstations were in place (and most of these for less than a year), the more significant curriculum development projects were still in their infancy, and discontent with Athena was high.

Athena was continued, at least in part, because it could not have been discontinued at that point without an implicit declaration of failure.

The next period of roughly six months (from January to June 1987) came to be known as "Athena's learning curve." While Professor Lerman and Dean Wilson were negotiating the new three-year extension with DEC and IBM, and Lerman headed a committee to plan Athena's next phase, Athena's managers looked for ways to accept what they felt they could not change. They reformulated students' mundane uses of Athena as acceptable as a first stage of involvement with the computer or as one element of a pattern of demand that also included more sophisticated applications. Thus reformulated, mundane computer use was more than tolerable, it was desirable. Widespread faculty disinterest in developing new courseware could be accepted if the metaphor of a thousand flowers were dropped and the focus shifted to the flagship projects. They made peace with the idea that most faculty members who wanted to use computers in their teaching would rely on commercially available software.

At the same time, there was some softening of the policies and practices that had most irritated faculty and students. Proposals that had been rejected because they used computer languages such as BASIC or Logo that were not "Athena-approved" got a second look, and many were now supported as exceptions to a too-strict rule. Athena no longer rejected proposals for support of faculty salaries during the academic year. In response to faculty's irritation with Athena's insistence on separating educational and research uses of the computer and undergraduate from graduate education, Athena announced that some additional workstations would be placed in faculty offices, where graduate students would of course have access to them.

Even in the reticent and bristling Department of Physics, the new accommodations were perceived as soothing. In 1988, the new chair of the Physics Department, Professor Jerome Friedman, remarked at a faculty meeting that "Athena had a learning curve, and I think they have a different policy now which is a much more reasonable one."

There were, of course, limits to how much leeway Athena had for its new policy of accommodation. Budgetary constraints dictated that the "wiring" of faculty offices to enable them to house Athena workstations would go very slowly. The new contract with DEC and IBM would leave little room for educational expenditures, with the result that Athena would devote most of its resources to installing and maintaining equipment and ensuring the smooth operation of the network. Policy reforms, such as the establishment of an educational outreach group, would be ignored, for the most part, in the practice of Athena's second phase. Nevertheless, certain of Athena's spending priorities did change. Recognizing that faculty and students were upset and genuinely disrupted by Athena's unreliability, Lerman decided in the last days of his tenure as director to concentrate on making the system more reliable and easier to use.

Turning the pejorative distinction between "two classes of people" into a basis for constructive action, Athena's policy makers proposed a new model of Athena as a two-tiered system. Faculty outside the School of Engineering who were interested in computers and education would be brought under Athena's umbrella. They would be accepted as "valuable and legitimate," in the words of the report Lerman wrote for the planning committee.[23] Also, they would receive certain network services. Nevertheless, their interests would be categorized as "lower end," in contrast to the "higher-end" uses of engineering workstations.

In order to make the two-tiered system work, Athena's architects knew they had to address a technical issue that had long been controversial: the question of Athena's operating system. DOS had shown resiliency and commanded faculty loyalty; UNIX had not overtaken it as rapidly as expected, nor had software applications capable of running on UNIX proliferated at the expected rate.[24] Moreover, during the early Athena years, the Apple Macintosh had grown in popularity in academic circles. It had become a major environment for commercially available educational software whose importance to MIT faculty Athena had underestimated. Such developments had taken Athena's architects by surprise; they were left with a technically advanced system that could not run most commercially available educational software. To solve this problem they proposed an immediately effective transition phase of operations during which there would be *two* Athena systems. One would be UNIX-based and dedicated to higher-end computing, primarily in the School of Engineering. The second, mainly DOS-based, would include the hardware and software preferred by faculty and students in the other schools. UNIX would be made easier to use, and software for converting DOS to UNIX would be devised.

During the transition phase it was anticipated that the cost of powerful computers would drop so that more MIT students could, perhaps with some subsidy, purchase their own. Within a few years, ownership of individual machines would become close to universal. By the end of the transition phase, Athena would become a complete computer utility—in Professor Dertouzos' words, "a telephone system." It would be physically integrated with MIT's new digital phone system, and anyone would be able, by plugging into it, to gain access to a range of Athena services, and certainly to the full range of lower-end services.

With their plans for a two-phase approach to a two-tiered system, Athena's designers believed they found a way to preserve the core of their original idea. By giving up what they now saw as the "romantic" extension of a full range of Athena services to all the schools, the "pure" vision of Athena could be frankly reserved for the School of Engineering, as its architects had originally intended. The wishes of the other schools would be respected until new technology or educational priorities led them to catch up.

## REFRAMING THE PROBLEM (1989–90)

In June 1988, Steven Lerman resigned as Athena's director and was replaced by Earl Murman, who had been a member of the Athena Executive Committee, chair of the faculty committee that reviewed curriculum proposals for the School of Engineering, and leader of Athena's flagship project in the Department of Aeronautics and Astronautics.

With new management, a new plan of action, and a new contract with DEC and IBM, the Athena system began to flourish in its new direction. By spring 1989, about six thousand different individuals had used Athena at least once, and over 90 percent of all MIT undergraduates used it on a regular basis, most often for word processing, electronic mail, and games. In addition, over fifty MIT subjects made some use of Athena each semester in classroom lectures, demonstrations, or problem sets. In order to handle the rising demand for its services, Athena streamlined its operation. It halved its original goal of two thousand workstations and concentrated on making the network services operate smoothly.

DEC, along with many other companies with UNIX products, had now commercialized several of the main technological developments stimulated by Athena, including the X Windows System and the Kerberos authentication system.[25] These and other Athena-based developments were reported to be major sources of new business for the computer industry. Considerable progress had been made toward creating the complete computer utility. It was now possible to use many different machines, including the Mac II, as Athena workstations. Lower-end terminals were installed in Athena clusters to provide for mundane uses. It was now possible to gain access to electronic mail by dialing up Athena through a modem and a dedicated phone line, or by plugging into a digital phone on the MIT system. It would soon be possible, via Ethernet hook-ups, for students and faculty to plug into the full range of Athena services, including graphics and X Windows, from remote terminals. Interestingly, one aspect of the complete computer utility has never developed as planned: UNIX has not become easier to use, but rather, in the words of Dertouzos, "has gotten harder and harder to use as its functionality increased. It is now the kitchen sink!"[26]

All of these successes were advanced by the Athena office as signs of educational success. They were also advanced as surrogates for any more systematic evaluation of Athena's educational impact.

It remained the case that very little new educational software was being developed by MIT faculty. With a few exceptions, mostly in the School of Engineering, emphasis had shifted to the use of such commercially available software packages as matrix-processing systems and spreadsheets. However, from the point of view of Athena's leadership, there was now considerable evidence that MIT's lost leadership in institutional computing had been restored. Thousands of visitors flocked to inspect Athena. Universities around the world monitored its progress, and its architecture and network technology were widely copied not only by universities but by a wide range of commercial enterprises.

During Athena's second phase, the administration established the new Institute Committee on Academic Computation for the 1990s and Beyond, with Dean MacVicar as its chair. Faced with the budgetary implications of a long-term future without external donor support, the administration, in the person of Dean MacVicar, took visible leadership of a group that included representatives of all the schools and of the undergraduate and graduate student populations. Athena's founders were represented by only one individual, Professor Dertouzos.

The committee's attention focused on MIT's total expenditure for computation in research, administration, and education, an expenditure that amounted to some $20 million in a total institute budget of about $400 million. Athena's expenditures came to about $6.2 million, including a yearly contribution of $2.4 million from MIT's general funds. In the face of such large numbers, MIT faced the future of educational computing as a massive investment decision. The committee reformulated the problem of the future of academic computing in these terms, emphasizing issues of opportunity costs, financing strategies, and fairness.

But the committee could not address these issues without turning, once again, to the problem of assessing Project Athena's educational impact. It discovered, as might be expected, that opinions about

Athena varied dramatically throughout the institute. Now, however, differences of opinion seemed to have crystallized around the schools, whose positions Dean MacVicar described as follows.

The position of the School of Engineering was essentially the position of Athena's founders. For them, retreat from Athena's original vision of MIT in the forefront was unthinkable. Professor Dertouzos, representing this view, believed that Athena should continue to promote educational development projects on state-of-the-art computers, maintaining a single operating system that would support machines from different vendors. It was his conviction that MIT,

> as a premier institute of technology . . . could not afford not to pioneer in exploring and using the new information processing technology; it could not afford to sit on its haunches for a decade, only to find out that some other place had successfully mined a major new technology, unless it was prepared to cede its leadership.[27]

The School of Architecture and Planning, with its computer resources laboratory linked to Athena and developed largely with Athena funds, displayed enthusiasm for MIT's continued support of academic computing. The School of Science retained a slight but significant interest in educational computing, preferring, however, to do its own thing in its own way. The Sloan School of Management, which had never seen Athena as addressing its problems, had developed its own, DOS-based, computing system for research and educational uses; nevertheless, it saw some "cross-platform connectivity and services" as desirable. The School of Humanities and Social Sciences, awakened to the large sums being spent on Athena at a time when it was having to reduce its own faculty, argued that these funds would be better spent on pressing needs such as faculty salaries and research support.

In the face of the conflicting views of the schools, the committee made further inquiries into Athena's effects on education. Although they recognized that Athena had "supported a large number of educational experiments some of which had won national or international awards and otherwise contributed to education," their endorsement of Athena as an educational experiment was ambivalent.[28]

In the end, they produced a carefully qualified endorsement of Athena, noting that the experimental program had taken many risks, succeeding in some respects and failing in others. They firmly endorsed the continued pursuit of MIT's leadership in academic computing, arguing, just as Dertouzos had, that MIT would be relegated to also-ran status if it permitted an erosion of its academic computing resources, educational initiatives, and leading-edge technical capabilities. In taking this position, the committee was resisting any pressure to undermine what had become an externally valued MIT resource. Project Athena now existed as a widely admired and imitated institutional computer system; the School of Engineering identified this leadership position with its own prestige, and MIT identified its prestige with the School of Engineering.

But since several of MIT's schools either had no interest in educational computing or had developed their own systems outside of Athena, these developments had to be reconciled with a decision to invest in MIT's continued development of an Athenalike system. To do this, the committee invented yet another version of the two-tiered system. It introduced as its principal educational strategy the idea of Basic Educational Services and Tools: services of broad interest to all parts of MIT, including electronic mail, an on-line teaching assistant service that could be used in any course, a computerized course catalog and registration service, and electronic access to scholarly databases at MIT and elsewhere. "Coherence" would be redefined to mean that users could gain access to Basic Educational Services and Tools not only through UNIX-based machines but through machines using DOS or Macintosh operating systems. In addition, in a section of its report that reflected the voice of Athena's challengers, the committee proposed that MIT support carefully targeted educational development projects in the computer environments favored by various schools or departments, "nourishing diversity . . . not only in content but in the form and feeling of computer use."[29]

Along with these recommendations, the committee recognized that the School of Engineering would continue, with funds it raised for itself, to pursue the original Athena model; it would develop state-of-the-art educational computing in a UNIX-based system that preserved coherence in Athena's original sense of the term. Implicitly, the committee seemed to be saying that the institute's priority of maintaining technological leadership would be justified by providing universal access to Basic Educational Services and Tools. In effect, the committee redefined "fairness" in educational computing. Provost Low's standard of fairness, aimed at avoiding a division between computer haves and have-nots, had led to treating Athena as a uniform good, making no distinction between types of uses or users. To the MacVicar Committee, "fairness" now meant universal access to a basic level of computer services that everyone in the MIT community could find useful.

The committee was careful to state that if budgetary choices had to be made, priority should go to these basic services. It estimated that the incremental costs of academic computing would range from a floor of about $6 million to a ceiling of about $12 million per year. The higher end of the range, which would maintain MIT's leadership position, would cover both the support of basic educational services and diverse educational development projects; the lower would cover basic services alone. As of this writing, in a climate of increasing fiscal austerity, a newly appointed president and provost of MIT have decided to continue MIT's support of Athena at a level below the committee's floor, sufficient only to maintain the basic network.

## CONCLUSION

### THE POLICY CONVERSATION

One of the most striking features of the story of Project Athena is the disjunction between the original intentions of its designing system and the meanings constructed for Athena in the context of its use. In contrast to the engineer-architects' expectations that Athena would be used for technically sophisticated and educationally innovative purposes, students used Athena mostly for such "mundane" purposes as electronic mail, word processing, and electronic games. Faculty, who were intended to see Athena as a liberating opportunity, often ignored it or found its coherent system an impediment to their preferred approaches to educational computing. The faculty champions of educational computing came to see Athena a trap for their younger protégés. Science faculty, who tended to see the computer only as a research tool, read Athena as an attempt by engineers to usurp control of the science curriculum. Perhaps most shocking to Athena's designers was that what they had conceived as a grand experiment in undergraduate education should be widely seen as a technological enterprise that was not about education at all.

These discrepancies between the original intentions of policy designers and the meanings constructed for a policy object in use are central to the idea of a "policy conversation." This term does not refer to a literal conversation; it is not a verbal interchange among individuals in a policy forum, which we call "policy discourse." Policy conversation is a metaphor for policy design seen as communicative interaction between designers and those who use or have a stake in the policy object. A policy object sent out into its larger environment functions as a message. Other actors in the environment who come into contact with that object must somehow make sense of it and figure out how to respond to it. The message of the policy object is not objectively contained in the thing itself, nor is it directly transmitted from the mind of the designer to the mind of the user.[30] Users and other stakeholders *construct* the meaning of the policy object. They in turn send messages back to the designing system by the ways they interpret, use, or otherwise respond to the deployed object. The exchange of verbal and/or action messages between designers and users of a policy object is central to the design process. Its quality is critical to design rationality.

As in literal conversations, the meanings intended by "speakers" in a policy conversation may be very different from the meanings constructed by "hearers." The intended users of a policy object may not "get" the meanings intended by the designers, and even when they do, they may prefer the meanings they themselves construct. So, in the early retirement case described in the previous chapter, the firms interpreted the state's 59er rule, which was originally intended to smooth the way for returning veterans, as a splendid way to gain state subsidy for the restructuring of their work force in response to the pressures of international competition. Similarly, in the Athena case we have observed that students who received Athena interpreted it as, among other things, a word-processing tool (though, in their view, a cumbersome and unsatisfactory one) for which they felt an urgent need, and they proceeded to use the system in that way. When Athena's designers first became aware of this pattern of utilization, they read its meaning in their own terms: not as information about the computer uses that were of most immediate interest to students, but as a perversion of their vision, a mundane use of the technically sophisticated system for which the designers held such high hopes. Similarly, many faculty members, especially in the School of Science, read the strictures of Athena's coherent system as an attempt to deprive them of their favored computers, languages, and applications as well as an affront to their intellectual and administrative autonomy as MIT faculty. Athena's designers initially read the scientists' angry reactions and subsequent avoidance of Athena not as a message about their preferences but as evidence of their failure to appreciate the beauty of the Athena idea.

We use the term "back talk" to refer to messages sent back to policy designers that surprise them by violating their taken-for-granted assumptions and tacit "action frames," telling them, in effect, that the policy object as perceived and used by other actors is different from the one they intended to design and deploy. Actors in a policy arena can listen, interpret, and respond to such back talk in many different ways. How they do so determines much about the reliability of a policy conversation—that is, the extent to which participants in the conversation reliably grasp the meanings intended by message givers and message receivers. In a policy conversation, as in a literal one, reliability of communication is distinct from the degree to which speakers and hearers agree with each other. The outcome of reliable communication is not necessarily a settlement of disputes; indeed, the better the participants understand one another, the more they may become aware of the depth of their disagreement. But reliable communication is a critical condition for the further inquiry that may result in acceptable policy adjustments, or even in pragmatic resolution of policy controversies.

At first, Athena's engineer-architects were inattentive to the back talk they received, denied it, or treated it as a failure of Athena's student and faculty users to appreciate or understand their work. But by 1987, after the PASG report had been submitted and MacVicar had communicated the results of her private inquiry, Athena's engineer-architects began to listen in a new way. Realizing that Athena had created an angry and explosive climate that threatened the very survival of the project, they adjusted their policies to accommodate the negative messages coming back from the field.

## ATHENA'S POLICY ADJUSTMENTS

Once policy designers become aware of a discrepancy between the meanings they intend for their policy object and the meanings actually constructed by its users, they must set about dealing with the discrepancy. They have three options for how to do so. They can accept the object as defined by its users and abandon their original intentions for it. They can try to force the users to accept the object as they originally saw and wished it to be. Or they can try to modify the object, adjusting their policies in such a way as to make the object acceptable both to themselves and its users. These options are best seen as continuations of the design process; they carry new messages that once again are open to interpretation and response, and the choice among them is central to the character of the continuing policy conversation.

The choice of policy adjustments faced by the Athena architects may also be conceptualized as a choice between marketing, negotiation, and co-design.

> 1) In *marketing* the policy designers treat the policy object as a product and other actors in the environment as a market for that product. They design with a model of the users in mind. But when the users express dissatisfaction with the product, or reject it—"exiting," as Albert Hirschman would say[31]—the designers

try to reshape the object in order to give it greater market appeal.

2) In *negotiation* designers and other stakeholders make competing claims on the policy object. When actors are dissatisfied with the degree to which their claims are met, they "give voice"—as Hirschman, again, would say[32]—to their dissatisfaction. In this case, the designers treat the expression of dissatisfaction as the sign of a political dispute, which they try to settle by negotiation with the aggrieved parties, giving and getting concessions in order to secure a satisfactory compromise.

3) In *co-design* the expression of dissatisfaction is taken as an occasion for cooperative redesign of the policy object. The designers seek to involve users and/or other actors in a collaborative design process, in which all parties accept one another as legitimate contributors to the shared design task.

In practice, of course, these three ideal types blend into one another. A negotiation may include periods of co-design, for example; conversely, co-design may give rise to disputes that call for negotiation. Or, as in the Athena story, policy designers may adopt different strategies of adjustment at different stages of the design process.

In Part 3 of our Athena story, Athena's designers read student and faculty back talk as a market signal that could have serious political consequences. They neither negotiated with their challengers and resisters nor engaged them in co-design. Their invention of the two-tiered system was a marketing strategy intended to neutralize the political threat to Athena's continued existence.

In Part 4 of our story, Athena's policy was reframed. This time, however, the MIT administration, aware of the long-term budgetary implications of an Athena without external funding, took a much more visible role in determining Athena's future. MIT's budgetary constraints were central to the dilemma that triggered the new round of policy adjustment. On the one hand, the MacVicar Committee accepted the position of Professor Dertouzos and the School of Engineering that MIT's leadership in academic computing must be sustained. On the other hand, the committee realized that this acceptance carried a high opportunity cost that would be especially painful for the other schools. In response to these conflicting imperatives, the committee adopted an approach to policy adjustment that combined negotiation and co-design, hammering out a new version of a two-tiered Athena system that focused on providing basic educational services for the MIT community as a whole.

Parts 3 and 4 are two distinct policy windows. In these key moments in the formulation of policy, we observe Athena's designers and administrators listening and accommodating to back talk that disconfirmed their expectations and revealed views that conflicted starkly with their own. In these windows we are able to observe policy adjustments that were in fact continuing the policy design conversation that had been under way for the better part of a decade. These adjustments followed a pattern of least change. The policy makers called a halt to their inquiries about Athena-in-use when they found what seemed like a workable accommodation that would enable Athena to proceed. Nevertheless, these successive, least-change adjustments did embody some institutional learning, did effect a pragmatic resolution of the controversies, and did result in an Athena system that could be declared, in several respects—widespread utilization by students and faculty, technological advance, commercial exploitation, international visibility—a success.

## FRAME-CONSERVATISM

Throughout the first turbulent ten years of Athena's existence, the cultural frames held by Athena's founders, challengers, and resisters remained remarkably constant. At the end of the period, these frames were essentially what they had been at the beginning.[33]

At a deeper level, then, the Athena story turns on a conflict of these frames, which correspond to two conflicting views of Athena's identity: a quest to regain MIT's lost technological leadership in institutional computing or an experiment in undergraduate education. This conflict first appeared in the early Athena debates, then, as Athena's difficulties began to surface, in the differing views held by Athena's protagonists and critics about how to interpret the flaws in its design, and, finally, at the end of our story, in the schools' divergent attitudes toward academic computing.

But although a significant number of Athena's observers, participants, and critics talked about this conflict from the earliest days, it was not obvious to Athena's designers. On the other side, Athena's challengers were not generally able to appreciate the importance of an advanced and coherent institutional network—what Athena's architects saw as its central idea. Or, when the challengers saw it, they did not grant it pride of place as an educational necessity.

Whether or not one sees Athena as having an identity conflict is largely dependent on whether or not one has faith that the world's front-running distributed computing system will yield, as an inevitable or likely consequence, positive educational change. This faith is of course a particular version of a more general belief that technological advances will inevitably have positive social consequences.

Athena's founders and champions had this faith. It justified their model of educational reform, and it underlay their belief that once the Athena network was in place a thousand flowers of educational software would be elicited and naturally selected in the traditional MIT way. The design problem as they framed it was to make their technical vision into a reality so that the desired educational consequences would follow. Even if they could not predict these consequences, they saw no reason to believe in a method that put desired effects first. For example, in a reaction to an earlier draft of this chapter, Professor Dertouzos wrote:

> At the bottom of this whole discussion lies, in my view, the basic question of how progress is achieved. There is hardly a person around that can accurately assess the societal benefits of television, synthetic drugs, radar, even gunpowder, decades or centuries after their introduction. Yet you seem to call for assessing the impact of a new technology *before* it is deployed, and accurately enough to guide its deployment. *Has this approach succeeded anywhere in the history of science and technology?*

In the end, it was the architect-designers' persistence in seeing their policy object through the lens of *their* intentions that provoked Athena's crisis of survival. Up to the point of this crisis the designers did not ask "What does Athena mean to its users?" but only "Did it work as we planned?" Policy intentions were taken as surrogates for outcomes on matters as small as Athena's support of faculty salaries and as large as the educational emphasis of the entire experiment. When the back talk was finally noticed, it was read as criticism of the designers' intentions for Athena rather than as manifestations of genuine pluralism within MIT as a social and cultural world. In all of these respects, the story of Athena illustrates a nonreflective policy conversation.

Athena's critics and skeptics lacked the implicit faith that social good would follow technical progress. Even as they became more diplomatic in their language—for example, when they worked on cooperative efforts to shape future MIT policy—the outlines of their differences with Athena's founders and champions remained clear.

Not surprisingly, the fundamental frame conflict persists at MIT. Protagonists and defenders continue to advocate and defend. Skeptics and resisters remain skeptical and resistant. Some of the challengers may have tried to promote a frame-reflective dialogue; if they did, it is clear that they did not succeed. Perhaps, as Professor Deutch seems to have believed, frame-reflection would have been incompatible with the visionary enthusiasm of Athena's champions. It is important to note that, had the founders not held to their faith—had they suggested, for example, that a coherent system might not work educationally in an institution that contained diverse computer cultures, or that technological instability might be incompatible with educational innovation—they might not have been able to strike the bargain with Athena's corporate donors.

The dividing line around which Athena polarized MIT is, of course, by no means unique to MIT. Rather, MIT mirrors a conflict of cultural metaframes in our society as a whole. But at MIT this larger social conflict takes on the character of a split between true believers and heretical doubters of a fundamental tenet in what amounts to an institutional religion about the role of technology in society. The Athena story, which exhibits the tenacity of these conflicting metaframes, reveals more about what MIT *is* than how it has changed.

# CHAPTER 6

# Homelessness
# in Massachusetts

In the early 1980s, a crisis of homelessness broke into public consciousness in the Commonwealth of Massachusetts, triggering an unfolding policy drama. For nearly a decade, between 1982 and 1991, state bureaucracies and advocacy groups would struggle to create a statewide program for the homeless. They would see homelessness through the lenses of conflicting interests and action frames, and their policy disputes would fester and bubble to the surface.

But the story we shall tell in this chapter is about more than institutional contention. It is also about cooperative policy design undertaken by a network of individuals who were able, at crucial moments in the drama, to bring to their roles a high degree of reflective inquiry. They did this in a prevailing climate of institutional antagonism, instability, and political pressure.

The policy designers in our story first joined together to orchestrate an unruly planning process in which a comprehensive program for the homeless was hammered out. Then, as their program moved from planning to implementation, they saw that it was being used by its recipients in ways they had not anticipated. Design flaws, in the form of gaps and contradictions, came to light. As they attempted to diagnose and fix these flaws, the policy designers learned that they must think differently about the very meaning of the problem of homelessness. But, at the same time, they became more intensely aware of a fundamental dilemma of policy and politics that they could not resolve. It was only at the end of the decade, in a radically changed state climate, that a coalition of program managers was able to invent new practices to unlock the stalemate that had paralyzed state policy.

The Massachusetts story exhibits a level of productive policy inquiry that goes beyond our two previous cases and thereby raises questions about design rationality and reflective policy practice critical to our larger argument. These questions are explored in the following chapter. In this one, we trace the story through its several stages: the first surfacing of the issue of homelessness, the development of the statewide program, the discovery of its flaws, and the attempts to fix them.

## PROLOGUE (1981–83): HOW DID THE PROBLEM OF HOMELESSNESS BECOME AN IDEA IN GOOD CURRENCY?

Historical revisionism tempts us to impose our present understandings onto events of earlier times. By the late 1980s, policy analysts distinguished many different types of homelessness, each with its own peculiar causality. But in the early 1980s, when homelessness first came to public attention, it was a blooming, buzzing confusion; there seemed to be no clear, consensual answers to the most elementary questions: Who were the homeless? How many of them were there? How did they come to be homeless? What should be done about them? Who should do it? Indeed, the very problem of defining the problem of homelessness was subject to intense debate and political struggle, since this question must influence who to count as homeless.[1]

At first, the tendency was to see homelessness as an emergency condition, temporary in nature, and—at least as the Reagan administration pictured it—relatively small in scale. Early responses to the crisis consisted of constructing or expanding emergency shelters. In New York, the court order that followed the National Coalition for the Homeless suit against the city led to the creation of hundreds of beds in large, warehouse-type shelters. In Boston, the two existing private shelters doubled their capacity. In many cities, the lack of a coordinated governmental response led grass-roots groups and religious organizations to step into the policy vacuum in order to keep people from freezing to death on the streets.

A strange feature of the crisis of homelessness that gripped the nation's cities in the early 1980s was that, as nearly everyone writing about the topic has since observed, homelessness was not a new problem. Modern American cities have always had their traditional skid rows (from the skid roads that served as skids for timber) such as New

York's Bowery, San Francisco's Tenderloin, and Boston's Combat Zone. Here, in single-room-occupancy units, alcoholics and drifters lived. Skid rows worked because of widespread tolerance for low-standard housing in zones of urban decay where, under conditions of weak public regulation, a free market could accommodate the homeless. The poor could survive, as Peter Marin has explained, through "hash houses, saloons offering free lunches, pawn shops, surplus clothing stores, and most important of all, cheap hotels and flop houses and two-bit employment agencies speculating in the kinds of labor (seasonal, shape-up) that transients have always done."[2] Even public facilities such as libraries became resources for skid row inhabitants. County jails, too, periodically dealt with them, and the police were key agents in the transition from street to jail.

In addition to the inhabitants of the skid rows, there have always been the mentally ill who roamed the streets, families evicted from their homes who for a time had no place to live, and hoboes who made homelessness a way of life and passed into American mythology as way-farers of the open road. Throughout history, a variety of names have been applied to those who lacked a home. In Kim Hopper's words,

> Victorian England would have recognized as homeless those whom its Elizabethan forebears would have hunted down as "masterless men." Each era would have readily identified the other's "vagrants." Late 19th-century America would castigate as "tramps" those whom New England colonists somewhat more delicately referred to as the "strolling poor." In the early decades of the 20th century, America's "hobo" performed the same economic functions as Canada's "bunkhouse man." And curiously, when in 1959 the *Saturday Evening Post* asked, "Will ours be the century of homeless people?" it had in mind not the dispossessed poor but the vast cohorts of political refugees of the time.[3]

In different periods, as Hopper goes on to point out, those who made up the "official roster of 'houseless poverty'" were put into different culturally sanctioned categories. Never, though, had the diverse populations that shared the condition of being without a home been subsumed under a *single* category. How was it that in the early 1980s a national policy crisis came to be defined in terms of the single aggregate category of homelessness? What was new?

First of all, there was the scale and visibility of the problem. Suddenly in large cities throughout the country thousands of men, women, and children wandered the streets with no place to go. No one knew just how many of them there were. Estimates ranged from a high figure of 2.5 million, advanced by the National Coalition for the Homeless, to a low range of from 250,000 to 350,000, proposed by the Department of Housing and Urban Development. Whatever the right number was, everyone seemed to agree that it was growing.[4]

Further, the people wandering the streets were not limited to familiar skid row stereotypes such as alcoholic bums, bag ladies, and "crazies." Some of them were families with children, and some of these were working-class families living, as the newspapers reported, in automobiles. Indeed, the streets seemed to be full of a bewildering variety of homeless people. A 1984 article listed the following: low-income families evicted for nonpayment of rent; victims of condominium conversion, urban renewal, or gentrification; the unemployed; battered women; the mentally ill who had been deinstitutionalized; and others cut off from federal programs who were unable, in a tight housing market, to find housing they could afford.[5]

What set the contemporary homeless apart from their historical antecedents was, then, in Hopper's words, "their sheer visibility, their manifest diversity, [and] the prevalence of evident (especially psychiatric) disabilities." But Hopper goes on in this passage to cite political struggle as a distinctive mark of the new homelessness:

> The forces contending on their behalf (homegrown champions and advocates from without) and the places in which that struggle is staged (the streets, the press and the courts) and the terms of both popular and scholarly debate on the problem and proposed solutions—in all these varied respects, today's homeless poor are set apart from their forebears.[6]

The very naming of the phenomenon of homelessness reflected a political struggle. The many different populations without fixed address were first lumped together under a single name by a loose coalition of grass-roots and advocacy groups that had organized to provide emergency shelter for them. This coalition had been searching for a common cause to mobilize its several constituencies. In the 1970s, welfare reform had seemed like a promising issue but had lost its appeal when efforts to restructure the welfare system failed. The campaign for affordable housing had also looked at first like a promising issue, but it had run up against budgetary intransigence, and its further progress seemed to depend on the difficult task of forging an alliance between advocates for the poor and promoters of working-class solidarity. The scandal of homelessness looked as though it could harness a new politics of compassion and shame—compassion for the plight of the dispossessed and shame at the inhumanity of national and local policies toward them. Homelessness, in sum, had political appeal.

In Massachusetts, as elsewhere in the nation at this time, a local version of the National Coalition for the Homeless was in the process of forming, drawing together the welfare rights movement, inner-city churches, shelter providers, nonprofit agencies, and other grass-roots groups, and strongly supported by the human services providers. Like other such groups, the Massachusetts coalition felt that it could get more political mileage by lumping together the several populations newly visible on the streets of the center cities. It deliberately adopted the socially constructed category of homelessness as a vehicle for political organization and public pressure.

In order to explain the emergence of a public crisis of homelessness in Massachusetts, however, we must also take account of electoral politics. In the early 1980s, Michael Dukakis began to campaign for a second term as governor, after four years in the political wilderness. Between his first term and his campaign for re-election, Massachusetts had been governed by Edward King, a Democrat turned Republican whose conservative social policies matched those of the Reagan administration. King and Reagan policies, together with Proposition $2\frac{1}{2}$ (a state law that limited taxes on local property to $2\frac{1}{2}$ percent of its assessed value), had decimated the state's human services budget. But the powerful coalition of human services advocates and providers had managed to survive these four dry years. Through their sophisticated lobby on Beacon Hill, they had made an alliance with State Senator Chester Atkins, chair of the Senate Ways and Means Committee, who kept the flame of human services alive during the King years by regularly supplementing King's budgets with outside items for human services.

By 1982, however, the human services coalition was vigorously campaigning for additional state support, and Dukakis knew that he could not be re-elected without their backing. He had been criticized in his first term as an unfeeling technocrat. Now he felt that he must show a caring, human side, and homelessness seemed just the right issue. He knew that media exposés had stirred up a great deal of political compassion for the homeless among the Massachusetts voting public. He and his wife, Kitty, shared these sentiments, and he had noticed the rising power of the newly formed Massachusetts Coalition for the Homeless, a group with strong ties to the broader human services coalition. This group had already persuaded the state legislature to grant rights of general relief for people without a fixed address, a move that was to have a major impact on the demand for welfare support.

Dukakis was primed to respond, then, when the Massachusetts coalition met, some months into his campaign, in the western part of the state. They were meeting to consider whether they should sue Massachusetts, as the National Coalition had earlier sued New York City, claiming a right to shelter and demanding that the state close the poverty gap (the gap between actual levels of welfare payments and minimally acceptable income levels). Only the local media covered the story, but Dukakis took notice. Shortly afterward, he had his transition team invite representatives of the local coalition to sit on committees that were planning a human services agenda for the new administration.

One of the advocates who participated in this event described, in an interview held several years after the fact, how the Massachusetts coalition had "pushed to Governor to act":

> Here this team was, trying to recruit the human services community who voted Duke out the first time. . . . So they had to get us involved or we might break their wonderful consensus. They [invited] us to sit on specific committees—first, onto the disability committee; but we said, Not enough! . . .
>
> It was during that power period between election day and the inaugural speech that the present structure for confronting the homelessness problem was designed. . . . we represented all those groups that they had been wooing to get back in.[7]

In the inaugural address he delivered in January 1983, Dukakis staked out the issue of homelessness. "Tomorrow morning in my office," he proclaimed,

> I will convene an emergency meeting of the new Cabinet, the Senate President and Speaker of the House, nonprofit organizations, civic and religious leaders and representatives of the Coalition for the Homeless. We will begin immediately to put together a statewide effort which will provide the necessities of life to those in desperate need.[8]

## STAGE 1 (1983–85): HAMMERING OUT A STATEWIDE PROGRAM

Once he was elected, Governor Dukakis set about planning his statewide program. As the coalition advised, he created three forums: the Advisory Committee made up of representatives of charitable institutions, advocacy groups, and human services providers; the Cabinet Working Group, to involve the heads of state agencies whose cooperation would be essential to the program; and the Interagency Task Force to work out the program's operating details.

## THE ACTORS

The main actors in these forums were the advocates, the local charitable and nonprofit organizations who made up the existing shelter system, and various members of the legislative and executive branches of state government.

The advocates included the Human Services Coalition, along with their supporters in the nonprofit organizations and state agencies, and the Coalition for the Homeless. The shelter system included two private shelters in Boston, Rosie's Place and the Pine Street Inn. Both were managed by competent and politically astute individuals. Kip Tiernan of Rosie's Place was a highly articulate person who had become something of an institution in the state. Both the advocates and the shelter providers saw as their principal ally in the legislature State Senator Atkins, who had been the "Man on a White Horse" for human services during the four lean King years. Atkins was a Yankee from Concord who had learned to "out-Irish the Irish" in the rough and tumble of Massachusetts politics.

Playing for high political stakes, the governor clearly intended to give his statewide program for the homeless high visibility and a privileged place in the state's bureaucracy. He appointed his wife, Kitty, and Bishop Harrington, a Catholic bishop from central Massachusetts, to head his Advisory Committee on the Homeless, and he assigned responsibility for it to his newly created Office of Human Resources (a move recommended to him by the Coalition for the Homeless). The commissioner of this office was Philip Johnston, a former legislator who had challenged the governor's policies during his first term and was reputed to know everyone of political importance in the state. Under him, the governor brought in Nancy Kaufman, a human services advocate and former director of a local Community Action Program, to coordinate the homelessness initiative.

Dynamic, compassionate, and politically savvy, Kaufman was an outsider who was rapidly becoming an insider to the state bureaucracy. She was put in charge of the Interagency Task Force, a job whose critical importance grew out of the fact that the governor had decided not to create a new bureaucracy for the homeless but to distribute his program among existing agencies.[9] This task force included representatives of all state agencies that might conceivably have a role to play in the statewide program: the Executive Office of Human Services (EOHS), the Department of Public Welfare (DPW), the Executive Office of Community Development (EOCD), the Department of Mental Health (DMH), the Department of Social Services (DSS), the Office of Elder Affairs, the Department of Public Health, and the Office for Children. Of these, the most important, at least in the early stages, were DPW and EOCD.

Because DPW had the lion's share of the money for homelessness and the most direct relationship to people on general or family emergency assistance, it was under the greatest pressure from the advocates to increase welfare benefits and funds for shelters, subsidies, and services. Dukakis had named Charles ("Chuck") Atkins, a manager with no previous human service experience or links to the advocates, to head this department.

EOCD had major responsibility for the state's affordable housing programs, including administration of the two hundred local public housing authorities and the Community Action Programs (CAPs). Amy Anthony was EOCD's executive secretary, and Langley Keyes, an MIT professor with a long history of involvement in affordable housing, was special assistant for policy development.

## How the Planning Process Worked

The governor invited eighty people to serve on the Advisory Committee, including members of the clergy, advocates, service providers, and representatives from foundations, businesses, and the helping professions. Foreshadowing the structure of his eventual program, he divided the committee into three working groups: emergency services, social services, and permanent housing. He attended some of the early meetings himself, leaving the leadership of the later ones to his wife.

Nancy Kaufman began her work as coordinator by gathering information at the grass-roots. Aware of the legacy of bitterness and distrust left over from the King administration, she bypassed state government. She convened meetings on homelessness in twenty-four regions of the commonwealth under the auspices of local, primarily antipoverty, nonprofit organizations. The atmosphere of these meetings was conveyed, some years later, by Langley Keyes:

> In the first year it was like a camp meeting. . . . We had endless committees, everybody was there, all kinds of subcommittees. I remember one at Pine Street where two people got up, one a lawyer for Sullivan Trust for Pine Street, who is an absolute genius at putting

this thing together. He said, "You know, if I was an alcoholic, I would have been out there on the street. I *was* out there. The only thing that changed my life was Pine Street Inn." A lot of people got up. I thought we were going to Praise the Lord and Keep the Powder Dry!

If Keyes likened the atmosphere of these meetings to a religious revival, Paul McGerigle, author of an early report on the homeless, compared the planning process to a floating crap game:

> Nobody planned this! There was no centralized planning process. Rather, it was a floating crap game at many levels. Nancy Kaufman and Lang Keyes were major players, and Nancy was indispensable, but there were dozens of other players . . . who were equally important at one time or another. For example, one of them got the Governor aside and got him to agree to do what he had said he wouldn't do. . . . One day, Kip Tiernan got up and blasted the Governor to his face!

In such an atmosphere and in the full glare of media attention, Keyes and Kaufman joined forces. They sought to clarify the problem of homelessness, gather information about it, and work out the structure of a comprehensive program. But their first priority was to "stop the bleeding," to get people off the streets.

In 1983, Massachusetts had only two state-supported shelters (Pine Street and Shelter, Inc.), one privately supported shelter (Rosie's Place), and one DSS-operated family shelter. No one had expected that the governor would actually promise to build more shelters. When he did make this promise, as Phil Johnston said the day after the governor's inaugural address, no one was prepared for the amount of interest it generated. By 1984, the state had put thirteen new small community-based shelters in place;[10] Rosie's Place and the Pine Street Inn had doubled their capacity, largely with state support, and two new one hundred-bed shelters had been created at Shattuck Hospital and Long Island Hospital. Eventually the state would have ninety shelters, sixty-five of them for families with children, each receiving 75 percent of its operating funds from DPW.

However, as one of the advocates later observed, the very scale of the state's emergency response to the homeless became a double-edged sword. "On one hand," she said, "they'd satisfy some group that was threatening their status quo; but on the other hand, the more they elevated the issue, the more they left themselves vulnerable to the question, Why aren't they doing more?"[11]

In the interest of doing more, even as the emergency shelters were being constructed, the governor's Advisory Committee published its 1983 *Profile of the Homeless*. The profile estimated that from eight thousand to ten thousand people were living in shelters or on the streets. Of these people, 30 to 40 percent had serious problems of substance abuse, and 25 percent were families with children (an estimate that by 1985 would grow much larger).[12] The report said that homelessness looked very different in different parts of the state. On Cape Cod, where there was a large population of homeless families, a peak in homelessness occurred every May 30. In the rural areas, there were the "invisible homeless." The profile also emphasized the importance of programs for preventing families at risk from becoming homeless, and it advocated construction of more affordable housing.

While the Advisory Committee gathered information, events beyond its control increased the public pressure on the Dukakis administration. The advocates, who had joined the governor in an uneasy truce, continued to stage protests and demonstrations, beginning with a sit-in in Phil Johnston's office the day after the inauguration. They continually threatened to break ranks with the governor if he did not live up to their expectations.

In the state legislature, Chet Atkins executed what one observer called a "brilliant broken-field run." Before any of the governor's agents quite knew what had happened, the governor's legislation, which had been narrowly framed to remove permanent address restrictions for General Relief recipients, turned into Chapter 450, the Act to Prevent Destitution and Homelessness. This bill, engineered by Atkins with the support of the advocates, encompassed the construction of emergency shelters, social services for families in emergency and transitional housing, and mental health services. What had begun as a $5 to $7 million piece of legislation grew to many times that amount. State officials felt had by Atkins, but, as one of them later observed, "it was too late to do anything about it because he was out there, and what were we going to do—say we were against the homeless?"

## POLICY CONTROVERSIES

At the time the governor made homelessness his highest human services priority, the commonwealth was entering a period of economic growth and budget surplus that would become known as the "Massachusetts Miracle." For a time, at least, the getting was good, and the statewide program for the homeless became an arena for competition over resources. Rancorous disputes soon erupted.

One of the first of these had to do with who the homeless were and what kind of problem they posed. Ellen Bassuk, a psychiatrist who had studied the homeless in Massachusetts shelters, claimed they were a new population, radically different from the unattached, middle-aged, alcholic men who had been familiar skid row types since the Great Depression.[13] They were younger, she believed; 90 percent of them suffered from mental illnesses that ranged from schizophrenia to severe personality disorders, and many of them were victims of the deinstitutionalization of the state mental hospitals. She saw homelessness mainly as a problem of adult individuals. To the extent that families were involved, they were mainly troubled, female-headed households—the "problem families" familiar to generations of social workers.

Bassuk's homeless were "mentally disabled and isolated from the support that might help to reintegrate them into society,"[14] and she saw the shelters trying in vain to replace not only the almshouses but the large state mental hospitals of the past. Homelessness was mainly a problem of mental illness, which had been allowed to fester and grow "primarily because the Federal and State governments never allocated the money to fulfill [the promise of the community mental health movement]."[15]

Advocates for the homeless violently disagreed. For them, the right to shelter was a universal entitlement, as they had claimed in their suit against the state, and the homeless suffered mainly from the absence of a home. Whereas Bassuk saw in the homeless pathologies that cried out for clinical treatment and social support, the advocates saw nothing more than the ravages produced in ordinary people by the intolerable conditions of life on the street.

This debate was to persist for the better part of a decade, attaching itself to a range of issues, from transitional housing for the mentally disabled to social services for the residents of shelters, hotels, and motels. What sharpened the edge of the debate was the advocates' fear that Bassuk would diffuse their pressure on the state to provide affordable housing for the poor. Indeed, some of them accused the bureaucrats of setting Bassuk against them for this very purpose.

Parallel with this long-running controversy was a policy dispute of another kind that arose between two state agencies, DPW and EOCD. This dispute also persisted throughout the 1980s, attaching itself over time to a variety of policy issues, but it was essentially a fight for control. Each of the two agencies tried to assert against the other the primacy of its own mission—seeking to hitch on to the larger purpose of the problem of homelessness.

DPW saw in homelessness an opportunity to fill the poverty gap.

This gap could be filled, in principle, by giving people either housing or more money. But giving welfare clients more money could create a highly visible problem of inequity in relation to the working poor and, as some people claimed, might reinforce the incentive to remain on welfare. If welfare clients got housing certificates, on the other hand, their combined resources could bring them above the poverty line even though their cash benefits remained the same. What DPW wanted, therefore, was to subsume housing subsidies under welfare policy in order to use them to fill the poverty gap. In this they were rather successful. In their battle with EOCD over who should get priority access to housing vouchers, DPW would eventually secure a compromise that set aside a significant number of housing subsidies for homeless families.

The "housers" in EOCD fought against DPW's efforts to make housing an extension of the welfare system. They insisted that homelessness was a housing problem and tried to use it to advance their own housing policy agenda. At the same time, they placed great importance on preventing families at risk (a number they estimated at sixty thousand to seventy thousand) from becoming homeless. They saw the existing homeless population as the tip of an iceberg of demand for affordable housing to which, in a tight housing market, private developers and builders would not respond. EOCD argued that the production of new housing must rise to the top of the state's social agenda, if the state were not to be swamped by families at risk of becoming homeless. Its strategy, too, turned out to be largely successful. In the mid- to late-1980s, the commitment of state funds to the production of affordable housing would take a leap forward, and the governor would often repeat the EOCD message that homelessness is basically a housing problem.

In addition to their competing efforts to hitch onto homelessness, DPW and EOCD came into conflict over two other policy issues: Who should get priority access to public housing and housing subsidies, and how should problem families be dealt with?

For two main reasons, DPW argued that the homeless should go to the head of the queue for affordable housing. First, DPW's chief, Chuck Atkins, had allied himself with the advocates who considered housing a God-given right. Second, DPW had no alternative but to deal with the homeless. Since the state legislation engineered by the advocates meant that a shelter could be used as an address from which to apply for welfare benefits, a homeless family denied access to state-sponsored housing would spill over into another part of the system where DPW would still have to provide them with shelter and services.

EOCD believed that priority for access to public housing should go to those families, mainly the working poor, who had waited patiently in line, often for years, and who were not likely to become problems to the public housing system. EOCD saw DPW's claim as a threat to the hard-won integrity of the public housing queues, which could be easily overwhelmed by an influx of homeless families. Housing was not an entitlement, they thought, but a scarce resource whose access must be controlled by clear eligibility rules.

The dispute about problem families played itself out along similar lines. DPW wanted to allow them to enter the state housing system or else give them housing subsidies. They were not as much of a problem as some agencies claimed, and if their behavior proved troublesome, they could always be referred for help to the DSS. In any case, if they were not admitted or subsidized, they would still be DPW's problem; they could not be institutionalized. EOCD asserted, on the contrary, that a few problem families could destroy the viability of a public housing project. EOCD had been working for fifty years to create an orderly system for moving people into subsidized housing. Problem families should be kept out, and if they managed to get in, they should be evicted. To this, DPW responded (in Nancy Kaufman's paraphrase), "We're glad you're good planners, but these people have priority needs."

## CONFLICTING FRAMES

These policy controversies, triggered by practical problems of resource allocation and program management, also expressed the actors' conflicting institutional action frames—and, beneath these, conflicting cultural metaframes.

The official frame, sponsored by the public agencies, saw housing as a scarce resource whose distribution was properly a matter for governmental discretion. The advocates, on the other hand, saw housing as a legal entitlement enforceable in a court of law. They insisted, in Kim Hopper's words, that "what is understood as legitimate need may be prosecuted as a warrant of entitlement."[16] These contrasting frames of discretion and entitlement underlay the highly visible policy controversy between the advocates and the bureaucrats.

Among the sponsors of the discretionary frame, however, there were conflicting views of the principles that should govern equitable rationing of scarce resources. DPW maintained that priority should be given to those in greatest need, the welfare clients, and that housing should be used to fill the poverty gap. Limited resources could be rationed based on people's position in a housing queue, EOCD's view of a fair and orderly way of exercising discretion. DSS argued that limited resources should be allocated based on the individual's ability to use them.

Different rules of distribution within the discretionary frame reflect different versions of underlying cultural metaframes—the metaframes of market, social welfare, and social control. These intellectual traditions are by no means peculiar to homelessness but are generally present in the structure of controversies over such issues as poverty, deprivation, and deviance. We shall present them first as ideal types. Then we shall go on to show how they are varied and combined in the institutional action frames sponsored by key actors in the homelessness story.

The core idea of the *market* frame is that, in competitive markets, supply responds to effective consumer demand through the mediation of price signals. In principle, effective consumer demand for housing, for example, leads suppliers to invest new capital in expanding rental or home ownership stock. Demand bids up the price, which attracts suppliers to the market. Excess supply eventually bids down the price until the market reaches a supply-demand equilibrium.

According to the market frame, the state's first response to market failure should be restorative. In the case of housing, the state may restore markets by supporting the supply of housing (made available by builders and developers) and/or the demand for housing exerted by low-income and homeless families. Economists favor this view of the world, even though it has a poor narrative fit with a special homeless population that lacks the ability to express need in the form of effective demand.

When effective demand is inadequate, the state's function is, as Langley Keyes expressed it, to "keep the homeless from falling out of the market." The state may do this in one or more of three ways: increase the level of housing subsidies, construct more affordable housing, or protect the availability of existing stock earmarked for low-income tenants. The first two strategies underlay EOCD's consistent efforts to use the visibility of homelessness to leverage new housing subsidies and construction programs; the third underlay its struggle to safeguard the integrity of its housing queues.

The *social welfare* frame rests on the assumption that markets are imperfect, and that a humane society must provide the needy with resources that enable them to survive and achieve social integration with the larger society. According to this view, all markets are embedded in society; when they fail, as Pope John Paul II's encyclical on markets proclaimed, collective social obligation must fill the gap. The state has an obligation to satisfy individuals and families who stand in need of shelter, services, and housing subsidies. However, the political will to meet human needs varies with swings between periods of compassion and stringency. For the social welfare profession, this means that when the gap between needs and resources cannot be filled with unrestricted cash grants or in-kind benefits, there is a professional obligation to help the most distressed clients gain access to the resources they need. It was on this basis that DPW argued consistently for giving priority in the allocation of resources to individuals and families who fell into the emergency category of homelessness.

Those who hold the social welfare frame take the individual as a starting point and tend to see the individual in wholistic terms. They emphasize the state's obligation both to respond to individuals' needs for material goods and to uphold the values of individual autonomy and choice. Clinically oriented human service professionals, such as Ellen Bassuk, build the imperatives of need satisfaction and autonomy into a way of framing the problems of mental illness and social disability, leading to a policy solution that combines the provision of housing with social services, therapy, and social supports.

The core idea of the *social control* frame is that individuals must comply with societal norms of appropriate, law-abiding behavior. In the pure version of this frame, a social problem is understood as one of changing the behavior of problem people. Society has a right to protect itself against individuals such as criminals and drug addicts, who are seen not as victims but as victimizers.

In the case of homelessness, the social control frame directs attention to the ways in which homeless individuals or families carry responsibility for their own plights. When disruptive tenants threaten affordable housing institutions, for example, then, as EOCD claimed, the need to preserve these institutions justifies the control of tenant behavior. If a unit in a public housing project has its toilets continuously overflowing because tenants throw garbage into the toilet bowl, then the manager is seen as having a right to warn the tenants against this practice, and to evict them if they fail to comply. Punishment and the regulation of behavior are the main themes of this tradition, which is mainly associated with political conservatism.

The pure metaframes of market, social welfare, and social control underlie the frame contest played out in the story of homelessness in Massachusetts, but a more accurate picture of the policy drama would show how these metaframes are subtly hybridized in the actors' institutional action frames.

How well, for example, do the core ideas of the market map onto EOCD's institutional action frame? EOCD deals with a population of low-wage workers and welfare clients for whom there is a gap between supply and effective demand. Filling this gap, created by market imperfections, can be justified only by some idea of need, which is alien to the pure market frame. The frame controversy related to markets has to do with the state's proper role: Should it transform need into effective demand? Should it do so by providing vouchers or cash grants to low-income consumers or by subsidizing suppliers through low interest rates or other means? EOCD's practice, which represents answers to these questions, reflects market ideas, but only in a hybrid way; social welfare ideas about need play a large part in it, though an implicit one.

In its pure form, the social welfare frame assumes that the obligation to meet human needs for survival and integration into the larger society should be met in a way that satisfies the value of individual autonomy—that is, by unrestricted cash grants. Thus, human needs should be met in a way that respects consumer sovereignty—an idea taken over from the market frame. In practice, human needs tend increasingly to be met by earmarked grants, such as food stamps, medical care, and housing vouchers. Earmarking involves the control of consumption, which derives from the social control frame.

Social control enters into the action frames of human service and welfare agencies in a variety of ways, some of them subtle and partly hidden. First, as already observed, providers of social services may seek to control their clients' behavior when it comes to be seen as problematic. In cases of child abuse or neglect, for example, parental rights may be severed. The power to safeguard the interests of the child is mediated through a system of laws backed up by a system of incarceration: negligent parents can be put in jail, and children can be put up for adoption or placed in foster homes. In the case of welfare, clients' rights to receive benefits can be made conditional on work or acceptance of social services aimed at promoting the clients' independence. Of course, the history of social welfare policy has been one of resistance to the introduction of these alien elements, as witnessed by the three hundred-year fight over the work requirement for welfare recipients.

In the period of our study, social control was not as much of an idea in good currency as homelessness. Its influence varied throughout the decade, depending on the social, economic, and political climate of the state. When the climate shifted from stringency to leniency, the social control frame receded and the social welfare frame advanced. But with the shift from affluence to constraint, the opposite occurred. As the context shifted, so did the balance of alien and core elements in the agencies' action frames.

Social control was close to the core of EOCD's action frame. EOCD fought for the integrity of the queues that regulated access to public housing and housing vouchers, for limits to housing subsidies, and for the importance of evicting problem families from public housing. But they advocated these measures more or less strongly depending on the political and economic climate, and tried as much as possible to delegate responsibility for social control to agencies other than their own.

DPW's position on social control was more elusive still. In their formal pronouncements they distanced themselves from any suggestion of it; in practice, they tried a variety of approaches to it. Although they tended to fudge the problem of drug addicts among the single homeless, they tried to turn homeless families with children over to DSS and persuade DMH to address homelessness as a problem of mental illness. As we shall see, neither agency was eager to comply with DPW's idea of a proper division of responsibility for social control.

Although the agencies could not exclude social control, neither could they make it so explicit an element of their practice as to undermine the core of their action frames. DSS and DMH tried, in the case of homelessness, to avoid responsibility for the execution of policies of social control. EOCD tried to keep the social control implications of its action frame implicit, and DPW incorporated social control in its action frame as an alien element, which it tried to mask.

## An Underlying Policy Dilemma

If we shift our focus from the action frames of individual agencies to the interplay of their action frames in the larger policy drama, we can see how the frames of social welfare, market, and social control entered into a policy dilemma that underlay the decade-long attempt to create a workable program for the homeless in Massachusetts.

The state bureaucrats had a powerful incentive to launch an effective statewide program. Only by doing so could they enable the governor to keep his inaugural promise to satisfy those in desperate need. At the same time, sensing the potentially limitless demands championed by the human services coalition, they had an equally powerful incentive to keep the governor from falling into a bottomless pit. They were committed to delivering a comprehensive statewide response to the crisis of homelessness, yet at the same time they saw homelessness as a Trojan horse that could undermine the integrity of their service systems. This policy dilemma expressed itself in conflicts of different kinds and at different levels of aggregation—first, and perhaps most of all, in the long-running conflict between the advocates and the state bureaucracy.

The advocates were quite aware of the policy dilemma confronting the state, but they saw it in their own terms. In the early 1980s they had embraced the political strategy of subsuming many different social problems under the single aggregate category of homelessness. Later on in the decade, however, that strategy seemed to them to contain a cruel hook. As one of the advocates put it,

> Calling the issue "homelessness" has become a problem, because, like any issue, it's only going to go as far as the public won't tolerate it and will scream about it. . . . We made a bandaid, which became part of the big bandage, and now it sits there and there's no way to make the fundamental changes necessary, given how things are structured. It's still "regulating the poor."[17]

Throughout the entire policy-making process, the homelessness and human services coalitions, operating from their entitlement frame, continually applied political pressure to the state. The bureaucrats, with their discretionary frame, continually tried to find a balance between giving in to the advocates' pressure and resisting it in the name of restraint and fiscal prudence.

The underlying policy dilemma also found expression in the conflict between DPW, which allied itself with the advocates, and EOCD, which led the resistance to them. In some cases the dilemma broke out in conflicts among subgroups within a single agency. At both DPW and DSS some factions spoke for the advocates while others spoke against "giving away the store," "cheating," and "abuse," which they associated with compliance to the advocates' demands. In some cases, finally, the policy dilemma found expression in conflicts within the consciousness of individual actors.

Those who sought to resolve the policy dilemma would advocate restraint in distributing resources, mandatory reciprocity on the part of those who received them, and the exercise of social control over those who abused them. But in the prevailing climate of political pressure, advocacy of restraint and reciprocity could be read as a failure of will to promote social justice, a reading especially poignant for a state administration committed to both efficient public management *and* humane treatment of the poor.

## THE STATEWIDE PROGRAM

The tensions implicit in this unresolved dilemma affected the decade-long process by which Massachusetts tried to determine its policy for the homeless. In the early 1980s, these tensions were lived out by the individuals who played key roles in the initial design of the comprehensive statewide program.

The designers of the statewide program operated in a network, a loosely coupled system orchestrated by Nancy Kaufman and Langley Keyes. They met in formal and informal forums. They shifted, at times, from one institutional role to another, and worked in a constantly changing, sometimes chaotic, policy environment. They were helped by the presence of certain constants: a policy arena in which the same configuration of institutional actors remained more or less in place and a policy object (the program to be designed) that served as a continuous focus of attention.

By 1984 it had become clear that the causes of homelessness were multiple and interactive, which greatly increased the complexity of program design. Nevertheless, the designers eventually agreed on a program rationale based on a view of homelessness as a "multidimensional human services issue."[18] Its conceptual structure depended on a typology of homeless people linked to an analysis of the different causes of homelessness, overlaid on a continuum of housing and welfare services that matched sequential stages of treatment. All services were to be organized around a few central principles: prevention, comprehensiveness, decentralized access, continuity of care, and differentiation by population, geography, and stage of passage through the system.

The designers distinguished three homeless populations—economic, situational, and chronic—each of which corresponded to a major cause of homelessness. The *economic homeless,* whom the media dubbed "the new homeless," were on the street because they could not find a place to live that they could afford. They had "dropped out of the market." They were poor, or nearly poor; they consisted mostly of families with children; and they were victims of a tightening housing market, the condominiumization of rental apartments, and the drying up of housing subsidies and supports. The *situational homeless* were households, often single women with children, that suffered from family turbulence or domestic violence. They were on the street, as Bassuk had argued, because of trauma or personal disorganization that made them unable to manage the process of finding and maintaining housing. The distinction between the economic and situational homeless was an attempt to take account of the polar positions taken by Bassuk and the advocates, as well as by the "housers" and the social service workers. In this debate, to caricature it, one side argued that people act crazy because they lack good housing, and the other that people lack good housing because they act crazy. As Langley Keyes has written, where one draws the line between the economic and situational homeless depends on where one stands in this debate.[19]

By 1984, in any case, all parties involved in the design of the statewide program were aware that homeless families were a major part of the problem of homelessness, and that their problems were very different from the problems of homeless individuals. These individuals were included in the category of the *chronic homeless* made up of bag ladies, vagrants, alcoholics, drug addicts, and other disoriented individuals, all of whom were traditionally described as "street people." All of them suffered from the disappearance of the skid rows of the central cities that had provided them, in earlier years, with a basis for marginal survival. For such people, it was generally recognized, housing would not be enough.

Against this typology of homelessness, the designers of the Massachusetts program arrayed a sequence of services: emergency services (shelter, food, clothing, and financial support), transitional services (housing and employment assistance, social and health services), and stabilization (access to permanent housing, employment, and social supports). The several homeless populations were expected to flow through the stages of this system. First they would go to emergency shelters, and then to transitional housing. Families would be temporarily housed in hotels and motels, where they would receive housing search services and counseling and, if they were eligible, gain access to vouchers for the housing subsidies that gave access to permanent housing.

The comprehensive program contained several further provisions. Transitional housing would be specially designed for the mentally ill, drug and alcohol addicted, or socially disabled. The state would provide large-scale funding for the construction of new affordable housing. Families at risk of becoming homeless would be offered preventive services, including emergency and fuel assistance, tenant advocacy, and counseling and negotiation aimed at preventing unnecessary eviction.

The administration of this multistaged program was to rely on a high level of interagency coordination since it would not have a bureaucracy of its own and would be highly decentralized. Service delivery would be delegated to a network of local conveners made up of public housing agencies, private shelters, and nonprofit organizations.

## STAGE 2 (1986–88): DISCOVERING THE FLAWS

The new statewide program was implemented piecemeal in 1984 and the years immediately following. By 1985, 320 homeless families occupied rooms in hotels and motels, and a pilot housing subsidy voucher program had been established on Cape Cod. Under the state's Section 707 program, 250 vouchers were issued to families, each covering the gap between 25 percent of household income and the actual cost of rental housing up to a limit of $500 per month. By 1986, 500 families were living in the hotels and motels on a steady state basis, and about 1,800 had moved from emergency to permanent housing. In this year, too, the state set up 27 local, small-scale family shelters. They were run by local nonprofit agencies, and the DPW paid 75 percent of their costs.

In 1987, the voucher program went statewide, with a total of 2,400 vouchers distributed to homeless families. From 1986 through 1989, 3,500 vouchers were so distributed. In the same period, prevention programs were initiated. DPW now had 28 housing services workers of its own and funded 18 staff members within regional nonprofit agencies to work with welfare families at risk of becoming homeless. DPW estimated that 450 families participated in its program, of which 405 were able to remain in existing housing. EOCD's estimate was that its prevention programs, budgeted at about $500 thousand annually, had helped to keep some 8,000 families in existing housing.

New affordable housing construction initiatives were taken by the governor and approved by the legislature in 1985. By 1987, some 3,400 units had been built under the state's Sharp and Teller programs, and 1,000 more were in the planning stage, while, under Section 707, 1,500 units had been built and 1,300 more were in planning. By 1988 a total of 3,000 units of low- and moderate-income housing were under development by EOCD, and the governor had announced an additional $7.1 million for the construction of affordable housing to serve 1,200 more homeless families.[20]

The state could now claim that its emergency housing system provided enough beds so that no one needed to remain on the street because of a lack of available places; that large numbers of families were now moving through the system, passing from emergency shelters to hotels and motels, receiving vouchers, and moving on to permanent housing; that preventive services were being provided to many tenants judged to be at risk; and that thousands of new affordable units were under construction.

Nevertheless, observers inside and outside the state bureaucracy still had much to complain about. The concept of a comprehensive program had proved difficult to sustain in implementation. The designers had learned, for example, that a system suited to homeless individuals was very different from one suited to homeless families with children. There were now, in the words of one observer, "two different shelter systems with nothing in common except health care," and the relatively simple program matrix became much more complex when individuals and families were distinguished within the types of homeless populations.

Some critics argued that, in any case, the scope of the state's program was inadequate. Paul McGerigle, for one, complained that the state had done little more than build more shelters and put more money into existing ones. He saw "no real system out there, except . . . a system of shelters." He thought the state could use three times the number of beds in hotels and motels, and that "the prevention system is not really real."[21] Many observers, in addition to McGerigle, criticized the state because, with a few local exceptions, it had still not integrated welfare, social, and housing search services into its emergency housing.

## PERSISTENT CONFLICTS

More than a few of these shortcomings were due to the program's administrative design, which overlay the budgetary priorities of homelessness on agencies whose primary missions were defined in other terms. This design had worked reasonably well in the early months of the crisis, when the statewide program held a place of privilege in the bureaucracy. But in 1984, homelessness lost its special place. Nancy Kaufman was asked to move from the Office of Human Resources in the governor's office to the Executive Office of Human Services, and the agencies, disgruntled by the compromises they had made when the program was ascendant, became less compliant.

Some observers felt that there had never been the real joining of the services needed to make the program work. For example, Irene Lee, coordinator of mental health services for the homeless, thought that the program's coherence depended on a powerful official like Phil Johnston who would go to each agency and ask, "Where is homelessness in your budget?" When Johnston stopped doing this, she thought, the program became "a jig-saw puzzle bedeviled by turf wars," and, as each institution began to see how the program's implementation threatened its traditional interests, conflicts that had arisen in the design phase surfaced anew. Five of these conflicts were especially significant:

1) The DSS and DMH tried as much as possible to distance themselves from the homelessness issue, and in the early years they

succeeded in doing so. At DSS, the director, Sandy Metava, made no secret of her belief that other needy groups, such as abused children, juvenile offenders, sexual offendees, incarcerated mothers, and children with AIDS, deserved priority. Until DSS was on a solid footing with these populations, she believed, it should leave the homeless alone. DMH, in turn, claimed that both its priorities and its distinctive competence lay in the administration of the state's mental health system. It resisted dealing with street people it considered unsuitable for therapy; even community mental health centers refused to accept the homeless as clients.

The reluctance of these agencies to join the program left critically important gaps in screening candidates for hotels and motels, providing social and mental health services, and creating special transitional housing for substance abusers, the mentally ill, and the socially disabled.

2) The legislature proved unwilling to fund preventive services at the level requested by the governor. In spite of the preventive activities undertaken by DPW and EOCD, the potentially overwhelming threat of families at risk of becoming homeless remained substantially unabated.

3) In 1986, the uneasy truce between the state and the advocates came apart as the advocates sued the state for $600 million to fill the poverty gap. A lower court judge ruled, much to the state's surprise, that the legislature could be compelled to provide a specific level of funding for the homeless. But this judgment was overturned by a higher court. In the course of the litigation, the state argued that in-kind goods like services and housing should be counted as part of the state's contribution to welfare recipients, and the advocates countered by demanding cash on the line. The suit would eventually be settled, at least as far as homelessness was concerned, by the state's agreement to earmark a certain number of housing certificates for homeless families.

4) The need to provide services to families in the shelters and hotels and motels triggered disputes over who should provide which services, how services should be defined and grouped, and whether support of families should be contingent on their willingness to accept services. Each agency and interest group had its own way of looking at these issues.

The housing search was a particularly thorny problem, since without it families could not be moved from transitional to permanent housing. As one observer remarked, "[The state] got them in there safe and sound under a roof, and then realized they weren't able to get them out." But of the several agencies that might have provided these services, none wanted to do so. Although DPW was perfectly willing to fund the services, it resisted delivering them; a 1973 policy decision that separated social services from cash support had effectively removed DPW from the social service business. DPW wanted EOCD to provide the services because it was closest to the housing market and the landlords, but EOCD refused to do so on the grounds that the housing search was inseparable from counseling and social services, both of which fell outside its expertise. EOCD wanted DSS to take on the job, but DSS begged off, arguing that welfare recipients would be threatened by the agency they saw as taking children from their families.

Eventually, the DPW got the CAPs to take on housing services as a separately funded program. Then EOCD, which financed the CAPs, agreed after all to accept overall responsibility for coordinating services. DSS agreed to provide social services in the hotels and motels; the CAPs took care of the housing search; and all-inclusive services were provided in the shelters.

5) The early struggles between EOCD and DPW over housing queues and problem families persisted well into the program's implementation phase. EOCD continued to defend its carefully planned system for access to limited affordable housing, while DPW continued to advocate that every welfare-eligible family should get a voucher, and that priority in the public housing queues should be assigned to families who fell under the emergency category of homelessness. Only with the partial settlement of the advocates' suit against the state, as stated, was EOCD forced to set aside a number of housing vouchers for the homeless and change its regulations to make homelessness an emergency category.

EOCD and DPW also came into conflict over the issue of "eviction for cause." The question was whether or not a family evicted from state-supported affordable housing for a cause like drug dealing still had the right to enter a shelter and receive a new voucher. If the answer was yes, EOCD saw itself having to readmit families it had already expelled to protect the viability of its housing. But DPW argued that families evicted from public housing would only fall back into the pool of homeless, welfare-eligible people that DPW would still be legally obliged to serve.

In general, EOCD tried to use the welfare system as a mechanism for controlling problem families in order to preserve the integrity of its housing stock. For example, when negligent tenants failed to pay the rent on time and their rent arrearages mounted up, EOCD wanted DPW to funnel welfare checks directly to landlords as "protective payments." Under Chuck Atkins, however, DPW resisted being drawn into the role of exercising social control over troublesome tenants, a role that Atkins saw as incompatible with DPW's primary obligation to meet its clients' needs.

## PERVERSE INCENTIVES

Between 1987 and 1989, as Nancy Kaufman and her colleagues tried to cope with service gaps and interagency disputes, all the actors involved in the statewide program became gradually aware of a new and overriding problem. As the resources the state poured into the program for the homeless kept increasing, so did the number of people in the system. Homelessness reconstituted itself.

The first sign of trouble was a 1987 state-sponsored study that pointed to the rising number of families in the hotels and motels.[22] In a system that had been designed to hold no more than two hundred or three hundred families, the number in 1987 approached six hundred. Although almost three times as many families had been permanently housed in FY1987 as in FY1986, new entries into the system were increasing at a faster rate than the exits. The author of the study sought the cause of this phenomenon in the state's policy of giving vouchers almost exclusively to families in the temporary shelter system, which had created "perverse incentives." She stated that families were making themselves homeless in order to gain entry to the hotels and motels: "This policy has had the unintended consequence of encouraging some desperate families to become homeless and enter an emergency shelter in order to access the scarce housing subsidies."[23]

In 1988, an EOCD working paper observed that, in spite of "the dramatic increase in rental subsidies for the homeless, the number of people entering the emergency shelter system continues to grow."[24] Although nine thousand people had received housing vouchers and had been placed in permanent housing, there were still approximately eighty-two thousand families on welfare, of which about two-thirds lived in unsubsidized units, with as many as twenty thousand of these doubled-up in apartments and at risk of becoming homeless. As families left the hotels and motels, they were replaced by others from this enormous backlog of at-risk welfare families.

By 1989, it had become clear just how homelessness reconstituted itself and how the state's policies created perverse incentives. Homeless families and tenants at risk, and the advocates, social workers, and landlords who dealt with them, had learned that entry into the shelters, hotels, and motels was the best or only way to gain access to long-term housing subsidies. Recognizing that vouchers were available only in transitional housing, many different kinds of people had learned to play the system. For example, a landlord might agree to evict a tenant so that the tenant could get into the housing pool; later, the landlord would rerent the same unit to the tenant. This would assure the landlord of a guaranteed income while at the same time providing the tenant with an attractive subsidy.

The rising numbers of families in the hotels and motels became the focus of a new state crisis.[25] The governor, already contemplating the presidential bid he would make in 1987, ordered his agency heads to get the numbers down. They responded in characteristically different ways. DPW quickly hired a staff of twenty-four to "blitz" the problem by pouring new services into the hotels and motels. Chuck Atkins was said to have screamed, "We gotta do something about the H and M numbers. It's my name that's going to be on the front page of the *Globe!*" EOCD decided to tighten its rules so as to give preference to tenants at risk, requiring that entry to a shelter, hotel, or motel could be gained only from a primary residence. But DPW's approach was directed exclusively at the problem of clearing the hotels and motels; it had no effect on inputs to the system. EOCD's approach depended on figuring out how to screen candidates as they entered the system, a task that raised the elusive problem of social control.

As key actors came to recognize the perverse incentives they had inadvertently built into their program, they also became newly aware that homelessness was closely coupled to substance abuse and family disintegration. They learned that 40 percent of the families in transitional housing were drug addicts. Battered women, abused children, and evicted families were found, in many instances, to be direct or indirect victims of substance abuse. Crack was rapidly coming to be seen as the critical problem. The system's managers were also being confronted by protests from city officials in working-class communities like Lynn, Malden, and Lawrence, where many previously homeless families torn apart by substance abuse were ending up. Lacking social and educational services, hampered by budgetary restrictions, these communities were scarcely able to cope with high concentrations of social pathology, and they were furious at the thought that the burden of the state's program for the homeless was being unfairly "dumped" on them.

Carole Johnson, an advocate who had moved over to DMH, where she now had responsibility for services to the homeless, spoke—in different terms than the advocates had used earlier—of Ellen Bassuk's study that showed "the profound isolation" of the homeless and their very high incidence of early childhood violence. Johnson talked of social disorganization and chaos so great that "we don't even have words to talk about it; it's like talking about black holes." But she was reluctant to make her views public. "If you start talking about this stuff," she said, "the State will exploit it to stop everything and just do group therapy!"[26]

The managers of the state's homelessness program began to reframe the problem of homelessness. In private, if not always in their public pronouncements, they recognized the magnitude, complexity, and diabolical character of homelessness as a bottomless pit in which they saw the pervasive effects of drugs, family disintegration, and social chaos. Many of them now sensed an urgent need to reduce the perverse incentives that led people to play the system. Many now saw it as legitimate to think in terms of social control—to evict problem families from state-supported housing in order to keep that housing viable, and to treat a client's willingness to accept housing search and social services as a mandatory condition for receiving housing subsidies. But, in the face of continuing pressure from the advocates and quarreling among the agencies, it was by no means clear how to achieve these objectives.

## STAGE 3 (1989–90): FIXING THE FLAWS

In 1988, Nancy Kaufman took a year's leave at Harvard's Kennedy School of Government. When she returned to the state in summer of 1989 as deputy commissioner of welfare under a new commissioner, she found things greatly changed.

Economic growth in Massachusetts had come to a virtual standstill, and revenues were falling well below expectations; and, as the state's fiscal condition deteriorated, political compassion for the homeless sank to a low ebb. Funds for the homeless were in short supply. No new funds for affordable housing were forthcoming, and existing sources of subsidy were disappearing. Section 707 funds and welfare set-asides were drying up, leaving only a trickle of federal money under Section 8. At the same time, the declining state economy had begun to produce some softening in the housing market, though no one could say exactly how much.

After his unsuccessful presidential run, the governor was back in the state. But with the much-vaunted Massachusetts Miracle turned sour, his credibility as a public manager had rapidly eroded. He was at loggerheads with the legislature over budget cuts and new taxes, and he was accused of having neglected the state's affairs, permitting the growth of a ballooning deficit that might have been avoided had the decline in revenues been detected in time and offset earlier by spending cuts.

In the roster of the state's homelessness program, some old players had left the game and some new ones had joined it. Although Amy Anthony remained as secretary of EOCD, Langley Keyes had returned to his professorship at MIT. Chuck Atkins had left DPW in 1987 and had been replaced by Carmen Camino-Siegrist.

When Kaufman returned to work under Camino-Siegrist as deputy commissioner for program operations in DPW, with responsibility for homeless programs, income maintenance, and field operations, she found the bottomless pit of homelessness still very much in evidence. The number of families in the hotels and motels still exceeded five hundred. But from her year away she brought back a new approach to the problem.

In a course on negotiation at the Kennedy School, she had found herself together with Kathy Mainzer, one of the leading advocates. The two women decided to make their term project the design of a negotiation game based on homelessness policy in the state. As Kaufman considered how she might somehow alter the predictable responses of the institutional actors who would sit around a negotiating table, it occurred to her that institutional roles had to be re-examined. Prevention was key, since for every twenty individuals categorized as homeless at any given time, there were eighty who were at risk of becoming homeless. If the revolving door and the perverse incentives were to be corrected, families needed to be discouraged from entering the system.[27] Kaufman knew that both EOCD and the local housing authorities were searching for a better way to verify homelessness, and that welfare workers were tired of accepting "notes from Mommy." It occurred to her that DSS might be induced to screen families who sought entry to the hotels and motels. Screening could then be based on risk to the health and safety of children, which was central to DSS's traditional mission, and the advocates would find it hard to fight such a proposal, since they could not know in advance how many families would be excluded by it.

Soon after returning to DPW, Kaufman had breakfast with Sandy Metava of DSS. In the early days of the statewide program, DSS had wanted to remain on the sidelines. Now Kaufman found that Metava responded positively to the idea that DSS should take on the job of screening family candidates for the hotels and motels, which she saw as a front door to DSS services. Overwhelmed by its caseload, DSS now saw the verification process as consistent with its mission, and realized that it could use that process as a check on the effectiveness of its own case management. Moreover, DPW now proposed to pay DSS for its services, which offered it a further incentive for participation at the same time that DPW gained a degree of control over the process.

The two women proceeded to work out the details of the new verification scheme. There would be three categories of risk: children in immediate danger; children at risk, though not immediately in danger; and children not at risk. Only families placed in the first two categories would get preferential access to housing subsidies.

Shortly after this successful meeting with Metava, Kaufman met with Amy Anthony and won her agreement to the new procedure. She then arranged for Camino-Siegrist to meet with Metava to close the deal.

There were now four women in the key state roles. They liked and trusted each other, shared a view of the statewide problem to be solved, and were ready to work together to solve it. Moreover, in their dealings with the advocates they were able to present a united front. Kaufman, herself a former advocate, had managed to maintain credibility with her old colleagues. Camino-Siegrist, a Hispanic mother who had raised three sons by herself, could credibly claim that she really cared about single mothers. At the same time, she could be tough—unlike her predecessor, Chuck Atkins, who lacked credibility with the advocates, had staked his tenure on an alliance with them, and tended to treat them deferentially. Camino-Siegrist favored strict screening of families for eligibility and demanded that the families reciprocate for subsidies by taking steps to improve their own condition.

After they had closed the "front door"—the hotels and motels—Kaufman and Camino-Siegrist decided to tighten up the "back door"—the family shelters. Families in the shelters were considered the more serious cases. They were formally limited to a ninety-day stay, the period for which the federal government reimbursed the state, but many of them habitually stayed longer. Now, in order to better manage the back door, DPW initiated a case management system under which families would first receive a ten-day notice and would then be reviewed. Camino-Siegrist, described by Kaufman as a "frustrated case worker," conducted these reviews herself.

When DPW checked on the status of families screened out of the hotels and motels or removed from the shelters, they found that many families had been able to find alternative housing for themselves or had chosen to remain doubled up with relatives or friends in existing housing. What was happening, in Kaufman's view, was that, although the state continued to experience an urgent need for affordable housing, the shelters, hotels, and motels were no longer perceived as the obvious route to housing subsidies. As a result, places in the hotels and motels no longer exerted so strong an attraction for families at risk of homelessness.

To be sure, the advocates continued at each step of the way to challenge the new restrictions. They objected to the new verification procedures, claiming that some families were frightened away because they feared the DSS would separate them from their children. They brought suit against DPW, claiming that its ninety-day time limit on stays in the family shelters was unfair. In response to this suit, DPW rewrote its regulations, basing them now on a criterion it regarded as more fundamental: the willingness of families to cooperate with DPW in improving their situations and searching out housing alteratives.

Because of the new state practices introduced in 1989–90, and perhaps to some extent because of the reduced availability of housing subsidies and the softening of the housing market, the number of families in hotels and motels dropped off sharply to 125 families in August 1990, compared to over 500 in the summer of 1989. By the same comparison, the total homeless caseload dropped from 1,066 to 678, and the total number of families served in the course of a year declined by 24 percent from 6,200 in 1989 to 4,700 in 1990.[28] There was a secondary benefit to this reduction in numbers: the small number of families now coming into the system could be "case managed," each family in its own terms.

When these lower numbers were placed in the context of the statewide program as a whole, the picture was one of substantial progress. Some sixty-five shelters for homeless families now existed in the commonwealth. Housing search services were integrated into the prevention program, and 25 percent of all family placements in permanent housing were managed in this way, with the result that from 1989 to 1990 about fifteen thousand families were transferred to permanent housing. Finally, the special transitional housing gap had been partly filled. In shelters run by the Department of Public Health, eighty beds had been created for families suffering from substance abuse. Stays in these shelters were limited to nine months, with DSS standing again as a threat if families did not cooperate with the state to work out viable arrangements for themselves.

# CONCLUSION

## POLICY DIALECTIC AND DESIGN CONVERSATION

The story of the development of homelessness policy in Massachusetts in the 1980s certainly fits our description of a policy dialectic. It was a drama of political contention in which elected officials, bureaucrats, and advocates competed to hitch on to the newly christened issue of homelessness in order to further their own policy agendas. It was a process of cooperative antagonism in which each of the key actors saw homelessness through the lens of its own action frame. It was also a symbolic contest in which conflicting frames expressed themselves both in policy controversies among some of the actors and in a policy dilemma shared, in various ways, by all of them.

The policy drama of homelessness was also a design conversation. The designing system constructed a policy object, the statewide program, and sent it out into the larger environment, accompanied by verbal messages about the object's meaning and intended use. But the object was picked up and interpreted by actors in the larger environment—homeless families, social workers, advocates, and landlords—who constructed their own meanings for it and used it in their own ways. They talked back to the policy designers, challenging their intentions and assumptions, and the designers listened.

The designers' discovery of the rising number of families in the hotels and motels led them to reframe the very phenomenon of homelessness, which they came to see as a bottomless pit, a self-reconstituting problem magnified by the very policies that had been intended to reduce it. This discovery revealed flaws in the design of the policy object, exacerbating the dilemma with which the state had struggled throughout the decade: how to meet the needs of the homeless and keep the governor's political bargain with the advocates, while at the same time remaining faithful to a policy of fiscal restraint that required the exercise of social control. In the light of this reframing of the problem of homelessness, and in a new climate of economic stringency and reduced political compassion, a coalition of agency heads reinvented their policy practices in order to correct patterns of behavior they now saw as responsible for their program's perverse effects.

The actors were constrained by the politics of the policy contest, by conflicting action frames that shaped their interests and restricted their openness to evidence, and by the vicissitudes of a shifting policy context. Within these limits, however, they managed to engage in design-rational inquiry. They did so especially at two policy windows: the first, in which they planned the statewide program, and the second, in which they detected flaws in their design and tried to correct them.

The Massachusetts story portrays a policy conversation that is reflective in ways largely absent from the stories of early retirement in Germany and Project Athena at MIT. First of all, between 1987 and 1989 policy practitioners in Massachusetts demonstrated, at least intermittently, a cumulative inquiry into the changing policy situation. A kind of background learning percolated through the whole policy arena. By the late 1980s, even the most committed advocates saw that substance abuse, mental illness, an absence of social supports, and the deterioration of the social fabric were central to the plight of the homeless, and that housing alone could not resolve that black hole. Similarly, all the key actors saw that the crisis of the numbers in the hotels and motels represented an influx of families at risk of homelessness who were making themselves homeless in order to qualify for access to housing subsidies. To be sure, advocates and bureaucrats interpreted this phenomenon in different ways. The advocates saw it as an exercise of legitimate entitlement, the bureaucrats as an abandonment of restraint that threatened to overwhelm the state's limited resources.

The Massachusetts policy conversation was reflective in a further sense. At each of the two policy windows, some of the actors listened to the back talk generated by their moves, reflecting on and learning from the results of their designing, and they tried to understand the conflicting action frames and interests that threatened to bring their policymaking process to a halt. In the early 1980s, Kaufman and Keyes worked out a compromise acceptable to contending factions in the governor's Advisory Committee, and in the late 1980s, Kaufman, together with her coalition, managed to unblock the policy design process that had been stuck on dead center. Critical to her success was the fact that she had distanced herself from her own position enough to inquire into the sources of stalemate in the state system as a whole and thereby set the stage for an invention that could unlock that stalemate.

### FRAME SYNTHESIS

Kaufman's invention embodied a synthesis of metacultural frames. To be sure, the synthesis lay wholly within the discretionary frame and did not include the advocates' view of housing as a God-given right. But with its metaphor of closing the front and back doors, it did yield a bottom-up resolution of the previously contending frames of social welfare, market, and social control.

The verification procedure based on children at risk funnelled housing vouchers to the neediest families, according to a principle of fairness derived from the social welfare frame. Social control was embodied in the screening procedures that prevented families at risk of homelessness from making themselves homeless in order to gain access to vouchers. Social workers helped families who were denied vouchers to find housing they could afford on the open market, which reflected a market-frame view of the state's responsibility to meet family needs for housing only when the market failed. Similarly, the invention by which Kaufman and Camino-Siegrist closed the back door of the family shelters permitted need-meeting for families in distress but set a limit on the duration of the state's provision of shelter. In both cases, subsidies or services were delivered to the neediest within a framework of social control set, first, by verification procedures that determined who the neediest were and, second, by procedures of review and contracting that required families to take steps to improve their own conditions—which meant arriving at the point of being able to satisfy their needs in the open market.

These frame-synthetic inventions also resolved the political dilemma that had bedevilled the governor throughout the decade: how to keep a human face turned toward the human services lobby while at the same time behaving like a prudent fiscal manager. Of course, the resolution's durability would depend on features of the context that lay beyond the governor's control: the political economy of stringency, which increased the likelihood of finding affordable market housing for the poor, and the climate of reduced political compassion for the homeless, which weakened the advocates' political clout. In a new political-economic context, the housing market might tighten up again, and a revitalized advocate group might come charging back into the arena, reactivating the policy controversy and, with it, the governor's dilemma.[29] Nevertheless, at least for a limited time, the coalition of state bureaucrats had invented a way to unblock that controversy and resolve that dilemma.

# PART III

# Toward Frame-Reflective
# Policy Conversation

# CHAPTER 7

# Design Rationality Revisited

We began this book by questioning reflection's place in policy practice, and by claiming, contrary to Hannah Arendt and the prevailing academic wisdom, that competent practitioners can reflect on the meaning of the policy-making game from a position within it. We suggested that policy controversies are frame conflicts that may be pragmatically resolved by reframing, and that such frame reflection is central to design rationality—the kind of limited reason that is feasible and appropriate in policy making. We set out to investigate these relationships in three case studies of policy-making practice.

Here we describe what we have learned. We present a fuller picture of design rationality, which has so far emerged piecemeal, and take up some of the questions it raises for an empirical epistemology of reframing:

1) How is frame reflection represented in the thought and action of policy practitioners? How shall we recognize it when we see it at work?

2) How is frame-reflective resolution of policy controversies possible in light of the relativist predicament?

3) How is it that situated policy controversies lend themselves to pragmatic resolution, although generic controversies, abstracted from particular policy situations, remain intransigent?

4) Situated, frame-reflective policy practice requires creating and maintaining conditions of mutual trust. How do such conditions operate, and how may they be achieved?

5) How can the picture of design rationality that we have derived from our three cases be applied more generally? How is it that we find frame-reflective resolution of policy controversies in some cases and not in others?

## DESIGN RATIONALITY SUMMARIZED

As we review the conception of design rationality that has emerged piecemeal in our case studies, we begin with the simplest possible case of designing, revisiting the sketch of designing we first presented in our description of German early retirement in chapter 4. We explore what rationality means in this case and how it differs from problem solving or search as models of rationality. We go on, then, to more complex layers of the policy design conversation, first introducing multiple actors and the communicative-political dimensions of designing, and then to action frames, frame conflict, and potential for frame reflection.

### THE SIMPLEST CASE OF DESIGNING

Here we have a designer, a situation in which the designer wants to make an object (however vaguely imagined), and the designer's materials. We might consider a sculptor working with clay, an architect sketching a prospective building, or an inventor tinkering with a mechanism.

A designer works with materials to produce an intended object and discovers that the materials resist, more or less, his attempts to impose his intentions upon them. In this process, the designer's intentions evolve. Design moves inevitably produce some unintended effects, which the designer may see either as flaws to be corrected or as happy accidents that suggest new opportunities. In designing, as distinct from instrumental problem solving, something is being made under conditions of uncertainty and complexity, so that it is not initially clear what the problem is or what it would mean to solve it.

Even in this simplest case of designing, there is a "conversation" between the designer and his materials. The designer is *in* the situation, influenced by his appreciation of it at the same time that he shapes it by his thinking and doing—in Dewey's words, "instituting new environmental conditions that occasion new problems."[1] As anthropologist Edmund Carpenter has written: an Inuit sculptor scrapes away at a reindeer antler with his knife, examining the bone now from one angle, now from another, until he cries out, "Ah, seal!"[2] As Ben Shahn has written about painting, "It is an intimately communicative affair between the painter and his painting, a conversation back and forth, the painting telling the painter even as it receives its shape and form."[3]

In such a design conversation, what does "rationality" mean? The designer's conversation with materials takes the form of seeing/moving/seeing. As the process goes on, the designer sees what he has made, listens (more or less) to back talk from the materials, and thereby constructs new opportunities or problems. Clearly, even in this simple case, design rationality involves reflection—on materials, seeing/moving/seeing, unintended effects, emergent intentions, and the form and character of the evolving object.

These are some of the simplest norms of design rationality:

• As the designer iteratively shapes her object, the problems she sets should be adequate to her appreciation of the possibilities and difficulties inherent in her materials. The problems she sets should be ones that she can eventually solve.

• Problem setting should take account of constraints and possibilities inherent in the situation, including conflicts, complexities, and uncertainties. The formulation of a design task or problem is inadequate if it rests on a model that excludes important features of the situation.

• Typically, an object's design involves many different values and variables, which tend to be interdependent—some of them mutually incompatible. Their meanings vary with shifts in local or global context. Initially, the designer may not have names for them. Hence, the designer's moves cannot produce only intended effects. The designer's continuing inquiry should incorporate the observed effects of her moves as she reformulates both her problem and her solutions in order to take fuller account of the observed complexity of the situation and its gradually discovered field of values and interests. These features are precisely the ones that make it appropriate to speak of design, rather than problem solving, search, or choice.

## THE COMMUNICATIVE-POLITICAL DESIGN DRAMA

As we move on to the second layer of complexity in designing, we see it as a social process in which first-layer processes are distributed among multiple actors—designers, would-be designers, recipients of the designed object, and other stakeholders. Each of them is in conversation with the evolving object and with a larger situation in which the other actors play their parts.

This layer of complexity also contains an external context, including the gallery of public opinion, whose shifts may change the meanings constructed for the object and for the values and constraints that determine how the object can or should be shaped.

Designing is a social process in two ways. First, the designer now becomes a "designing system," a coalition of actors, individual or institutional—for example, the architect-engineers of Project Athena, or the state bureaucrats who forged the Massachusetts statewide program for the homeless. Interactions within the designing system may be, in varying degrees, cooperative or antagonistic. Second, the designing system sends its object out into a larger environment—the larger arena of MIT, for example, or Massachusetts politics–where other actors see, interpret, and respond to it. The social design process now becomes a drama enacted in an arena—an image that captures policy design as well as the collective design of such artifacts as buildings or industrial products.

Social designing is necessarily communicative. Because the actors shape the object through their more-or-less organized interactions, they must communicate with one another, sending and receiving messages in the form of words and actions. These messages include design moves and responses to the object in situations of use. Although vagueness and ambiguity may at times serve useful purposes—for example, by softening disagreement or deferring conflict—the designers cannot effectively make something together unless their communications achieve at least minimal reliability. All first-layer processes—setting problems, seeing/moving/seeing, detecting back talk, interpreting design flaws, fixing flaws, recognizing emergent intentions—must now be carried out through communications that work reliably only if participants are able to test the meanings of the messages they receive, and anticipate and test how others will interpret the meanings of *their* messages.

The social design process is inevitably political. The designing system is a coalition of actors who have their own interests, freedoms, and powers. If that coalition fragments, as the state actor fragmented in the later stages of the early retirement case, the designing system becomes an array of antagonistic parties whose interactions no longer qualify as designing. From this consideration comes the requirement of "double designing," which is to say that substantive design moves must not threaten the integrity of the designing coalition.

The conversation between a designing system and its larger environment is inevitably political. When an object moves across this boundary, the back talk delivered from the policy environment to the designers may carry messages of protest and rejection, such as the protest stirred up by the first embodiment of Project Athena, or the advocates' angry reactions to attempts by Kaufman, Camino-Siegrist, Anthony, and Metava to "close the front and back doors." Such reactions may signal differences of interpretation that trigger contention, leading, in turn, to negotiation or the formation of a new design coalition.

Context dependency also becomes salient at the second layer of design complexity. Shifts in the larger context can affect the meaning of every element of the design process, as happened in both the German early retirement and Massachusetts homelessness cases with the shift from an economic climate of relative sufficiency to one of stringency. Awareness of these shifts may open up policy windows, creating opportunities for the detection and correction of design flaws, or for the perception of new meanings and policy intentions.

The second-layer design process can now be understood as a "four-body problem," in which a designing system interacts with a policy object, but also with other actors in the environment (who also interact with that policy object). The whole policy conversation now also is in interaction with an external context, whose changes can affect the meanings, strategies, moves, and requirements of that conversation.

At the second layer of design complexity, as at the first, reflection is central to design rationality. Now, however, the objects of reflection expand to include the designing system's communication with other actors in the policy drama: the messages sent and received, the interpretations constructed for them, and the tests of such interpretations. All three of our cases—early retirement, Athena, and homelessness—hinge on the controversies triggered by the constructed meanings for policy objects that were unintended by the objects' designers. A second group of norms for design rationality derive from the expanded scope of the designers' reflective inquiry to include their communications with one another and with other actors in the larger policy environment:

> • As a consequence of the structure of the task in which they are engaged, the members of a designing system should seek to arrive at agreements about the problems they are trying to solve and the character and content of the policy object they are trying to shape. Hence,

appropriately rational designers strive for reliable communication. They probe the meanings that lie behind the messages they receive from other designers, and probe other designers' interpretation of the messages *they* receive. They strive for convergence of meaning, at least about what is to be made, even though they may, at any given time, hold different views about the reasons for making it.

• Because policy designing is double designing, the designers' moves must meet both the substantive requirements of problem-setting and -solving and the requirements, political and interpersonal, of sustaining the design coalition. This is partly a matter of keeping in mind the instititutional and individual interests of other members of the coalition, but also of creating and maintaining a level of mutual trust sufficient to sustain cooperative inquiry.

## FRAME DIFFERENCES, FRAME CONFLICTS, AND FRAME REFLECTION

At the third layer of complexity, the design tasks and criteria of design rationality we have already described remain present, but they are complicated by issues arising from the actors' conflicting action frames. Contention enters into the policy design drama because the actors are more or less autonomous individuals and institutions with their own freedoms, powers, and frame-generated interests. As we have pointed out, there are four main ways of dealing with contention: by its continuation or escalation; by a marketing strategy, as in the third stage of the Athena story, in which the designers reshape their object to suit the needs, interests, or wants of other actors in the larger environment; by negotiation, as in the later stages of the early retirement story, in which the contending parties try to arrive at mutually satisfactory compromise; or by co-design, as in the final stage of the homelessness story, in which the contending parties become members of a reformed designing system for the purpose of redesigning the policy object. In co-design, the cooperative side of their cooperative-antagonistic relationship prevails.

Each way of coping with contention has its own criteria of rationality or effectiveness. From the point of view of the contenders, escalating contention can be seen in terms of the effectiveness of strategies of attack or defense. Rationality in marketing has to do with the designers' ability to understand the market they serve and their effectiveness in inventing and testing new versions of their policy object in order to satisfy the market's needs, wants, or interests. Negotiating rationality may be described, as noted earlier, in terms of the negotiators' effectiveness in converting win-lose to win-win situations of joint gains.

In the case of co-design, design rationality calls for frame reflection in three respects, all of which appear in the Massachusetts story:

> 1) The designers may reflect on the changing problematic situation, reframing the problem in order to take account of their new understandings. In the homelessness case, the actors' background learning, their gradual awareness of new features of the policy situation, expressed itself in a shift of metaphors. At first, the actors spoke of "stopping the bleeding"; later, they began to speak of homelessness as a "bottomless pit," a "self-reconstituting problem," and a "black hole." Each actor undertook this reframing for himself—beginning, perhaps, with the controversy between Ellen Bassuk and the advocates—but over time, individual reframings tended to converge on a shared view of the policy situation.

> 2) The designers may reflect on the blockage of their policy-making process. Nancy Kaufman used a negotiating game to simulate the state's policy making for homelessness and explore how it had become stuck. She and her colleagues reflected on the state of play in the policy drama, which led them, in turn, to reflect on the frames the actors brought to that drama and to speculate on moves that might reconstitute the design coalition in such a way as to unblock policy inquiry.

> 3) In close connection with their reflection on the policy-making process, the designers may reflect on the policy object and its associated practices, seeking to understand the frame conflicts that underlie their dilemmas and controversies. Co-design depends upon the ability of at least some of the actors to inquire into the intentions and meanings of other actors involved with them in controversy; and it is here, as we have seen, that situated frame reflection comes into play.

A third group of design-rational norms have to do with frame reflection:

> • Members of a designing system should reflect on the meanings that underlie policy back talk in order to detect unanticipated design flaws or opportunities. Through such reflection they may become aware of controversies, in the light of which they can redesign the poli-

cy object or reframe the values and purposes built into their formulation of the policy problem.

• Designers should reflect on their transactions with the policy environment, exploring how, as in Project Athena, their own actions may have provoked back talk or how, as in the case of homelessness, their actions may have contributed to a dilemma in which they are caught up. Transactional reflection opens up ways in which the designers may rethink the strategies, assumptions, and frames that underlie their design moves.

• Designers should reflect on background learning of the kinds illustrated in both the Athena and the Massachusetts cases. Awareness of new "facts" may lead to and justify a revision of the designer's model of the policy situation and, with this, a reframing of the policy problem that more closely approximates the discovered reality of that situation.

• When the policy-making process is stalemated by controversy, the designers should reflect, as Nancy Kaufman did, on the structure and politics of that process, seeking a pragmatic resolution of controversy through marketing, negotiation, or co-design.

• The effectiveness of co-design may depend, as in the Massachusetts case, on the designers' ability, through situated frame reflection, to invent new features of policy objects or practices that synthesize elements of their conflicting action frames.

## THE FUNDAMENTAL STRUCTURE OF DESIGN RATIONALITY

In describing the three layers of design complexity, we identify one underlying structure of design rationality:

1) There is always a process of making something out of materials, and under conditions of uncertainty and complexity.

2) This means that intentions are always, to some degree, emergent. The designer must be able to form new intentions on the basis of her discovery of the evolving nature of the design situation in which she is engaged.

3) The designer is always in conversation with the design situation. Design rationality is always, in part, a function of the conduct of that conversation, as the designer seeks to grasp the meanings of his moves, and of others' responses to his moves, and to embody his interpretations in the invention of further moves.

4) There is always a process of problem setting and solving, which can be evaluated in terms of its adequacy to the emerging intentions, values, and interests of the designer and other stakeholders in the design, and by reference to features of the design situation discovered through design inquiry.

These basic elements are present in each of the three layers of design complexity. In the second layer, where designing takes the form of a cooperative-antagonistic drama, design rationality become communicative and political. In the third layer, where communicative interactions are complicated by frame conflicts, design rationality expands to incorporate frame reflection.

## FRAME REFLECTION?

Our story of homelessness in Massachusetts presents no evidence of explicit, top-down frame reflection of the kind that we undertook as we constructed the metacultural frames of need, market, and social control. Kaufman, for one, reflected explicitly on a number of things—including the crisis of the numbers, the task of closing the front and back doors, and the policy stalemate—but she did not explicitly reflect on the action or metacultural frames held by actors in the policy arena. How, then, could she and her colleagues work out a synthesis of conflicting metacultural frames?

Possibly, metacultural frames were never explicitly in the actors' minds at all. Perhaps the agency members of the new coalition thought only about specific practices and their likely outcomes, and tinkered with a variety of elements that had existed all along in the agencies' institutional action frames. If so, the actors' "frame synthesis" would have contained nothing new; the pure metacultural frames would have existed only as artifacts of *our* imagination.

As we have already observed, the action frames of agencies, such as DPW and EOCD, *were* hybrids of the frames of social welfare, market, and social control. Throughout the early stages of our story, however, the dominant voice of each institutional actor emphasized one or more these particular metacultural frames at the expense of others. The advocates emphasized entitlement; DPW, social welfare; and EOCD, the market and social control. We have also seen that as the actors became aware of the crisis of the numbers and its causes, and discovered the overwhelming impact of the crack epidemic, their understanding of the problem of homelessness developed toward a view that *combined* the metacultural frames of social welfare, market, and social control. In their reframed problem, with its image of closing the front and back doors, and with the practices they invented to bring that image to reality, they did join together elements of the frames to which they had previously given separate and unequal emphasis.

We suggest that the coalition members reflected on metacultural frames through the medium of specific problems and practices and in this sense engaged in *situated* frame reflection. Perhaps it is a prejudice, Platonic in origin, to assume that the thinking that leads to frame synthesis must operate at the highest level of the policy ladder—to assume that because *we* abstract metaframes from the materials of policy-making practice, others can reflect on them only at that highly abstract level. In the Platonic dialogues, Socrates draws out and makes explicit the taken-for-granted assumptions, principles, and values that underlie the arguments of his interlocutors. He does so in order to reveal gaps and contradictions in their reasoning and to construct the general and abstract Forms (of piety, virtue, and the good, for example), whose definition is usually the manifest purpose of the Platonic dialogues.

We suggest that the Platonic mode of reflection—climbing a ladder of abstraction in order to make taken-for-granted assumptions explicit—is a particular mode of reflection, not the only possible mode. To assume the contrary is like assuming, in the very different domain of physics or mechanics, that mechanical principles such as the lever, or Newton's laws, can be understood only by studying the equations that correspond to these principles, rather than by playing with mechanisms that embody them. But it is well known that people who are unable to write the canonical equations for Newton's laws are sometimes able to manipulate physical objects as though they understood these laws; whereas students who are adept at manipulating the equations are sometimes unable to recognize the real-world phenomena that embody them.[4] Perhaps with mechanisms, as with policies, it is the very language of reflection that gets in our way. This language suggests that we must climb *up* the ladder of abstraction in order to reflect *on* the contents of the levels below. But metacultural frames are embedded in our habits of thought and action. As we attend to the material at hand, we may succeed in reflecting *through* it to frames that are implicit in our understanding *of* it. Those who are adept at climbing up the ladder of abstraction are not necessarily better equipped to reflect on metacultural frames than those who have acquired a feel for the frames built into concrete materials and practices.

## IMPLICATIONS FOR THE RELATIVIST PREDICAMENT

Our story of homelessness in Massachusetts tells how situated policy controversies were reframed and pragmatically resolved through frame reflection. But we claim in chapter 3 that awareness of multiple and conflicting frames poses a dilemma of epistemological relativism. Different frames, we argue, cause us to notice different facts and make us receptive to different arguments, and there is no frame-neutral basis for choosing among them. How, then, did the protagonists of our story avoid the relativist trap? To this question we propose two distinct but closely connected answers.

First, in spite of their general dispositions to notice different facts, the sponsors of conflicting metacultural frames may also be struck by similar perceptions of their policy situation. Over the decade in which our story of homelessness policy unfolded, for example, the key actors discovered, through a kind of background learning, that many families at risk were being drawn to declare themselves homeless by the attractive prospect of gaining access to permanent housing subsidies. Similarly, these actors became aware of the morass of substance abuse and social chaos that surrounded the social phenomenon of homelessness. In spite of—indeed, through the lenses of—their different frames, they became aware of these social facts. The "same" facts, which they interpreted in very different ways, led them all, nonetheless, to reframe the problem of homelessness, and their different but family-resembling reframings set the stage for the frame synthesis they eventually achieved. In Project Athena, too, the actors came to share similar perceptions of at least one feature of the policy situation, although here it stimulated neither frame reflection nor frame synthesis. The anger and disaffection of students and faculty came eventually to be accepted as a social fact by individuals who held radically different views of Athena.

In a somewhat different sense, shared perceptions of the policy situation also help to explain how some actors in the policy drama of homelessness—especially Nancy Kaufman—could put themselves in the shoes of other actors whose views of homelessness were very different from their own. Kaufman was able, for example, to adopt the points of view of EOCD, DSS, and the advocates. Although she worked for the state, she had once been an advocate. She did not share the advocates' view of housing as an entitlement, but she did share their empathy with the homeless and at least a part of their anger at the social injustice of homelessness. Over the decade, as coordinator of the statewide program, she had intimate contact with the perceptions, arguments, and politics of people from EOCD and DSS, and she could readily imagine how each group would probably respond to a wide range of circumstances. In fact, her views on the issues of homelessness were by no means wholly different from theirs. She could see the point of EOCD's concern to protect its housing queues, evict its problem tenants, and increase the state's supply of affordable housing. She understood DSS's need to fulfill its primary mission and empathized with its sensitivity to the fears it inspired among welfare clients.

The ability Kaufman displayed was not one of mapping, or translating, from one actor's frame to another's, but one of finding in her own experience the counterparts of their several views. She was like a method actor who could learn to play others' roles because her own experience was linked in so many different ways to theirs.

We propose, then, that the relativist predicament was not a fatal impediment to reciprocal frame reflection in the homelessness story because the actors' conflicting frames did not *wholly* color their visions of the policy situation. The conflicting frames that led them to notice different facts and stubbornly cling to different arguments nevertheless left room for some of them to be struck by the same salient features of the policy situation—which, on the one hand, caused them to reframe the problem of homelessness in family-resembling ways and, on the other hand, enabled them to enter into one another's viewpoints on the basis of experiences they held in common.

## SITUATED RESOLUTION OF
## POLICY CONTROVERSIES

When policy controversies are abstracted from the situations in which they arise, as in academic discourse, they are removed from the pace and pressure of the policy arena, but they exist in a kind of vacuum where it is hard to imagine how they might ever be resolved. Conflicting metacultural frames, detached from any particular action setting, seem to be frozen at the metacultural level. In the homelessness story, however, we have found not only a pragmatic resolution of policy controversy but one that worked by effecting a synthesis of conflicting metacultural frames. What is it about situated policy practice that lends itself to such a process and makes such an outcome possible?

When policy controversies are situated in the fruitful mire of an actual policy arena, a great variety of processes open up and many different kinds of outcomes become possible.[5] Policy inquiry may bog down. The actors may become embroiled in endless contention, driven round in circles by an underlying policy dilemma that lies beyond their capacity for inquiry, as in the recent controversies about abortion and the disposition of toxic wastes. It may also happen, however, that when policy inquiry is blocked by controversy, further inquiry removes the blockage. This may happen via marketing or negotiation, even though underlying metacultural frames remain in conflict, as we have seen in the case of Project Athena. But the blockage may also be removed by a process of co-design that leads to reframing, as in our Massachusetts case.

Situated policy inquiry may be conducive to the resolution of frame conflicts in several ways. First, the inquirers tend to have an overriding interest in getting something done. Like Kaufman and her colleagues, they tend to have a powerful incentive to make something happen, even though they may have very different ideas of what that something is. Second, situated policy controversies provide informational richness and variety on which actors may draw to invent strategies of pragmatic resolution. In the Massachusetts case, the circumstances under which families tried to gain access to the hotels and motels, the specific mission of DSS and the overload it experienced in 1989, the particular life experience of Camino-Siegrist, the vagaries of federal reimbursement criteria, the regulatory and judicial environments—all played productive roles in the coalition's thinking.

Third, situated controversies lend themselves to pragmatic resolution because the action frames that operate in such controversies tend to be complex variants of pure metacultural frames. The heads of DPW, EOCD, and DSS could invent mutually acceptable policy practices without a wrenching re-examination of their agencies' missions and principles because the elements of their invention were already present in their institutional action frames, even though the agencies' earlier, conflictual positions had given priority to some of these elements at the expense of others. What is more, because institutional action frames are only loosely coupled to the beliefs of individual actors, situated policy controversies contain slack that individuals may exploit in order to improvise pragmatic resolutions of their controversies.

Fourth, situated policy controversies exist in local and global contexts whose shifts may foster their pragmatic resolution. In the Massachusetts case, as noted, the state's economic decline and ballooning deficit undermined political compassion for the homeless and weakened the position of the advocates. Furthermore, the changing cast of characters in the policy drama—especially, the substitution of Camino-Siegrist for Atkins—set the stage for a new approach to the policy problem. Yet the effectiveness of the coalition's inquiry also hinged on the fact that certain contextual elements held constant. The statewide program remained in place throughout the decade, serving as an anchor for learning and redesign. Several of the key actors in the policy arena—especially Kaufman, the principal orchestrator of the program—remained in pivotal positions for nearly a decade, with ample opportunity to reflect on the program's design flaws and the policy stalemate that had prevented the contending agencies from removing those flaws. It was this combination of change and continuity between 1987 and 1989 that set the conditions for productive policy inquiry and culminated in the new coalition's frame-synthetic invention.

Finally, the prospects for pragmatic resolution of policy controversies are enhanced not only because those controversies are situated in policy practice but because actors in the arena jointly engage in a process of policy design in which each actor is obliged to interact and communicate with the others. The actors' different ways of perceiving, interpreting, and valuing, rooted in their conflicting frames, tend to be revealed by their design moves. Consider, for example, how both DPW and EOCD revealed their underlying action frames by their responses to the issue of housing search, and their different ways of dealing with the problem of the rising numbers of families in the hotels and motels.

In such cases, the actors may be struck by their different views of a policy issue; and when they are so struck, they have an opportunity to test their construction of one another's views. This is very much like what goes on in an architectural design studio, where different designers can reveal, by their visible design moves, both how they understand the design situation and how they interpret the meanings of one another's utterances. In a design process, each party reveals his view of the object, and perhaps also his interpretation of the other's messages. So long as the parties are jointly committed to making an object, they find it difficult to avoid dealing with their differences of perception and interpretation. They are continually objectifying their differences. At the same time, the concrete situation, the materials, and the object in transition give the actors hooks on which to hang their attempts to invent adjustments that may resolve their differences—at the limit, synthesizing elements of their conflicting frames.

In contrast, when a policy controversy is not situated, and when the actors do not engage in co-design, then they are under no compulsion to converge on agreed-upon action, and they lack the aids to communication that co-designing provides.

## MUTUAL TRUST

The situated frame reflection described in the homelessness case is a process of cooperative inquiry. However much it may have depended on the initiative and creativity of Nancy Kaufman, it could not have been developed, and the practice inventions that resulted from it could not have been implemented, without the active participation of Camino-Siegrist, Metava, and Anthony. What made this feat of cooperative inquiry possible?

The four women who made up the new coalition of agency heads constituted an informal public forum, continuing a pattern of informal networking that had existed since the early days when Keyes and Kaufman joined forces to build consensus around the statewide plan. In the later stage, as in the earlier, the operation of the informal network depended on relationships of mutual trust.

The four women trusted one another to invent cooperative linkages across the boundaries of their previously warring agencies, and they did so in a political climate that was in many ways conducive to mutual suspicion. They could easily have feared that joining in a cooperative enterprise might threaten their respective positions, loosen their holds on bureaucratic territory, or make them vulnerable to political retribution—especially if one of them were to go public with their informal deliberations. To exhibit trust in such a context is to be prepared to act as though your counterparts will behave cooperatively in spite of the risk that they may not do so and in advance of evidence that reveals how they will behave.[6] Mutual trust is a virtuous circle of anticipation and action whose initiation always requires a leap of faith beyond the available evidence.

On what bases were the four women able to create a behavioral world of mutual trust in a bureaucratic and political climate conducive in so many ways to mutual suspicion? We cannot know the answer to this question, but we can engage in some informed speculation. Let us consider, to begin with, what the women held in common. They seem to have liked each other and to have held one another in mutual respect. They shared a working knowledge of the operations of bureaucracies, central and local, and a practiced understanding of political in-fighting. They emphathized with the plight of homeless and disadvantaged families, but they also shared a wariness of the potentially bottomless human services agenda.

Most important, perhaps, they shared a respect for civitas in the policy-making process, a disposition to work toward the larger purposes of state government, to "solve the Governor's problem," as Keyes and

Kaufman both expressed it. This respect for civitas led the four women to embrace both horns of the governor's policy dilemma: to respond to the needs of families at risk, but to do so in ways that were consistent with prudent management of the state's resources. A commitment to tackling the governor's problem, the "whole problem," meant, in Kaufman's words, meeting the needs of the 20 percent of families who found themselves homeless at any given time, while also keeping the remaining 80 percent of families at risk from falling out of existing housing. Civitas, the participants' commitment to solving what they shared as a vision of the whole problem, fulfilled two crucial functions: it provided them with a basis for mutual trust, and it gave them a place to stand from which to engage in reciprocal reflection.

Friendship, mutual respect, solidarity, and civitas may override prevailing norms of win-lose bureaucratic or political behavior. Even these pre-existing conditions of mutuality may fail, however, if the antagonisms of a policy arena overflow into the forum in which reciprocal frame reflection is attempted. Breaches of trust are not unusual. When they occur, the participants' ability to repair them depends on their ability to act in such a way as to restore mutual confidence, by communicating second-order messages—above and beyond the face value of what they actually say and do—from which their counterparts can infer the reliability of the temporary world they jointly inhabit. The basis of mutual trust lies not only in shared purposes and values, but in shared competences to create behavioral worlds conducive to the leap of faith on which trust depends.

The special conditions of policy inquiry created and sustained by the coalition of agency heads suggests certain features of the idealized policy discourse described in chapter 3: notably, Habermas's ideal speech situation and John Forester's image of a civic, republican discourse. We lack the data to explore to what degree the four women managed to conduct a dialogue characterized by "truth, freedom, and justice." That they may have approximated this ideal is suggested, however, by the fact that although they headed agencies with recent histories of institutional antagonism, they were able to generate enough mutual trust to work out a joint policy invention that synthesized elements of their agencies' conflicting action frames.

## THE GENERALITY OF DESIGN RATIONALITY

The picture of design rationality sketched in this chapter is incomplete in several respects. We have discussed only a few of the norms represented in our case studies (saying nothing, for example, about the operation of prototypes and exemplars in policy design), and our brief discussions only scratch the surface (books could be written, for example, about rationality in marketing, negotiation, and co-design). In neither of these respects shall we try here to remedy the incompleteness of our sketch of design rationality. Our purpose is more limited. We have tried to show how the ideas of policy design conversation and design rationality can respond to the inadequacies of prevailing models of rational choice, politics, and negotiation; to suggest how these ideas can account for the situated inquiry of reflective policy practitioners; and to explore their complex connections to the reframing of intractable policy controversies.

There is a third kind of incompleteness in our account which we cannot wholly ignore, however: the fact that it derives from only three case studies. It is true that these cases represent widely different policy domains and settings—suggesting, for example, that our findings may be relevant to policy making within institutions as well as across institutions in the public sphere. Nevertheless, the generality of our view of design rationality remains an open question; a different sample of public policy cases might suggest a different view.

We believe that our account of design rationality should be tested against many additional cases of policy making, preferably cases observed at close range over long periods of time. It may be useful, however, to consider at this point what it would mean for our picture of design rationality *not* to be generally applicable. We can envisage two kinds of exceptions to it, lying at polar extremes of a spectrum that ranges from order to chaos and from harmony to contention. At one extreme, the policy situation would present a high degree of order and a virtual absence of contention. There would be no policy dialectic, no controversy, and minimal uncertainty. The model of rational choice would have its greatest applicability here, and the factors that require a policy design perspective (and with it, design rationality) would be least in evidence.

At the opposite pole, the policy situation would be so polarized, contentious, and chaotic that policies could only be understood as consequences of antagonism and chance. Policy design would be inapplicable to this situation—or applicable only in a Pickwickian sense.

Although these caricatured extremes are unlikely to be found in the actual world of policy making (the second, perhaps, somewhat more likely than the first), it is not hard to imagine cases that would be enough like them to count as exceptions to our account. Between these extremes, however, there is a vast middle range where the conditions of policy dialectic and design conversation hold; and where they hold, it seems to us, the three layers of design-rational norms will be applicable. First, messy problematic situations will have to be converted to manageable policy problems, and policy objects will have to be constructed under conditions of complexity and uncertainty. Second, policy makers will be called upon to reach agreements in a policy arena that combines antagonism and cooperation, and will therefore need to strive for reliable communication.

As to the third layer of design complexity, which introduces norms of frame-reflective policy inquiry, some further discussion is in order. What reasons are there to believe that reflection on the frames involved in interpreting the meanings of policy objects, the problems of policy situations, the blockage of policy-making processes, are *generally* appropriate to the broad middle range of policy practice? We have touched on the answer to this question in the previous section, but we take it up at greater length here. We see four distinct but complementary arguments for the general relevance of frame-reflective policy inquiry. We derive these arguments from the potential for miscommunication among policy actors, from the actors' (often unrecognized) transactions with the policy environment, from the need to detect and correct design flaws, and from policy stalemates and pendulum swings. We consider each of these in turn.

## THE COMMUNICATIVE IMPERATIVE

All parties involved in a policy design conversation have a rational interest in the reliability of their communications, both within the boundaries of a designing system and in that system's interactions with the larger policy environment. When these communicative processes are unreliable, policy makers run the risk of missing the point of one another's messages or misreading others' interpretations of policy design moves.

A dramatic example of such miscommunication has come up recently in the form of a review of the Cuban Missile Crisis conducted by its Soviet and American participants. Just after the last of these meetings, on January 14, 1992, Robert McNamara, secretary of defense under presidents Kennedy and Johnson, said in an interview with the *New York Times* that "the actions of all three parties [Americans, Russians, and Cubans] were shaped by misjudgments, miscalculations and misinformation."[7] McNamara went on to say that in 1962 the Soviet Union had sent short-range nuclear weapons to Cuba, and that Soviet commanders there were authorized to use them in the event of an American invasion. According to McNamara, the Americans knew nothing about the presence of these weapons on Cuban soil, and the Soviets did not expect American nuclear retaliation.

According to Andrei Gromyko, who was Soviet foreign minister during the crisis, the Soviets had sent nuclear warheads to Cuba "to strengthen Cuba's defensive capability," because they believed a U.S. invasion of Cuba was probable. McNamara reported, on the other hand, that "we had absolutely no intention of invading Cuba, and therefore the Soviet action to install missiles was based on a misconception—a clearly understandable one, and one that we, in part, were responsible for." Moreover, McNamara found it "inconceivable . . . that we would have thought, if we were the Soviets, that we could have fired the tactical nuclear warheads with impunity." In a nuclear age, McNamara concluded, such mistakes—misjudgments of the other side's intentions and of the meanings the other side constructs for one's own actions—could be disastrous: "It is not possible to predict with confidence the consequences of military action by the great powers. Therefore, we must achieve crisis avoidance. That requires that we put ourselves in each other's shoes."[8] But what would it have taken for Soviet and American high officials to have put themselves in each other's shoes *in 1962?* Under the stress of confrontation, and in the face of overwhelming risks, they would have had to explore how what seemed inconceivable to them could nevertheless have seemed natural—indeed, obvious—to the other side. Each side would have had to question its understanding of the other side's position, overcoming its blindness to the other's way of framing the policy situation. Each would have had to consider on what assumptions, on what view of the world, the other side's apparently senseless actions might actually make sense to them.

Turning from the high drama of the Cuban Missile Crisis to the more ordinary policy-making stories of our three case studies, we have also noted both the price actors in the policy arena sometimes paid for their unreliable communications and the benefits they gained when some of them were able to put themselves in the shoes of their antagonists, co-designers, or intended beneficiaries.

It is true that policy designers are sometimes less concerned with trying to grasp how other actors see the policy object than with imposing their own design intentions. They may persist in ignoring policy back talk or treating it as mere perversity, not because they are blind to others' views but because they seek to exert unilateral political control over others. Unless the policy discourse is one of overwhelming dominance, however, designers of a policy object are simply unable to take complete control of a policy environment. The success of their enterprise depends on other parties choosing to behave in certain ways. Just to this extent, the designers live in a world of distributed powers, which requires them to enter into a communicative relationship with their antagonists. Just to this extent, like the actors in the Cuban Missile Crisis who might have more reliably reduced the risk of catastrophe by putting themselves in one another's shoes, they have a rational interest in creating a frame-reflective policy conversation.

## Transactional Effects

On several occasions we refer to transactions in which institutional actors contribute to shaping a policy environment that shapes *their* subsequent moves. In *Institutions Rediscovered,* James March and Johan Olsen also mention such effects, noting that "actions taken as a result of *beliefs about an environment* [our emphasis] can, in fact, construct the environment. The classic examples are found in self-fulfilling prophecies and the construction of limits through avoidance of them." They further observe that, "when environments are created, the actions taken in adapting to an environment *are partly responsive to previous actions by the same actor, reflected through the environment* [our emphasis]."[9] They point out that institutions often try to control the processes by which meanings are constructed for events in the policy-making process, making strategic use of symbols not merely to confuse the weak but to establish an interpretive order that conforms to their systems of belief.

March and Olsen also recognize, as we do, that the more powerful the actors are, the more they may be able to impose their beliefs and preferences on others, without taking into account their own contribution to creating the environment in which they find themselves. But when actors face a hostile environment and are *not* able to control the beliefs held by others in that environment—as we found to be true of the protagonists in our case studies—then these actors have a rational interest in discovering how their own beliefs may have led them to undertake actions that helped to create the environmental conditions by which they are constrained.

If policy makers are to pursue such a rational interest, they must probe how they could have been at least partly responsible for engendering the reactions they receive from other actors in the environment. Once they see, for example, that the antagonism of other actors is possibly, at least in part, of the designers' own making (as McNamara said of the Americans' responsibility for the Soviets' belief in the likelihood of an American invasion of Cuba), then they have a strong incentive not only to project themselves into the point of view of the others but to reflect on the interests, intentions, and beliefs that shaped their own prior actions.

This can be a very painful step. We usually find it convenient to see our environments as imposed upon us by external forces rather than as byproducts of actions of our own for which we must take responsibility. It is difficult to reflect on our own transactional responsibility for the world around us, especially when the world we have helped to create turns against us. It is much easier to consider how we might cope more effectively with the other's antagonism. Nevertheless, we have a rational interest not only in putting ourselves in other people's shoes, but in discovering and taking responsibility for the frames that shape our own contributions to an antagonistic environment.

## DESIGN FLAWS

In our case studies, flaws in the design of policy objects were manifested in patterns of behavior—for example, the German firms' proactive use of the 59er legislation, the MIT students' and faculty's avoidance of Athena or use of it for "mundane purposes," and the tendency of families at risk of homelessness to enter the hotels and motels in order to gain access to long-term housing subsidies. We argued in these instances that policy makers had a rational interest in discovering how such patterns of behavior made sense to those who manifested them, for in so doing the policy makers would be more likely to correct the design flaws they had detected. Like a teacher who tries to "give reason" to her pupils, seeking out the sense that underlies their apparently senseless questions, policy makers have a rational interest in giving reason to the apparently perverse behavior of their intended beneficiaries.[10]

But in order to "give reason" to the patterns of behavior manifested by other actors in the environment, policy makers must be able, again, to put themselves in their shoes, entering into their ways of framing the policy situation and constructing meaning for the policy object. More generally, the productive interpretation of design flaws requires an awareness of multiple constructs of reality. As Robert Heilbroner has written, the main task confronting the sponsor of a policy position begins as he or she "works through the implications of a prevailing belief system, considers the consequences that spring from its implications, and *examines the conceptual scheme for its compatibility with other constructs of reality*" [our emphasis].[11] Contrary to Joseph Gusfield, who maintained, as we noted in the introduction to this book, that practitioners cannot afford to consider the action frameworks inherent in other "possible worlds," Heilbroner argues, as we do, that policy practitioners ought to reflect across the frames implicit in multiple constructs of reality.

Such constructs may be the ones held by different actors in the policy arena, or they may consist in new frames that have come into good currency and older ones that have fallen into disrepute. In our discussion of Hirschman's account of the reconstruction of the economies of Eastern Europe, we point out that, in order to remain viable, radical reforms must often accept elements of the frames they have displaced. In both kinds of cases, the correction of design flaws depends on the designer's ability to reflect across different ways of framing policy situations.

## STALEMATES AND PENDULUM SWINGS

Of course, there is no guarantee that the hybrid frames generated by reflection on multiple constructs of reality will be internally coherent. Isaiah Berlin has observed that there is "no necessary compatibility" of all accepted truth. For example, the conservative and radical visions of scarcity both contain abiding truths, which are incompatible. Similarly, "The future is dominated by the past," and "The future transcends the past," express two commonly held views that are in conflict, though each contains an abiding truth.[12] The effect of constructing hybrid frames that more adequately reflect the full reality of a problematic situation may be to bring fundamental dilemmas—conflicts of abiding truths—to the surface.

There are many different ways in which a situated policy controversy may be unblocked so that policy making inquiry can go forward. But some ways of going forward remain caught up in underlying dilemmas. Although pragmatic agreements are reached and policy adjustments are made, the process still lurches from one side to another and the disputants may remain profoundly dissatisfied. Our analysis of Project Athena at MIT suggests how such a process may work: pragmatic agreements and adjustments mitigated an underlying policy dilemma without eliminating it.

In the Massachusetts case, on the other hand, policy positions and practices were reframed in such a way as to combine elements of the conflicting frames of need, market, and social control, and the resulting policy solution gained the wholehearted support of previously contending agencies. Even in this case, however, there was the distinct possibility of a future shift of context that would enable the advocates to return to center stage with their "entitlement" frame intact, thereby reactivating the underlying policy dilemma.

Perhaps what was done was the best that could be done at the time; it certainly allowed the policy-making process to go forward. In the future, however, it may be possible to design a policy to which the several parties, including the advocates, can give their support on the basis not of their earlier views but of views they might come to hold through reciprocal frame-reflection stimulated by shared awareness of a persistent, underlying dilemma.

## THE ARGUMENTS FOR FRAME REFLECTION TAKEN TOGETHER

Our several arguments for the general relevance of frame-reflective policy inquiry are constructed around the central idea of a reflective policy conversation. Participants in such a conversation must be able to put themselves in the shoes of other actors in the environment, and they must have a complementary ability to consider how their own action frames may contribute to the problematic situations in which they find themselves.

If policy makers are to communicate reliably with their antagonists and reliably interpret flaws in the design of policy objects, they must be able to "give reason" to other actors in the environment, which means entering into the action frames that inform multiple constructs of reality. The very act of giving reason means that policy makers must also be able to reflect on the action frames that underlie the transactions through which they may have helped to promote miscommunication or exacerbate design flaws.

Similarly, in order to contribute to the reframing of policy dilemmas, policy makers must be able to reflect on the action frames held by their antagonists. Even to recognize the existence of such dilemmas, policy makers must be able to reflect on their own action frames: they must overcome the blindness induced by their own ways of framing the policy situation in order to see that multiple policy frames represent a nexus of legitimate values in conflict.

# CHAPTER 8

# Conclusion: Implications for Research and Education

I f one accepts our principal theses—policy making as dialectic, conversation, and design; policy controversy as frame conflict; pragmatic resolution of controversy through the exercise of design rationality—then what follows for research, assistance, and education? What kinds of research are likely to be helpful to policy practitioners? What kinds of assistance do they need in order to conduct design-rational practice? What kinds of education will best prepare them for their jobs?

These questions bring us back to the issue with which we began our book: the relationship between the world of policy practice and the world of the policy academy. We pointed out in our introduction that under prevailing conceptions of the actual and proper relationships between these two worlds, practice loses twice. First, practitioners are said to be unable to reflect in any systematic or rigorous way on the meanings of the game they are playing—unable to reflect on the game from a position within the game. Second, those researchers who *are* said to be capable of reflecting systematically and rigorously on the game of policy making—but from a position well outside it—tend to produce results more congenial to the standards of interest and rigor favored by other academic researchers than to the standards of practical utility favored by practitioners.

This double loss suggests a version of the dilemma of "rigor or relevance." In a previous book, Schön described this dilemma in the following terms:

> In the varied topography of professional practice, there is a high, hard
> ground where practitioners can make effective use of research-based theo-
> ry and technique, and there is a swampy lowland where situations are con-
> fusing "messes" incapable of technical solution. The difficulty is that the
> problems of the high ground, however great their technical interest, are
> often relatively unimportant to clients or to the larger society, while in
> the swamp are the problems of greatest human concern. Shall the practi-
> tioner stay on the high, hard ground where he can practice rigorously, as
> he understands rigor, but where he is constrained to deal with problems
> of relatively little social importance? Or shall he descend to the swamp
> where he can engage the most important and challenging problems if he
> is willing to forsake technical rigor?[1]

To this formulation of the dilemma we now add: on the high ground, systematic reflection on the meaning of the policy-making game, minimally useful to practitioners; in the swamp, involvement in the game, without access to reflection on its meaning.

We approach this dilemma through our notion of design rationality, which attributes to practitioners a capability for reflective inquiry in and on the practice situation—as well as on the effectiveness of their strategies of action, the meaning of the back talk generated by their design moves, the action frames that underlie the controversies in which they are involved, the stalemates and pendulum swings in which they are caught up. We see competent policy practitioners as reflective inquirers—researchers, of a sort—*within* the policy-making game, and our norms of design rationality set a framework within which policy practice may be appropriately rigorous.

Yet design rationality is an ideal whose achievement in practice is, at best, uneven. For every Nancy Kaufman, there are many practitioners who would not be able to produce, or perhaps understand, her kind of reflective policy practice. Moreover, as we have already observed, the concrete situations conducive in some ways to the pragmatic resolution of policy controversies tend in other ways to impede the exercise of design rationality. Crisis, pressure, and sheer busyness militate against reflective inquiry, and the level of antagonism that frequently exists among actors in the policy drama works against cooperative policy designing.

How, then, might policy practitioners be helped to become reflective, design-rational inquirers? Through what forms of education or assistance, and in what types of settings? What kinds of research can enhance reflective policy inquiry? Finally, what norms of validity and rigor, if any, are applicable to it?

Traditionally, we look to the university-based schools of public policy and the policy research institutes for help in matters of research, assistance, and education, institutions that traditionally regard policy practitioners as their natural constituents. What kinds of research are the schools of public policy carrying out? How are they attempting to assist and educate practitioners?

Like most contemporary professional schools based in the research universities, the policy schools are in a period of searching, if not agonizing, reappraisal. A recent review article by Professor Laurence Lynn describes the work of these schools and the debates in which they are involved.[2] While we disagree with Lynn's proposed redirection of the policy schools, his portrayal of them helps to clarify the implications of our own perspective for research, education, and assistance.

## LAURENCE LYNN'S CRITIQUE OF THE SCHOOLS OF PUBLIC POLICY AND MANAGEMENT

Lynn highlights the differences between the newer and the older schools of public policy and management. He points out that the older schools of public administration have tended to serve a clientele of midlevel bureaucrats in federal or local government and have therefore focused on the execution of policies, the day-to-day management of public agencies, the carrying out of ordinary functions of service provision or regulation.[3] On the other hand, the newer schools of public policy, like the Kennedy School of Government at Harvard University, have aimed to serve a clientele of high-level elected officials and bureaucrats and have emphasized both policy formation and the strategic action of public agencies, adding "responsibility for goal setting and political management to the traditional responsibilities of public administration."[4]

This conception of public management strongly overlaps what we have called *policy practice,* for it is, at least in part, through their participation as actors in the policy arena that public managers set goals, and it is through their day-to-day management of agency operations and politics that they shape policies-in-use. True enough, policy practitioners, in our sense of the term, represent a far more inclusive class than managers in the executive branch of government. The policy makers who have figured in our cases include not only elected officials and managers of public agencies, but also advocates for interest groups, judges, and other stakeholder representatives such as union officials or heads of management associations. Moreover, our case studies include nongovernmental policy-making institutions such as MIT. Public managers, as described above, are only an important subset of the larger group that we call policy practitioners. Nevertheless, Lynn's review is broadly applicable to policy practice in our sense of the term.

Lynn addresses two main questions: how the policy schools should establish the intellectual content of their field, and how they should teach. He claims that the newer schools of public policy, following the example of prestigious schools of business administration like Harvard's, have taken a principled position that their teaching and research should, in the words of Graham Allison, first dean of the Kennedy School, "start from problems faced by practicing public managers."[5] Hence, the research strategy of these schools has been to accumulate cases of public management problems, with the aim of describing *practice wisdom* and identifying *best practice.* But, along with other critics of the new policy schools, Lynn finds this strategy wanting.[6] He believes that policy academics have lost their ability to take a critical stance toward practitioners because the practitioners have higher status than the academics and occupy positions of importance not only as clients of the policy schools but as members of their faculties. As a consequence, he argues, the academics have lost their intellectual independence and have thereby suffered a loss of conceptual clarity.[7]

As Lynn sees it, the scholarly plight of the newer schools of public policy has its roots in an "epistemic predicament." He distinguishes three forms of policy knowledge: *experiential knowledge,* the identification and documentation of best practices; *craft knowledge,* empirically derived rules of policy practice that make no formal claim to general validity although they are governed, in Lynn's view, by some criteria of validity; and *true statements,* general propositions subjected to empirical tests of a formal or quasi-formal kind.[8]

As far as true statements are concerned, Lynn claims there is "virtual unanimity within the public policy community" that social science methods are inadequate to the complexity of real-world policy making and are capable of producing, at best, "trivial truths of little value in improving practical wisdom."[9] In the public management literature, he believes, general and empirically tested true statements are few and tenuous, while the heuristic principles of craft knowledge proliferate. However, these principles tend to be mutually contradictory, noncumulative, not generally applicable, and nontestable. In the evolving public management literature of the 1980s, he laments, "the balance between art and science seems to have been tipping in favor of *art* [our emphasis]."[10]

Lynn's conclusion is a version of the dilemma of rigor or relevance:

Not having to be bound by conventional academic standards of intellectual value was, of course, a goal of many of the founders of the public policy schools. By shaking off "the dead hand of social science," as one of the field's mentors put it, the schools' faculties could pursue a deeper, more socially significant, and more resonant truth. The problem with such freedom from conventional standards, however, is that it may be difficult to discern if there are any standards at all.[11]

Clearly, Lynn believes that the policy academics have sold their scholarly birthright for a mess of practice pottage. Faced with the dilemma of rigor or relevance, he comes down on the side of rigor, arguing that policy academics should refrain from "canvassing yet another generation of practitioners for pearls of wisdom and documenting still more self-serving claims of managerial derring-do."[12] Rather, he proposes, policy researchers should try to discover nontrivial general rules by mining "adjacent fields" of social science—such versions of economics as the theories of games, principal-agents, transaction costs, and collective action and public choice. But he does not try to show how such theories may lead to the development of knowledge that is both consistent with norms of scholarly rigor *and* useful to policy practice.

Lynn refers only indirectly to the educational side of the predicament of the policy schools, but his main line of thought seems clear enough. Lacking knowledge that is rigorous, generally applicable, consistent, *and* useful, the schools cannot teach it. Instead, most of them have adopted a dual approach to education that mirrors their underlying model of professional knowledge. On the one hand, they educate students in microeconomics, quantitative analysis, and selections from existing theories of politics, organizations, and institutions—subjects closely linked to prevailing models of rational choice, politics, and negotiation. These subjects are taught early in the student's career as essential components of the policy curriculum. But Lynn, at any rate, makes no very strong brief for their practical utility.

The policy schools also teach the substantive details of a great variety of policy issues—for example, health, environmental protection, criminal justice, defense, and education. Beyond this, most schools recognize important policy "skills" or "arts" of making wise policy judgments, implementing policy, and conducting negotiations—which they teach by the case method, in imitation of some of the most prestigious business schools, or (especially in the growing field of negotiation) through the use of games and simulations. But if Lynn is right in the "epistemic dilemma" he poses, what can be derived from teaching based on cases or simulations?

# OUR PERSPECTIVE ON THE RELATIONSHIP BETWEEN POLICY PRACTICE AND THE SCHOOLS OF PUBLIC POLICY

We agree with Lynn's critique of normal social science and his disparaging view of the heuristic principles that result from attempts to codify practice wisdom. But we do not join him in concluding that scholars should turn from "best practice" to the enticements of "adjacent disciplines." We believe that the poverty of much academic policy research is due not to its emphasis on practice, but to the inadequacy of implicit models governing the kinds of lessons drawn from practice. If such lessons are heuristic principles, then they are likely to be noncumulative, mutually contradictory, and untestable.

We believe that policy researchers should seek first to understand policy practice—not to draw from it rules of effective policy making, but to describe and explain the kinds of inquiry in which policy makers engage. Policy researchers should focus on the substantive issues with which policy makers deal, the situations within which controversies about such issues arise, the kinds of inquiry carried out by those practitioners who participate in controversy or try to help resolve it, and the evolution of the policy dialectic within which practitioners play their roles as policy inquirers.

## COLLABORATIVE RESEARCH INTO POLICY PRACTICE

Policy academics who adopt these foci should collaborate with practitioners, recognizing that competent policy practitioners are reflective inquirers who become, at their best, frame-reflective researchers into their own practice situations. Practitioners like Dean MacVicar in Project Athena, or Kaufman and Keyes in the story of homelessness in Massachusetts, seek to understand the nature of the problematic situations in which they find themselves, the meanings of the messages communicated through words and actions in policy conversations, the sources of controversies and dilemmas with which they are confronted, the nature and causes of the flaws they discover in the policy objects they design, and the impediments that arise to block the flow of the policy design process. If policy academics want to build a better understanding of policy practice in a way useful to practitioners as well as appropriately rigorous, then they must not bypass the research in which practitioners are already engaged. If they disregard what practitioners already know or are already trying to discover, they are unlikely either to grasp what is really going on or to succeed in getting practitioners to listen to them.

Typically, policy analysts in the academy do not collaborate with practitioners. They tend rather to hook on to a policy issue and conduct their analyses in retrospect or in parallel with the ongoing decision making by which policy makers deal with that issue. Lindblom in his most recent book deplores this tendency, which he calls the "do-it-all-for-them" model of policy analysis: the tendency of analysts in the academy to "substitute their vision of scientific problem solving for a *cooperative policy* [our emphasis] in which professional prober—a social scientist or researcher—joins with functionary in probing."[13] Lindblom envisages many different ways in which policy-oriented analysts might "assist functionaries who possess their own distinctive competences," short of "doing it all for them."[14] He points out that

> one might call on an analyst for a body of fact; another might call on the analyst for a synthesis of conditions that run beyond the functionary's scope; still another might, for example, ask the analyst to criticize pieces of the functionary's own analysis.[15]

As Lindblom seeks to open up the category of policy assistance, he does not focus on policy controversies or on frame-reflective policy inquiry. He does not propose (though he might well approve) the kind of cooperative action research that we believe to be most critical to a desirable future working relationship between practitioners and researchers in the policy field. In the normal world of policy practice, reciprocal frame reflection is, if not a rare event, at least an unusual one; and under the normal conditions of threat, stress, hostility, and distrust, actors in the policy arena, left to their own devices, often remain stuck in the morass of controversy or even make things worse. Hence, we propose cooperative policy research of the following kinds.

Policy researchers and practitioners might undertake projects aimed at learning from success—carefully studying examples of policy practice identified, preanalytically, as most effective. Such studies would seek to make explicit the criteria implicit in such preanalytic judgments of success. They would focus on processes of policy inquiry as well as on the structural conditions that elicit or demand more effective inquiry. In the field of economic and social development, notable studies of this kind have been carried out by Albert Hirschman.[16]

Academically based policy researchers might collaborate with practitioners in studying policy issues, such as the reform of education or health care. Studies of this kind are most useful when they are frame-reflective—that is, when they examine the controversies that arise around such issues and construct the frames that underlie them—and when they are situational, in the sense of examining the forms controversies take in different policy situations, and the different trajectories of inquiry to which they give rise.

Policy academics and practitioners might collaborate in the retrospective study of policy controversies, cycling back to communicative interactions central to those controversies, as in the Cuban Missile Crisis research to which the previous chapter refers.

Finally, academics and practitioners might collaborate in conducting frame-reflective studies of policy designing in process. Collaborative inquiry of this kind would occur at policy windows, when policy-making inquiry is blocked and actors in the policy arena are locked in stalemate. This is the kind of collaborative study that Nancy Kaufman arranged for herself when she made use of her year at the Kennedy School to design a negotiating game that took as its starting point the then-current state of play in the Massachusetts policy arena.

In such collaborations with practitioners, policy academics could fulfill two main functions. First, they could help with the difficult process of reciprocal frame reflection. Working from the careful construction of a record of practitioners' doing and thinking, they could help practitioners construct the frames that underlie their own policy positions, including the complexities and ambiguities of those frames and the (sometimes elusive) relationships between individual and institutional belief systems. They could also help the participants enter into the frames of other actors in the arena—helping them to construct, for example, how others see and interpret the policy object, or how they have interpreted the meanings of messages sent out by the designing system. From such starting points, policy academics might go on to help practitioners reframe a policy problem or to make and evaluate inventions that synthesize elements of conflicting frames, as in the Massachusetts story of closing the front door. They might make explicit the elements of a frame synthesis implicit in existing policy inventions, or diagnose the blockage of an ongoing process of policy inquiry.

Second, policy academics could help practitioners to create conditions for mutual trust, including help in repairing the breaches of trust that inevitably occur under conditions of threat and pressure. For example, the researchers might help surface dilemmas of participation that practitioners experience but find difficult to make explicit. Or the researchers might help the practitioners publicly test assumptions they may be making about their counterparts but are unwilling to risk testing out loud. At a deeper level, help might take the form of educative demonstration and dialogue through which the practitioners might learn how better to create conditions of mutual trust for themselves. The researcher's job would be to advance these norms of behavior by espousing and demonstrating them, in order to gain the participants' willingness to suspend, little by little, the normal patterns of behavior that inhibit cooperative, reciprocal frame reflection.

The combination of these functions defines a consultative policy research role that is not as yet formally recognized or, if it exists in practice, has no counterpart in theory and little or no professional legitimacy. Such a role, which might be called *frame-reflective consultation,* would combine and transform elements of existing disciplines and practices. It would include policy analysis of a frame-reflective kind, of the sort we have illustrated in the analysis of our three cases, but undertaken in a setting very close to the actual policy arena; and it would include facilitative intervention of a kind practiced, in various ways, by some mediators, process consultants, and educators, which demands an ability to contribute to the development of a behavioral world conducive to mutual trust.

The combined work of frame-reflective policy analysis and educative intervention would be tested not so much by its acceptability to other analysts as by its utility to practitioners who seek to reframe policy problems and make frame-synthetic inventions. Through their participation in such a cooperative process, the policy academics would gain, first of all, the satisfaction of helping practitioners generate usable knowledge, but they would also gain a far more intimate and engaged involvement in real-world policy practice than they could ever achieve by the more familiar route of historical reconstruction.

Competences for frame-reflective policy analysis and educative consultation are rarely combined in one person. Conceivably, the role of frame-reflective consultant might be played by more than one person, each specializing in one type of assistance and possessed of some feeling for the other's contribution. Ultimately, a practice of frame-reflective policy consultation might give rise to the formation a new profession analogous to the post–World War II development of the professions of policy analysis and organizational development.

## THE RESEARCH-POLICY-PRACTICE TRIAD

Exclusive focus on the collaboration of policy researchers and practitioners fails to take account of a critically important distinction between kinds of practitioners. We have focused on policy practitioners as designers of policy, but this focus ignores day-to-day practice in fields affected by policy—for example, producing and managing low-income housing, or providing social services to children at risk. When the two types of practice are distinguished, we become aware of a triadic relationship of research, policy, and practice,[17] which is central to many policy controversies.

Everyday practice occurs in a policy environment that may be friendly, neutral, or hostile to practice. At any given time, there is no a priori reason to assume that one of these effects is dominant, or that the policy-practice frontier is stable over time. Often, however, there is a tendency for policy to be unfriendly to practice because of a tension between the conflicting imperatives of autonomy and accountability: policy makers allocate resources to practitioners in exchange for their accountability to policy objectives, which runs the risk of reducing professional autonomy.

A good example of this tension lies in the field of children's services. Family support work is concerned with keeping children in their own families whenever appropriate, employing preventive strategies to avoid family disruption. By contrast, child protection policy, when "stripped of some of the more cozy or therapeutic language, is still about the policing, by the state, of child-rearing practice in the family."[18] Professionals in the voluntary child care sector want to act as family support workers rather than agents of social control charged with monitoring families' child-rearing practices. The relationship between policy and practice is friendly when policy asks the professional to render the kind of service he or she *wants* to perform; the more policy is believed to reflect prevailing practices, the more likely it is to be acceptable to practitioners. Increasingly, however, as governments have relied on contracting out services to voluntary child-care agencies, and as these agencies have become financially dependent on government contracts, the state has pressed social workers in the voluntary sector to pay more attention to child protection and less to family support work. In such cases, policy becomes unfriendly to practice.

More generally, friendly or unfriendly relationships between policy and practice can be understood in terms of conflicting imperatives of practice. There is a legal imperative to follow the law as understood in the legislation; a consensual imperative to do what is feasible, given both the consensus and the existing conflicts in the social world for which the legislation was designed; and finally, a bureaucratic imperative not to endanger one's position within a given agency. In the case of the conflict between child protection and family support work, there is a conflict between the legal and consensual imperatives.[19]

Policy research plays a role in such conflicts. While much policy research is free-standing and critical of policy, a substantial amount of it is commissioned by oversight agencies concerned with monitoring practice. Such agencies use the tools of evaluation to provide themselves with the information they need to assure accountability. In practice, as Chapter 1 points out, such commissioned research has won the reputation of being a killer because it always turns against the reforms that inspired it, resulting in the pessimistic view that nothing works—a finding often used politically to discredit policies and disclaim professional practice. Such evaluative research is not designed to help practitioners perform better but to evaluate whether their activity is worth doing in the first place. Low marks threaten the financial viability of the professional service.

From the practitioners' point of view, it is easy to see how they may be caught between policy and research, both of which are unfriendly to practice. This leads them to defend themselves, thereby making problems of trust and learning increasingly intractable. If we adopt the perspective of a policy researcher or designer, we become aware of their versions of the general predicament. Within the triad, each actor gives priority to a different field of constraints: for policy makers, it is the political environment; for researchers, peer review and funding; and for practitioners, the clienteles they directly serve. But as each actor addresses the problems internal to its own practice, it alters the environments of the other actors; and the story looks different depending on whose point of view one takes.

The triadic model surfaces issues that must be addressed if we are to develop a collaborative framework that permits the three types of actors to reflect on their own practice and recognize their transactional effects on one another. It is here that we find an intersection between frame-reflective practice, on the part of policy designers and everyday practitioners, and frame-critical policy analysis.

In order to carry out the kind of cooperative inquiry we propose, we believe it will be necessary to create new institutional arrangements that bring together the three key actors in our triad. Cooperative inquiry between the practitioner and researcher is incomplete if it fails to include the policy environment in which it is embedded.

## SETTINGS FOR COOPERATIVE RESEARCH IN POLICY PRACTICE

An institutional setting appropriate to the cooperative inquiry of researchers, policy makers, and practitioners must be optimally distant from the front lines of a policy arena.

When Nancy Kaufman took her year's leave at Harvard's Kennedy

School of Government, for example, she distanced herself from her role in state government, moving from the heat of the policy arena to the relative cool of academe; however, she brought the problems of her work place with her and used her time in the academy to think in new ways about them. More generally, an optimally distant setting must be close enough to the actual policy situation so that a practitioner can move in and out of it with ease, yet distant enough from it so that she is protected from its pressures, threats, and distractions. An optimally distant setting offers a retreat, where the players can gain insight into the game, while also being able readily to return to it.

Kaufman's year of leave was not wholly without precedent in Massachusetts circles. In the homelessness case, representatives of state agencies, the legislature, the human services lobby, and the advocates not infrequently came together in informal networks to talk about their turbulent policy-making process, and were sometimes able to work out solutions to problems that had seemed insoluble when addressed within the official forums of state government. However, they generally did so without the assistance of policy academics. If policy makers, practitioners, and academics are to come together on a more regular basis to engage in collaborative action research, then they will need access to optimally distant settings like the one Kaufman created for herself. Possible sponsors of such settings might include the policy schools, free-standing policy institutes, and the small firms and partnerships that practice mediated negotiation. Each of these possibilities has its strengths and weaknesses.

Like consulting firms, mediation organizations are close to the reality of contentious policy practice. But with this closeness comes the pressure to produce short-term results, a pressure often exacerbated by the demands of financial viability, which makes it difficult for practitioners to reflect on and extend the boundaries of their own practice. Nevertheless, as we have observed, mediators sometimes go beyond their theory, helping their clients to transform their understandings of their own interests. Perhaps such things just happen, or perhaps the mediators in such cases reveal skills they are unable to describe. In either case, this growing profession may evolve, on the basis of its acknowledged but unexplained accomplishments, toward a more conscious, systematic theory and practice of frame-reflective consultation.

Policy institutes are subject to demands for the production of relevant, usable policy-analytic knowledge. Yet they tend to define their work in terms of policy studies or evaluations, to which their educative or consultative services tend to be subordinated. Their members tend to be trained in analytic, or substantive programmatic, competences, rather than in educative consultation.

Academic policy analysts have the freedom to step back from the immediate demands of actual policy situations, and their institutional role encourages them to engage in theory building. Yet their distance from policy practice and subjection to disciplinary norms tend to keep them from engaging in collaborative action research. In order to create a multidisciplinary corner where they could join with policy makers and practitioners, they would have to develop their capabilities for both educative consultation and frame-reflective policy inquiry.

Of course, all forms of retreat are vulnerable. There is always the danger that ideas and inventions incubated in a retreat will dissolve as practitioners re-enter the policy arena, unless they manage to carry over some of the ways of thinking and acting developed in the retreat. More fundamentally, perhaps, there is no guarantee that, even within an optimally distant setting and with research assistance of the kind we have described, the participants will be able to engage in reciprocal situated frame reflection. The impediments of pre-existing antagonism, institutionalized distrust, and limited capability for inquiry would still remain. An optimally distant setting, and the collaborative inquiry that might occur within it, can only increase the likelihood that such impediments may be overcome.

## VALID INFERENCE AND APPROPRIATE RIGOR IN REFLECTIVE POLICY INQUIRY

We have advocated our proposals for cooperative, frame-reflective policy research on the basis of their relevance and utility to policy practitioners. But we have not as yet discussed what it means for such research to be valid and appropriately rigorous.

Clearly, all such research is concerned with causal inferences, which are inevitably built into the design and redesign of policy objects. In Massachusetts, for example, when Keyes and Kaufman revised their view of the underlying causes of homelessness, they gave far more importance to the crack epidemic and the breakdown of social order in disadvantaged families and neighborhoods. In Project Athena, when the engineer-architects adjusted Athena's policies, they based their adjustments on inferences about the causes of student and faculty disaffection.

Researchers like Laurence Lynn, who deal with the dilemma of rigor or relevance by coming down on the side of rigor, argue that all such "practice wisdom" is fated to be anecdotal, untestable, and not generally applicable. But such a position rests on a model of causal inference borrowed from normal social science. Normal social science seeks to establish general, objective causal relationships among pairs of variables according to a schema of causal inference, $Y = F(X)$, where $Y$ is a variable that defines effect and $X$ a variable that defines cause. To show that $Y = F(X)$ is true, one needs to show that values of $Y$ are *uniquely determined* by the values of $X$, which means that one must first obtain the values of $X$ and $Y$ across a wide range of variance, and then show that the values of $Y$ vary with changes in the values of $X$.[20] Normal social science distinguishes between two kinds of validity: the internal validity of a causal inference within a given situation, and its external validity for situations beyond the one in which it was generated.[21] In both cases, the normal science schema of causal inference depends on the isolation of distinct variables, the observation of a wide range of instances of their occurrence, and the elimination from the experimental setting of any confounding variables—all conditions that are difficult or impossible to achieve in an actual policy situation.

## SITUATED CAUSAL INQUIRY

Situated policy inquiry makes use of a different schema of causal inference, and the associated meanings of *validity, rigor,* and *generalizability* differ from their analogues in normal social science.

Consider, for example, in the case of Project Athena at MIT, the question of Athena's support of faculty salaries. Dean Wilson firmly believed that Athena had a policy of supporting academic-year salaries for faculty engaged in developing new courseware, while members of the School of Science, especially the Physics Department, just as firmly denied that Athena had such a policy. As Schön and Turkle discovered at the time of this dispute, the Athena Executive Committee had formally approved Athena's support of academic-year faculty salaries, but the committee charged with reviewing proposals from the School of Science chose not to follow this policy, apparently at the urging of the then-dean of that school. Moreover, even after the School of Science Review Committee reversed itself, faculty members continued for some months to believe that Athena would not support faculty salaries, and Dean Wilson never tried to discover how the policy he had personally approved could have been seen in a different way by members of the School of Science.

What caused the conflicting views of Athena's policy to arise and persist in spite of easily available evidence that could have resolved the conflict? The answer offered by Schön and Turkle took the form of a causal story. It referred to actions, contrary in intention, taken first by the Athena Executive Committee and then by the School of Science Review Committee, under the influence of the then-dean of science. It also referred to a disposition, shared by Dean Wilson and by certain members of the School of Science, to stick to their initial interpretations without further probing.

The validity of this story was supported not by statistical correlations of dependent and independent variables, but by a causal tracing of events. For example, Dean Wilson's strong view of Athena's policy was traced back to the executive committee meeting at which he claimed the initial policy decision was made. The perceptions shared by members of the Physics Department were traced back to specific actions on proposals taken by the School of Science Review Committee; these, in turn, were traced back (via interviews with committee members) to directives they received from the then-dean of the School of Science.

What makes such causal tracing feasible in any particular instance is a broadly shared background model of how decisions are usually made and acted upon, how decision-making bodies interact at different levels of an institution, how authority is exercised, and how attitudes toward issues and policies are formed and sustained. For anyone familiar with how a place like MIT works, it is more or less clear how to guide a specific causal tracing, and it is equally feasible to imagine and seek out data that could be used to test the causal story that results from that tracing. For example, the evidence gathered by Schön and Turkle was accessible to all of the actors involved in Athena at the time of the dispute, and most of it was explicitly known to members of the School of Science Review Committee. It would also have been possible to specify and seek out evidence that, if it could be found, would disconfirm Schön and Turkle's causal story. For example, one might have tested whether or not the documented actions of the various committees were actually executed as they were remembered, whether or not key individuals had actually made and communicated the decisions attributed to them, and whether or not one or more of the parties to the disagreement actually knew what they claimed not to know at the time. Members of the review committee might have denied that they rejected proposals containing requests for coverage of faculty salaries, or they might have produced an example of a School of Science proposal that contained such requests and was nevertheless approved for funding.

Just as a plumber with a good working knowledge of household plumbing can trace the causes of a leak, so anyone familiar with the workings of a place like MIT can make and test a causal tracing of institutional events.[22] In the policy as in the plumbing situation, moreover, the actors can perform on-the-spot experiments by which to test their causal tracings or background models. They may carry out such experiments, for example, through the very actions by which they try to solve the policy problems they have identified. So, for example, the creation of Athena's "two-tiered system," which was intended to respond to student and faculty disaffection, succeeded in achieving a certain degree of institutional harmony, and thereby also confirmed the designers' diagnosis of their marketing problem. In the homelessness case, Kaufman's diagnosis of the stalemated policy-making process was confirmed, in part, by the policy invention which brought DSS into the field as an active partner and thereby helped to unblock the process. Policy design moves can serve a dual function. If they work to solve the problems they are intended to solve, they may also confirm the causal tracings on which they were based.[23]

Policy inquirers may continue to probe the validity of their causal inferences, considering and testing alternative causal stories and occasionally uncovering new evidence that leads them to change their minds. They do not continue indefinitely, however. They tend to stop inquiring, at least temporarily, when they arrive at a causal account on the basis of which they can set a policy problem that is both adequate to the facts and values they have learned to recognize in the situation and plausibly amenable to solution through the means at their disposal.[24] The stopping rule they generally employ, in short, is to stop when they have set a problem they can solve.

Sometimes, of course, conflicting causal attributions are unresolvable by any means available to policy inquirers. But such extreme cases do not obviate the general schema that defines valid and rigorous causal inquiry in policy situations.

## REFLECTIVE TRANSFER

Normal social science aims at producing externally valid propositions, which it conceives as "covering laws"—propositions that are probably true of all the instances to which they are applicable in principle. The causal schema, $Y = F(X)$, where values of $Y$ are uniquely determined by values of $X$ across a wide range of variance, represents the structure of such a covering law.

As Lynn points out in his review of the literature on public policy and management, valid covering-law generalizations of the normal social science variety tend to be few and tenuous. Significant generalizations, potentially useful to practitioners, tend to be externally invalid. They falter on the basis of differences in context from one situation to another, or from one time to another. Generalizations asserted with the caveat "all other things being equal" tend to fail in practice because other things are never entirely equal in all relevant respects. Covering-law generalizations that do prove relatively invulnerable to empirical disconfirmation usually turn out, as Lynn notes, to be "trivial truths, of little value in improving practical wisdom."[25] On the other hand, situation-specific, case-based studies of practice, whether in public policy or other fields of social action, tend to be dismissed by critics of normal social science persuasion because they do not produce externally valid generalizations. The causal inferences contained in these studies tend to be denigrated as "merely anecdotal," or, in Lynn's words, "*sui generis* contributions," or, still more fatally, "practice lore."[26]

We believe that such criticisms misconstrue the kind of generalizability appropriate to situated practice knowledge. Competent policy designers, like designers in other fields, do learn from their own past experience and from their vicarious experience of other people's practice, which means that they do, in some fashion, generalize from the particular situations in which they have been involved, or about which they have heard or read. But their generalizations are not covering laws. While policy designers may, on occasion, espouse general principles or maxims for heuristic or rhetorical purposes, their principal mode of generalization from past experience fits the schema we call "reflective transfer," by which we mean the process by which patterns detected in one situation are carried over as projective models to other situations where they are used to generate new causal inferences and are subjected to new, situation-specific tests of internal validity.

The patterns carried over from one situation to another by reflective transfer may be formulated in many different ways and at different levels of abstraction. For example, someone familiar with the Massachusetts experience of policy formation for the homeless in the late 1980s might have carried over to New York City's homeless policy predicament a very specific version of the self-reconstituting problem of homelessness that had become, by then, so painfully obvious in Massachusetts. Or at a higher level of abstraction, what might be carried over from the Massachusetts experience to a new policy situation might be a pattern of "perverse effects," in which policies guided by one set of intentions yield undesired effects of another order through the mediation of social learning. From the experience of the Athena case, one might carry over to the next version of Athena an exemplar of multiple, robust computer cultures, each of which is likely to ignore a centrally designed computer system or turn that system to its own purposes; or one might carry over, more generically, the cautionary example of a designing system that mistakes its glowing intentions for "reality."[27]

Although competent policy designers tend to treat each practice episode as a unique case, they are able, through reflective transfer, to carry over learning from one unique episode of policy design to others. Like a good medical clinician or architectural designer, the policy practitioner builds up a usable repertoire of unique cases. Once a case has entered into a practioner's repertoire, he may be able to *see* a new case *as* that familiar one, the familiar one now functioning as an exemplar for inquiry into the new one.[28] The practitioner does not subsume the two cases under a general proposition. When confronted with a new situation, he scans the repertoire of cases derived from past experience to see whether the new situation is similar to one or more of these without being able to say, at this point, "similar with respect to what."[29] But from the understanding achieved in the earlier case, he may construct a variation appropriate to the new one—an initial, situation-specific understanding that serves as a starting point for a new round of on-the-spot testing. In such seeing-as, the inquirer enters into a transaction in which both the pattern carried over from an earlier situation and the understanding formed in the new one are transformed.

Competent policy designers, like competent practitioners of many different sorts, tend to be virtuosos at reflective transfer. They have accumulated a great variety of practice experiences, which they are able to hold loosely and deploy as projective models for new situations. For them, each new practice episode functions, in part, as preparation for the next project. Their ability to carry over experienced patterns from familiar to unfamiliar situations suggests the "metaphorical capability" that Aristotle, for one, valued above all other intellectual abilities.[30]

## IMPLICATIONS FOR THE EDUCATION OF POLICY PRACTITIONERS

The dual model of education adopted by most public policy schools is a variation on the curriculum created by the Veblenian bargain referred to in the introduction—the normative professional curriculum of the research universities: first, classroom education in the relevant basic and/or applied science; then, a practicum whose ostensible purpose is to help students learn to apply classroom knowledge to the everyday problems of practice.[31] In the policy schools, the relevant basic knowledge usually consists of microeconomics and microeconomic approaches to policy analysis, coupled with courses in the political and institutional process of policy making, and specialized courses that deal with particular policy domains. Often, the practicum consists in the use of case teaching to educate students in the skills or art of solving policy problems. More recently, many schools have developed practicumlike courses aimed at teaching skills of negotiation and mediation through the use of cases, games, and simulations.

In the first part of this dual policy curriculum, one can discern the influence of the three prevailing models of policy rationality: choice, politics, and negotiation. The second part of the curriculum, the use of case teaching, generally rests on a rationale first developed in the Harvard Graduate School of Business, whose teaching traditions have inspired many of the newer public policy schools. It is the idea that students can develop a generic problem-solving ability, in policy making as in management, through the careful analysis of many cases that force the student to take the position of an actor faced with a difficult decision.[32]

We believe that the first part of the dual policy curriculum can be useful for policy practice that conforms to the model of national choice. To the extent that practitioners confront relatively clear-cut policy choices, they will find it useful to have mastered microeconomic approaches to policy analysis. But such events are few and far between and represent, as our case analyses strongly suggest, a very small fraction of the terrain of policy practice.

As to the second component of this curriculum, the arts of policy judgment, political manipulation, and negotiation certainly exist and may be at least partly communicable through skillful teaching based on practice cases or simulations. But policy cases and simulations tend to be geared to decisions rather than to the framing of problematic situations that makes decision possible, or to the actions by which decisions are implemented. As this book argues, the arts of policy choice, politics, and negotiation do not cover all of the competences critical to policy design. Most especially, they do not cover frame-reflective approaches to policy controversies. How, then, should the policy schools help students acquire the problem-setting, problem-solving, communicative, and frame-reflective dimensions of policy design capability? Recall some of the key elements of this capability:

- Civitas—the disposition to try to solve "the Governor's problem";
- Contribution to the creation and maintenance of a climate of mutual trust among policy inquirers;
- The ability to put yourself in the other party's shoes—to discover where they are coming from—in personal and institutional terms, including especially the action frames that shape their interests;
- Double vision—the ability to act from a frame while cultivating awareness of alternative frames;
- Appreciation of the necessarily political character of policy design without the cynicism that often attaches to such an appreciation;
- The skill of inventing new policy modifications and practices, with an eye to resolving frame conflicts.

We know of no existing educational program that aims at the development of these capabilities. Clearly, some people do learn to acquire them, but very little is known about how they can be taught. We may be justified, therefore, in suggesting an approach of our own.

The competences listed are policy-specific versions of a generic design capability; and education for designing is an issue with which many professional schools, not only the schools of the traditional design professions, are grappling. For example, education for engineering design has re-emerged as a topic of lively debate in schools of engineering, now that the movement to incorporate engineering in applied physics has worn thin and the development of new products and manufacturing systems has been identified as a factor critical to success in international competition.

What we know of design education comes mainly from the design professions, and especially from the schools of architecture, where the dominant tradition is that of the design studio.[33] In this mode of professional education, whose origins antedate the professional schools of the research universities, students learn to design by doing it. Together with other students, they undertake design projects under the guidance of a studio master or coach. They work in a studio setting that, with the help of media such as drawing and modelling to scale, represents the world of practice—a virtual world of designing where the student can practice at low risk, work at her own pace, and go back and look again. In a design studio, students acquire an artistry of design for which no teachable theory exists; they are helped to learn designing by doing it, before they know what designing is.

The generic conditions of the design studio constitute a practicum that becomes reflective when students are encouraged to reflect on the understandings they bring spontaneously to design projects, as well as on the meanings of their coaches' words and actions, and when their coaches reflect on the theories and processes they bring to their own demonstrations and descriptions, as well as on the understandings and puzzlements revealed by their students' attempts at designing.[34]

Increasingly, schools of architecture have sought to marry the traditions of the design studio with the traditions of the research university. They have tried to expose students to certain bodies of systematic knowledge that are seen as crucial to professional competence—for example, knowledge of soil mechanics, construction technologies, structural engineering, and energy conservation. The problem of design education has been increasingly defined as one of making a marriage of artistry and applied science, though few schools of architecture are currently satisfied with the means they have employed to effect such a marriage.

The problem of education for policy designing might be framed as one of creating a reflective practicum in policy making, suitably married to courses in systematic knowledge useful for policy design. To our knowledge, no such reflective practicum exists apart from the settings some policy makers do actually manage to create for themselves, in which they learn to acquire the capabilities we describe and illustrate. Drawing mainly on the features of these work situations, we can identify what some of the features of a reflective policy practicum would be.

A reflective policy practicum would immerse students in a problematic policy situation where problems are not yet well defined, perhaps where multiple, conflicting problem settings clamor for attention. Students would be placed within a virtual policy arena, where a variety of institutional actors and interest groups are in contention over the shaping of a new policy object or the reshaping of an existing one. The field of action would be politically charged. Means would have to be found to represent critically important features of the policy context—economic, political, and cultural. Students would function as members of a designing system and would experience ambiguity and conflict over who is "in" or "out" of that system. They would be charged with the task of shaping, or reshaping, a policy object, which they would send out into a larger policy environment. They would be confronted with responses to that object that embody different constructions of its meaning by its users or by other actors in the environment. They would be faced with back talk whose meanings they would need to probe.

Controversies would arise. Shifts in the meanings of policy would occur in the process of implementation. Shifts in the larger context would create policy windows in which new rounds of designing would become possible. Under these conditions, students would be asked to engage in reflective policy design and coached in its exercise.

Such a policy design practicum would incorporate enormous complexity and pose serious problems of representation and compression. A year, or decade, of policy-making experience would need somehow to be represented and compressed in a practicum whose scope and duration were made to fit within the tolerable limits of an educational career. Such an exercise would be daunting, but it would not lie wholly beyond the capabilities of existing methods and technologies. In order to produce appropriate materials, the schools might extend and deepen their use of the cases, games, and simulations that teachers of negotiation and mediation have already developed; or they might make double use of action research collaborations with policy practitioners, constructing simulated design situations based on those collaborations.

At least two new elements would have to enter into the teaching of such a reflective policy practicum. First, students would need to be helped to learn the task of frame reflection. Frame-critical policy analysts could play a useful role in this process, but they would have to learn to extend their usual modes of analysis to include the kind of situated frame reflection that we have illustrated in the previous chapter— the invention of policies and practices that synthesize elements of conflicting frames. Second, students would have to be helped to learn how to contribute to the development of the kind of mutual trust that is necessary to sustain frame-reflective inquiry in situations of controversy.

The creation of such a reflective policy practicum would require a significant leap from current educational practice in the policy field— no less a leap than from conventional policy analysis to frame-reflective policy consultation. Indeed, these two movements would be mutually reinforcing, as new forms of collaborative research among policy makers, practitioners, and researchers would support the development of materials suited to the development of a reflective policy practicum. We believe that the magnitude of the leap is justified by what is at stake: our need to develop a capability for reflective conversation in policy design in order to deal more effectively with policy controversy.

# Notes

## INTRODUCTION

1. Hannah Arendt, *The Life of the Mind,* vol. 1, *Thinking* (New York and London: Harcourt Brace Jovanovich, 1971).
2. Arendt, *Life of the Mind,* p. 93.
3. Ibid., p. 193.
4. See Gregory Vlastos, *Socrates: Ironist and Moral Philosopher* (Ithaca, N.Y.: Cornell University Press, 1991).
5. Ibid., p. 197.
6. Ibid., p. 199.
7. Ibid., p. 94.
8. Joseph Gusfield, *The Culture of Public Problems* (Chicago: University of Chicago Press, 1981), p. 192.
9. See Albert O. Hirschman, *Development Projects Observed* (Washington, D.C.: Brookings Institution, 1967), p. 29.
10. We should note, however, that Hirschman limits his argument against reflection to the first stage of development projects. In the later stages, he argues, the "problem proneness of action" becomes evident and reflective problem solving becomes imperative. The potential for reflection arises, in Hirschman's view as in our own, when in the course of the political drama of policy making the weaknesses of action frames reveal themselves in the form of design flaws.
11. Renata Mayntz, director of the Max Planck Institute, proposed this argument in the course of a colloquium in honor of sociologist Tom Burns at Edinburgh in 1981.

12. Jon Elster, *Ulysses and the Sirens: Studies in Rationality and Irrationality* (Cambridge, England: Cambridge University Press, 1979).

13. Thorsten Veblen, *The Higher Learning in America: A Memorandum on the Conduct of Universities by Business Men* (B. W. Huebsch, 1918; New York: Hill and Wang, 1957).

14. Schön has argued this case at some length in *The Reflective Practitioner* (New York: Basic Books, 1983).

15. This point is well discussed in a recent review of the public policy and management literature by Lawrence Lynn, discussed in chapter 8.

16. Gusfield, *Culture of Public Problems,* p. 193.

17. William Perry, *Forms of Intellectual and Ethical Development in the College Years* (New York: Holt, Rinehart and Winston, 1970).

## CHAPTER 1. INTRACTABLE POLICY CONTROVERSIES

1. Charles Murray, *Losing Ground: American Social Policy 1950–1980* (New York: Basic Books, 1984).

2. See Francis Fox Piven, *Politics of Turmoil: Poverty, Race and the Urban Crisis* (New York: Vintage, 1975).

3. See, for example, Peter Marris and Martin Rein, *Dilemmas of Social Reform: Poverty and Community Action in the United States* (London: Routledge, 1967); Francis Fox Piven and Richard A. Cloward, *Poor People's Movements: Why They Succeed and How They Fail* (New York: Pantheon, 1977); Charles Murray, *Losing Ground*; and Robert Haveman, ed., *A Decade of Federal Antipoverty Programs: Achievements, Failures, and Lessons* (New York: Academic Press, 1977).

4. James Q. Wilson and Richard J. Herrnstein, *Crime and Human Nature* (New York: Simon and Schuster, 1986).

5. See Arthur R. Jensen, *Straight Talk About Mental Tests* (New York: Free Press, 1981).

6. Leon J. Kamin, "Is Crime in the Genes? The Answer May Depend on Who Chooses What Evidence," review of *Crime and Human Nature,* by James Q. Wilson and Richard J. Herrnstein, *Scientific American* 254, no. 2 (February 1986): 22–27.

7. Kamin, "Is Crime in the Genes?" p. 24.

8. James Q. Wilson and Richard J. Herrnstein, Letter to the Editors, *Scientific American* (May 1986): 5–6.

9. Wilson and Herrnstein, Letter, May 1986, p. 5.

10. *Scientific American,* Letters (May 1986), p. 7.

11. Lester Thurow, *The Zero-Sum Society* (New York: Basic Books, 1980).

12. Harold Lasswell, *A Pre-view of the Policy Sciences* (New York: Elsevier, 1971).

13. Richard Nathan, *Social Science in Government* (New York: Basic Books, 1988).

14. See, for example, Harvey Leibenstein, *Beyond Economic Man* (Cambridge, Mass.: Harvard University Press, 1976); Thomas Nagel, *The View from Nowhere* (New York: Oxford University Press, 1986); Kenneth Bouldilng, *Beyond Economics: Essays on Society, Religion, and Ethics* (Ann Arbor: University of Michigan Press, 1968).

15. Nathan, *Social Science in Government.*

16. Peter deLeon, "The Contextual Burdens of Policy Design," *Policy Studies Journal* 17, no. 2 (Winter 1988–89): 297–309.

17. See, for example, Charles E. Lindblom, *Inquiry and Change* (New Haven: Yale University Press, 1991), pp. 186–87.

18. See, for example, Leland Neuburg, *Conceptual Anomalies in Economics and Statistics: Lessons from the Social Experiment* (Cambridge: Cambridge University Press, 1989).

19. See his *The Asymmetric Society* (Syracuse, N.Y.: Syracuse University Press, 1982)

20. Coleman, *Asymmetric Society,* p. 168.

21. Ibid., p. 168.

22. See Jeffrey L. Pressman and Aaron Wildavsky, *Implementation* (Berkeley, Calif.: University of California Press, 1973).

23. Douglas Yates, *The Ungovernable City* (Cambridge, Mass.: MIT Press, 1980), p. 5.

24. Michael Lipsky, "Turning the Problem of Implementation on Its Head," in *American Politics and Public Policy: Essays in Honor of Jeffrey Pressman,* ed. Michael Lipsky (Cambridge, Mass.: MIT Press, 1978).

25. James March and Johan Olsen, *Rediscovering Institutions* (Glencoe, Ill.: Free Press, 1989). In opposition to this view, March and Olsen advocate a view of politics that, in their words, emphasizes "the relative autonomy of political institutions, the possibilities for inefficiency in history, and the importance of symbolic action to an understanding of politics" (p. 9). Chapter 3 says more about this.

26. This question has been a subject of study in its own right, especially in the context of "prisoners' dilemma" games. See, for example, Hayward Alker (1980) and Richard Campbell and Lannig Snowder (1985).

27. Charles E. Lindblom, "The Science of Muddling Through," *Public Administration Review* 19 (Spring 1989).

28. Coleman, *Asymmetric Society,* p. 168.

29. Lawrence Susskind and Jeffrey Cruikshank, *Breaking the Impasse* (New York: Basic Books, 1987).

30. Susskind and Cruikshank, *Breaking the Impasse,* p. 17.

31. Ibid., p. 192.

32. Ibid., p. 120.

33. David Laws, informal memorandum, MIT (December 1991).

34. Michael Wheeler, "Regional Consensus on Affordable Housing: Yes in My Backyard?" *Journal of Planning Education and Research* 12, no. 2 (Winter 1993): 143.

35. Deborah Stone, *Policy, Paradox and Political Reason* (Glenview, Ill.: Scott, Foresman, 1988), p. 171.

## CHAPTER 2. POLICY CONTROVERSIES AS FRAME CONFLICTS

1. The term is taken from Sir Geoffrey Vickers, *The Art of Judgment: A Study of Policy Making* (London: Harper and Row, 1983). He uses it to mean "a set of readinesses to distinguish some aspects of the situation rather than others and to classify and value these in this way rather than that" (p. 187).

2. The following discussion is based on Donald A. Schön, "Generative Metaphor: A Perspective on Problem Setting in Social Policy," in *Metaphor and Thought,* ed. A. Ortony (Cambridge: Cambridge University Press, 1978).

3. Quoted in Jewel Bellush and Murray Hausknecht, eds., *Urban Renewal: People, Politics, and Planning* (New York: Doubleday Anchor, 1967), p. 62.

4. Peggy Gleicher and Mark Fried, "Some Sources of Residential Dissatisfaction in an Urban Slum," in *Urban Renewal: People, Politics, and Planning,* ed. J. Bellush and M. Hausknecht (Garden City, N.Y.: Doubleday, 1967), pp. 126–35.

5. William Gamson has argued that, in symbolic contests over meaning, frames with greater cultural resonance tend to prevail. But this can only partly explain the outcomes of symbolic contests, because "losing" frames may also have deep cultural resonance. William A. Gamson, *The Strategy of Social Protest* (Homewood, Ill.: Dorsey Press, 1975). It is worth noting that the image of housing blight as a disease has a long history, going back to the Reform Era, when rundown urban tenements had a strong *literal* association with such diseases as tuberculosis.

6. It should give us pause, of course, that "social prophylaxis" has had so strong an appeal for Fascist regimes such as those of Stalin, Hitler,

the rightist dictatorships of the Third World, and the many different national groups passionately devoted to "ethnic cleansing" in the newly re-Balkanized regions of Eastern Europe.

7. Our use of the idea of framing is radically constructivist, in the sense described, variously, by Jean Piaget, Nelson Goodman, Ernst Von Glazersfeld, and others. This use of the idea is very close to the usage of the proponents of the sociology of knowledge, such as Mannheim, and very different from the usage of authors like Tversky and Kahneman, who make use of frames to refer to the rhetorical cast put on a proposition (for example, whether one describes a risky investment in terms of the losses it might incur or the benefits it might produce) and who maintain, alongside *their* use of frames, a robust belief in the frame-independent objectivity of the social world.

8. Thomas Kuhn, *The Structure of Scientific Revolutions* (Chicago: University of Chicago Press, 1962).

9. Richard Rorty, *Philosophy and the Mirror of Nature* (Princeton: Princeton University Press, 1979).

10. Rolf Goetze, housing policy memorandum, Boston Redevelopment Authority, 1974. Mimeo.

11. See James March and Johan Olsen, *Rediscovering Institutions* (Glencoe, Ill.: Free Press, 1989). See also Mary Douglas, *How Institutions Think*.

12. Versions of the nature-nurture debate and more complex hybrids of these underlying cultural metaframes have recently arisen in connection with the revived discussions of the problems of the "underclass" in American society. So, for example, William Julius Wilson has called attention to the degree to which the destructive behavior of individuals in minority communities, along with conditions associated with poverty and racial discrimination, must be held responsible for phenomena typically associated with the most disadvantaged neighborhoods inhabited mainly by minority populations. Wilson's position has figured in debates that revolve around conservative and liberal approaches to poverty in American society, and Wilson himself has argued for a more complex and clear-sighted study of the underclass that is not blinded by either traditionally conservative or traditionally liberal perspectives. William Julius Wilson, *The Truly Disadvantaged: The Inner City, the Underclass, and Public Policy* (Chicago: University of Chicago Press, 1987).

13. This formulation is taken from Michael Polanyi, *The Tacit Dimension* (New York: Doubleday, 1967). See, for example, chapter 1, "Tacit Knowing," p. 16.

14. Chapter 7, following our case studies of policy controversy, re-examines the meanings of "frame reflection" and "frame construction" and

suggests that situated frame reflection need not require the explicit, verbal construction of institutional action or metacultural frames.

15. This distinction is a version of the distinction between "espoused theory" and "theory-in-use"; see Chris Argyris and Donald A. Schön, *Theory in Practice* (San Francisco: Jossey-Bass, 1974).

## CHAPTER 3. RATIONALITY, REFRAMING, AND FRAME REFLECTION

1. See Walter Isaacson, *Kissinger: A Biography* (New York: Simon and Schuster, 1992).
2. Albert O. Hirschman, "Good News Is Not Bad News," *New York Review of Books* (October 11, 1990): 20.
3. Most economists believe that, in order to effect the transition to a free market economy, the pressures toward centralization must be resisted. When they are successfully resisted, however, there is an obvious danger that high and sustained unemployment will destabilize the political regimes. With this danger in mind, a group of Harvard and MIT economists has observed that, "even on narrower economic grounds,"

> there is no reason to believe that the unfettered market outcome would be best, and several reasons to believe that the rate of unemployment, that would be produced by unfettered markets forces, would actually be too high. Too many firms may go bankrupt. . . . Firms may fire too many workers. . . . High unemployment tends to stay.

(Oliver Blanchard et al., *Reform in East Europe* [Cambridge, Mass.: MIT Press, 1991], pp. 82–84.)

4. Kurt Wolff, "The Sociology of Knowledge and Surrender-and-Catch," in *Beyond the Sociology of Knowledge: An Introduction and a Development* (Lanham, Md.: University Press of America, 1983).
5. Karl Mannheim, "The Ideological and the Sociological Interpretation of Intellectual Phenomena," in *In Karl Mannheim*, ed. Kurt H. Wolff (New York: Oxford University Press, 1971), pp. 130–31.
6. Kurt Wolff, "Sociology of Knowledge," p. 11.
7. Karl Mannheim, letter to Kurt Wolff, 1946. In Wolff, *Trying Sociology* (New York: Wiley, 1974), pp. 558–59.
8. Harold J. Bershady, ed., *Max Scheler: On Feeling, Knowing, and Valuing* (Chicago: University of Chicago Press, 1992). Quoted in Kurt Wolff, "Sociology of Knowledge," p. 11. From Max Scheler, *Die Wissenformen und die Gesellschaft, Gesemmelte Werke,* band 8, ed. Maria Scheler (Bonn und Munchen: Francke, 1960), p. 363. Translated by Kurt Wolff.

9.  See, for example, Richard Rorty, *Philosophy and the Mirror of Nature* (Princeton: Princeton University Press, 1979).

10. See Reddy, "The Conduit Metaphor," in *Metaphor and Thought,* ed. A. Ortony. Reddy suggests the evocative image of a "tool-maker's paradigm" according to which different individuals, living in very different environments, would interpret the "same" instruction for tool-making in terms of the materials of their different environments, ending up with radically different tools.

11. James G. March, "Model Bias in Social Action," *Review of Educational Research* 42, no. 4 (Fall 1972): 413–29.

12. Thomas Kuhn, postscript to the second edition of *The Structure of Scientific Revolutions,* p. 200.

13. The term is Howard Raiffa's. See his *Art and Science of Negotiation* (Cambridge, Mass.; Harvard University Press, 1982). We note, however, that a disputant's ability to imagine possible outcomes of negotiation may also be frame-dependent.

14. Kuhn, postscript, p. 200.

15. Ibid., pp. 200–201.

16. Ibid., p. 201.

17. Ibid., p. 202.

18. Ibid., p. 202.

19. Ibid., p. 204.

20. Jurgen Habermas, *The Theory of Communicative Action* (Boston: Beacon Press, 1984), p. 102.

21. Seyla Benhabib has pointed out that Habermas's ideal speech situation, which she discusses in the context of communicative ethics, places less emphasis on rational agreement than on procedures. These procedures sustain "the processual generation of reasonable agreement . . . via an open-ended moral conversation. . . . It is not the results of the process that count, but the process for the attainment of such judgment which plays a role in its validity." "Afterword: Communicative Ethics and Current Controversies in Practical Philosophy," in *The Communicative Ethics Controversy*, ed. Seyla Benhabib and Fred Dallmayr (Cambridge, Mass.: MIT Press, 1990), p. 345.

22. Benhabib, afterword, p. 352.

23. Ibid., p. 358.

24. Ibid., p. 363.

25. See Jurgen Habermas, *Knowledge and Human Interests,* Part 3 (Boston: Beacon Press, 1968).

26. John Forester, "Envisioning the Politics of Public Sector Dispute Resolution." Cornell University, 1989. Mimeo.

27. See Thomas Nagel, *The View from Nowhere* (New York: Oxford University Press, 1986).

28. Forester, "Envisioning the Politics of Public Sector Dispute Resolution."

29. Hannah Pitkin, "Justice: On Relating Private and Public," *Political Theory* 9, no. 3 (August 1981): 327–52.

30. Forester, "Envisioning the Politics of Public Sector Dispute Resolution," p. 44.

31. See David Braybrooke and Charles E. Lindblom, "The Strategy of Disjointed Incrementalism," in *A Strategy of Decision: Policy Evaluation as a Social Process* (London: Collier-Macmillan, 1963).

32. Charles E. Lindblom and David L. Cohen, *Usable Knowledge* (New Haven: Yale University Press, 1979).

33. See John Dewey, *Logic: The Theory of Inquiry* (New York: Holt, Rhinehart and Winston, 1938); and *The Public and Its Problems: An Essay in Political Inquiry* (Chicago: Gateway Books, 1946).

34. Charles E. Lindblom, *Inquiry and Change: The Troubled Attempt to Understand and Shape Society* (New Haven: Yale University Press, 1991).

35. Ibid., pp. 35–36.

36. Ibid., p. 47.

37. James March and Johan Olsen, *Institutions Rediscovered* (New York: Free Press, 1989), pp. 13–14.

38. Ibid., p. 126.

39. Ibid., p. 142.

40. Ibid., pp. 170–71.

41. Both preceding quotes are from ibid., pp. 63, 62.

42. Albert O. Hirschman, *The Strategy of Economic Development* (New Haven: Yale University Press, 1958).

43. Albert O. Hirschman, *A Bias toward Hope: Essays on Development and Latin America* (New Haven: Yale University Press, 1971).

44. Albert O. Hirschman, *The Rhetoric of Reaction: Perversity, Futility, Jeopardy* (Cambridge, Mass.: Belknap, 1991).

## CHAPTER 4. EARLY RETIREMENT IN GERMANY

1. *Sud Deutsche Zeitung* (October 11, 1992).

2. Victor Turner, *Dramas, Fields and Metaphors: Symbolic Action in Human Society* (Ithaca, N.Y.: Cornell University Press, 1974), p. 133.

3. Ibid., p. 17.

4. See Peter deLeon, "The Contextual Burdens of Policy Design," in

*Policy Studies Journal* 17, no. 2 (Winter 1988–89): 297–309. DeLeon refers here to Nelson W. Polsby, *Political Innovation in American Politics* (New Haven: Yale University Press, 1984); John W. Kingdon, *Agendas, Alternatives, and Public Policy* (Boston: Little, Brown, 1984); Davis B. Bobrow and John S. Dryzek, *Policy Analysis by Design* (Pittsburgh: University of Pittsburgh Press, 1987); Ernest R. Alexander, "Design and the Decision Making Process," *Policy Sciences* 14 (1982): 279–92; and Ralph Hambrick, "A Guide for the Analysis of Policy Arguments," *Policy Sciences* 5 (1974): 469–78.

5. Herbert Simon, *The Sciences of the Artificial* (Cambridge, Mass.: MIT Press, 1976).

6. For treatments of designing in architecture consistent with this description, see John Habraken, *The Appearance of the Form* (Cambridge, Mass.: Atwater Press, 1988).

7. Donald A. Schön and Glenn Wiggins, "Kinds of Seeing and Their Functions in Designing," *Design Studies* (Spring 1992): 1.

8. We adapt for present purposes the distinction between espoused and theory-in-use first presented by Chris Argyris and Donald A. Schön in *Theory in Practice* (San Francisco: Jossey-Bass, 1974).

9. Michael Lipsky, *Street-Level Bureaucracy* (New York: Russell Sage Foundation, 1980).

10. See John Kingdon, *Agendas, Alternatives, and Public Policy*, in which the idea of "policy windows" was first discussed.

## CHAPTER 5. PROJECT ATHENA AT MIT

1. In spring 1986 the Project Athena Study Group, an institute faculty committee headed by Professor Jean DeMonchaux, then Dean of the School of Architecture and Planning, mandated a study of the educational impact of Project Athena on four MIT departments: architecture, civil engineering, physics, and chemistry. We were the principal investigators on this study. Other members of the study team included Brenda Nielsen, M. Stella Orsini, and Wim Overmeer. See Sherry Turkle and Donald A. Schön et al., "Project Athena at MIT," unpublished manuscript, May 1988.

2. Professor Michael Dertouzos, personal communication to the authors, June 1992. Dertouzos' view of coherence was not necessarily shared by the other architects of Project Athena. All of them shared the vision of a system of common interfaces, about whose specific form, however, they may have held differing views. According to Dertouzos, Professor Moses hoped that all MIT work stations would

speak the computer language LISP. In the event, again according to Dertouzos, the group settled on UNIX as an operating system that could be implemented "in a reasonable time and on a mass scale."

3. In later communications, Dertouzos has made it clear that in his view, there are no "educational first principles" or "societal master plan" to guide processes of institutional change in the areas of technology and education. All there could be was the intention to "educate our students the best we can by exploiting new technologies." Personal communication to the authors, November 30, 1992.

4. Joel Moses, "Computers and Education," report to MIT School of Engineering (1982), p. 12.

5. Ibid., p. 1.

6. Michael Dertouzos, "Report of the Ad Hoc Committee on Future Computational Needs and Resources," MIT, 1979, p. 66.

7. Dertouzos, personal communication to the authors, June 1992.

8. Dertouzos in his 1979 report had described the network in remarkably modern terms: "At the hardware level, this network consists of cables and interfaces that make possible the transmission of digital data among the computers and ports that are interconnected by the network. At the software level, users may, through appropriate commands: send electronic mail and messages to other users; use computational resources at other sites including special and unique peripheral devices; look at the information generated by other users, provided they have given their permission; access databases central and communal to MIT, such as MIT news, coming events, and the MIT catalog." In "Report of the Ad Hoc Committee," p. 69.

9. As noted earlier, UNIX was not originally seen by Athena's architects as the coherent system of choice. Dertouzos points out, in a recent communication to the authors, that "UNIX was not an ideal put on the MIT pedestal by the founders, but rather the best available crutch! Faced with the practical difficulty of achieving uniformity at higher levels, we had to settle for the minimal possible commonality."

10. Dertouzos, "Report of the Ad Hoc Committee," p. 10.

11. There is some question about whether or not Low was the only driving force behind this decision. Dertouzos mentions, in his November 30, 1992 communication to the authors, that he and Dean Wilson reached this conclusion independently, and that he believes MIT's then-president, Paul Gray, was keen on it as well.

12. DEC agreed to give the institute over 300 terminals, personal computers, and graphics stations and 63 VAX 11/750 and 11/730 minicomputers over a two-year period, and about 1,600 advanced person-

al computers in the following three years. IBM would provide 500 personal computers in the next two years and another 500 advanced single-user systems the following year. Together, the two manufacturers committed nearly $50 million in equipment, staff, maintenance, and other support for Project Athena. Dertouzos points out (personal communication, November 30, 1992) that "the decision to have two disparate worlds of DEC and IBM was largely necessitated by these companies' fear of mixing their people and products together. Naturally, we hoped they would blend."

13. Joel Moses, "Computers and Education," p. 12.

14. Wilson's comment was made at a special meeting of the Athena Executive Committee in spring 1987.

15. "Interim Status Report of Task Force on Education and Computers," March 14, 1979.

16. Dertouzos, "Report of the Ad Hoc Committee."

17. Edward Balkovich, Steven Lerman, and Richard P. Parmelee, "Computing in Higher Education: The Athena Experience," *Communications of the ACM,* ACM/IEEE Joint Issue, 28, no. 11 (November 1985): 1214–24.

18. This was out of $20 million that MIT pledged to raise "to support the design and installation of the distributed computing system and curriculum development projects." (See Earll M. Murman, "Introduction: The Athena Project—Goals, Philosophy, Status and Experience," Paper presented at the Nordic Conference on Computer Aided Learning in University and Higher Education, Trondheim, Norway, June 19–22, 1989). Professor Lerman reports, in a private communication, that there were debates in the Athena Executive Committee over how much of the $20 million should be allocated to curriculum development per se.

19. Abelson, memo to the Project Athena Study Group, MIT, 1988, p. 2.

20. Dertouzos, personal communications to the authors, June 1992 and November 30, 1992. Dertouzos makes clear that he had invented these terms earlier, in the context of debates over machine intelligence, and only later applied them to controversy over Athena.

21. Committee on Academic Computation for the 1990s and Beyond, "Computation and Educational Community: A Background Paper," June 15, 1990, p. 9.

22. Margaret MacVicar, personal communication to author, 1988.

23. Steven R. Lerman, "Three Year Plan for Project Athena," Draft, April 26, 1988.

24. Dertouzos points out (personal communication, November 30, 1992)

that he, for one, had never wanted to "freeze on *one* operating system," but that he had nevertheless "ended up caving in to that alternative in order to ensure even a minimal coherence." He reflects that "in the compromises that reality forces upon us, we end up with a system that is beyond our original conception. This dynamic has an inevitable intrinsic randomness that could propel a project toward unanticipated successes or disasters."

25. Kerberos was designed to maintain system security and integrity without centralizing system resources. The X Window System was a joint development by Scheifler of LCS and Getty of DEC/Athena.

26. Personal communication to the authors, November 30, 1992.

27. Dertouzos, personal communication to the authors, June 1992.

28. Committee on Academic Computation for the 1990s and Beyond, "Computing for Education at MIT: Final Report," background paper, MIT, 1990, pp. 7–9.

29. "Computing for Education at MIT: Final Report," pp. 6–7.

30. The idea that meanings may be directly transferred from one mind to another via words or other media has been happily labelled "the conduit metaphor" (see Michael Reddy, "The Conduit Metaphor," in *Metaphor and Thought*, ed. A. Ortony [Cambridge: Cambridge University Press, 1978]). Against the conduit metaphor, Reddy proposes "the toolmaker's paradigm," according to which each of us is isolated, as it were, in a slightly different environment and, on the basis of the repertoire available to him in that environment, must construct the meanings of the messages he receives.

31. Albert Hirschman, *Exit, Voice, and Loyalty* (Cambridge, Mass.: Harvard University Press, 1970).

32. Ibid.

33. To cite only one example of this frame-constancy, we note that Professor Dertouzos introduced the September 1991 issue of *Scientific American*—devoted to communications, computers, and networks— in language strongly reminiscent of his 1979 MIT report:

> The authors of this issue share a hopeful vision of a future built on an information infrastructure that will enrich our lives by relieving us of mundane tasks, by improving the ways we live, learn and work and by unlocking new personal and social freedoms. . . . A growing opportunity has attained critical mass as a result of a twofold serendipity: dramatic improvements in the cost-performance ratios of computers and of communications technologies. . . . This relentless compounding of capabilities has transformed a faint promise of synergy into an immense and real potential.

# CHAPTER 6. HOMELESSNESS IN MASSACHUSETTS

1. If the homeless were defined, for example, as those without a fixed address, this would exclude skid row residents who lived in a single-room occupancy or "cage" or cubicle hotels. If homelessness were defined as the absence of private space, then families in a family shelter or hotel or motel would be included among the homeless. If the definition of the homeless included those living in sufferance in someone else's home, then it would include about 2.5 million families at risk of being homeless because they are involuntarily doubled up. See Christopher Jencks, *The Homeless* (Cambridge, Mass.: Harvard University Press, 1974).

2. Peter Marin, "Helping and Hating the Homeless: The Struggle at the Margins of America," *Harper's Magazine* (January 1986).

3. Kim Hopper, "Homelessness Old and New: The Matter of Definition," *Housing Policy Debate* 2 (May 14, 1991): 760–61.

4. A 1984 National Bureau of Economic Research (NBER) study supported the smaller estimate. The study took off from the assumption that the proportion of time homeless persons had spent in shelters could be used to estimate the proportion of time they would spend in shelters in the future. Using data from a New York City survey, NBER estimated the time spent in shelters and welfare hotels for persons currently in shelters and for persons currently on the street. Then, using HUD's 1983 survey of shelters, NBER estimated the national population of the homeless, concluding that HUD's much-maligned 1983 estimate was roughly correct.

   In *Down and Out in America: The Origins of Homelessness* (Chicago: University of Chicago Press, 1992), Peter Rossi estimates that in Chicago two to three times more people were homeless at some time during 1984 than were homeless on any given night; on this basis, following the HUD estimate, more than 1 million might be homeless over the course of a year.

5. Nancy Kaufman, "Homelessness: A Comprehensive Policy Approach," *Urban and Social Change Review* 17 (Winter 1984): 21–26.

6. Kim Hopper, "Homelessness Old and New," p. 758.

7. Interview with the homeless advocate Carole Johnson, spring 1989.

8. Michael Dukakis, Inaugural Address to the Massachusetts Senate, January 6, 1983 (Senate document #1, p. 283).

9. As one member of his administration put it, "Homelessness is not a condition but a state of mind. . . . There were so many facets to it, you couldn't treat it as one entity. Rather than separate them out as a

new bureaucracy would do, better to plug them back into existing services, put people back into communities, keep homelessness from becoming chronic." Quote from interview with Irene Lee, who later coordinated an outreach team for the mentally ill homeless, March 17, 1989.

10. Kitty Dukakis had helped in this. When it was discovered that an anti-aid amendment barred nonprofit agencies from access to state funds for the construction of new shelters, she stimulated the creation of a fund for the homeless, which the Boston Foundation agreed to house, and helped raise $1 million to begin its work.

11. Interview with Carole Johnson, 1990.

12. The best national estimate is that in a typical week in 1987, 2.1 percent of the homeless were married couples with children, and 14.2 percent were families headed by a single adult, usually a mother. See Martha Burt, "Developing the Estimate of 500,000–600,000 Homeless People in the United States in 1987," in Cynthia Taeuber, ed., *Conference Proceedings for "Enumerating Homeless Persons: Methods and Data Needs,"* U.S. Bureau of the Census, March 1991.

13. Ellen Bassuk, "The Homelessness Problem," *Scientific American* 251, no. 1 (July 1984).

14. Ibid., p. 44.

15. Ibid., p. 48. Rossi and Burt estimate that the proportion of mentally ill among the homeless is about one-third. Jencks argues that "if America still ran its mental hospital system the way it did in the 1950s, . . . as many as half might be locked up." He points out that "the proportion of working age adults with disabling mental illness who live outside institutions roughly doubled between 1960 and 1980" (Jencks, mimeo, pp. 43 and 46).

16. Hopper, "Homelessness Old and New," p. 773.

17. Interview with Carole Johnson, 1990.

18. Nancy K. Kaufman, "Homelessness: A Comprehensive Policy Approach," *Urban and Social Change Review* 17 (Winter 1984): 21–26.

19. See Langley Keyes, "Housing and the Homeless," Working Paper HP #15, MIT Center for Real Estate Development, March 1988.

20. For sources of these estimates, see "Homeless Families: A policy paper prepared by the Office of Human Services," 1987; Cindy Brach, "The 707/Welfare Program Housing Homeless Families," Executive Office of Communities and Development Memorandum, July 1987; and Nancy Kaufman, "Helping the Homeless: The Massachusetts Experience," *Harvard Public Policy Review* 6, no. 1 (Spring 1989).

21. Interview with Paul McGerigle, 1990.

22. Ibid.
23. Ibid., p. 6.
24. EOCD Working Paper, Fall 1988.
25. Other states later encountered similar problems. For example, a *New York Times* article of November 1, 1990, reported that while advocates for the homeless were criticizing the city's apartment lottery program for welfare and working poor families because it "takes apartments that had been set aside for the homeless away from the families who need them most," Mayor Dinkins was pointing out that "unintentionally, an incentive for people to use welfare hotels has been created. Families are frequently entering our city shelter system in order to find a permanent apartment. We do not want doubled-up families to make themselves homeless in order to find city housing." Thomas Morgan, "Advocates for the Homeless Fault Housing Plan," *New York Times,* November 1, 1991, section B.
26. Interview with Carole Johnson, 1990.
27. What Kaufman discovered at this point was paralleled, some years later, by the discoveries of others. In a *New York Times* article, July 12, 1992, by Celia Dugger, Nancy Wackstein, formerly Mayor Dinkins's director of the Office on Homelessness and Single Room Occupancy Housing, thought back over her tenure in that job: "I thought that if you just provided 8,000 units of permanent housing for a couple of years, you'd address the problem. I failed to understand that the universe of potential homeless families is very large. There are probably 200,000 ill-housed welfare families in the city." The article goes on: "That simple insight made Ms. Wackstein understand that the city had to regulate the number of people coming into homeless shelters. The unspoken reason that the city made people stay in shelters a long time before they got housing was in fact, she said, to discourage more ill-housed people from checking into the system." Celia Dugger, "Memo to Democrats: Housing Won't Solve Homelessness," *New York Times,* July 12, 1992, p. 22.
28. Statistics on Homeless and Prevention Caseloads, Department of Public Welfare, 1990.
29. The resolution of policy controversies and dilemmas is vulnerable to contextual factors in addition to the possible resurgence of the advocates. At the time of this writing, an article in the *Boston Globe* records the fact that the Department of Public Welfare, "faced with a burgeoning number of homeless families living in welfare motel rooms that cost the state more than $2000 a month in rent, has opted for the first time to rent apartments for such families until they find permanent homes" ("State Opts for Fewer Motels for Homeless," by Jordana Hart, November 15, 1992). This article goes on to say that "the number of

homeless families living in state-funded motels and hotels has almost tripled over the past year, [to the level of 278 families] according to welfare data, partly due to drastic cuts in rent subsidies for permanent housing."

## CHAPTER 7. DESIGN RATIONALITY REVISITED

1. John Dewey, *Logic: The Theory of Inquiry* (New York: Holt, Rinehart and Winston, 1938), p. 8.

2. Edmund Carpenter, *Eskimo* (identical to *Explorations,* vol. 9 [Toronto: University of Toronto Press, 1960]), pp. 66–67.

3. Ben Shahn, *The Shape of Content* (Cambridge, Mass.: Harvard University Press, 1957), p. 49.

4. This phenomenon has recently captured the imaginations of researchers interested in physics teaching and the education of engineers. See, for example, Eleanor Duckworth, *"The Having of Wonderful Ideas" and Other Essays on Teaching and Learning* (New York: Teacher's College Press, 1987), and Andrea di Sessa, "Learning about Knowing," in *Children and Computers,* ed. E. L. Klein (San Francisco: Jossey-Bass, 1985).

5. In the entirely different context of genetics, the Nobel Prize winner Barbara McClintock has observed that, contrary to the so-called central dogma of molecular biology—according to which the gene is understood as a fixed, unchanging unit of heredity—the development of an individual organism, such as an ear of corn, poses a very different situation:

> There's no such thing as a central dogma into which everything will fit. It turns out that any mechanism you can think of, you will find—even if it's the most bizarre kind of thinking. Anything . . . even if it doesn't make much sense, it'll be there. (Quoted in Evelyn Fox Keller, *A Feeling for the Organism: The Life and Work of Barbara McClintock* [New York: W. H. Freeman, 1983], p. 179.)

6. For further discussion of this point, see Charles F. Sabel, "Studied Trust: Building New Forms of Co-operation in a Volatile Economy," in *Industrial Districts and Local Economic Regeneration*, ed. F. Pyke and W. Sengberger (Geneva: Institute for Labor Studies, 1992).

7. Martin Tolchin, "U.S. Underestimated Soviet Force in Cuba During '62 Missile Crisis," *New York Times,* January 15, 1992.

8. Ibid.

9. James March and Johan Olsen, *Institutions Rediscovered* (Glencoe, Ill.: Free Press, 1989), p. 47.

10. We borrow the phrase *giving reason* from Jeanne Bamberger and Eleanor Duckworth, "The Teacher Project: Final Report to the National Institutes of Education," Massachusetts Institute of Technology, 1979. Mimeo.

11. Robert Heilbroner, "Analysis and Vision in the History of Modern Economic Thought," *Journal of Economic Literature* 28, no. 3 (September 1990): 1097–1114.

12. Isaiah Berlin, *The Crooked Timber of Humanity: Chapters in the History of Ideas* (New York: Vintage Books, 1992). See, especially, chapter 1, "The Pursuit of the Ideal."

## CHAPTER 8. CONCLUSION: IMPLICATIONS FOR RESEARCH AND EDUCATION

1. Donald A. Schön, *The Reflective Practitioner* (New York: Basic Books, 1983), p. 42.

2. Laurence E. Lynn, Jr., "Public Management: A Survey" (Draft paper prepared for presentation at the Fourteenth Annual Research Conference of the Association for Public Policy Analysis and Management, Denver, Colo., October 29–31, 1992). University of Chicago, 1992. Mimeo.

3. As an illustration of this focus, Lynn quotes one of the standard texts of public management, J. Steven Ott, Albert C. Hyde, and Jay M. Shafritz, *Public Management: The Essential Readings* (Chicago: Nelson-Hall, 1991): "Public management focuses on public administration as a profession and on the public manager as a practitioner of that profession. . . . Public management focuses on the managerial tools, techniques, knowledges, and skills that can be used to turn ideas and policies into programs of action . . . [for example,] position classification systems, recruitment and selection procedures, management by influence, budget analysis and formulation, supervisory skills" (p. 1).

4. Mark H. Moore, "A Conception of Public Management," in *Teaching Public Management* (Proceedings of a Workshop to Assess Materials and Strategies for Teaching Public Management, Seattle, Wash., May 9–11, 1984), pp. 1–12.

5. Graham T. Allison, Jr., "Public Management: Are They Fundamentally Alike in All Unimportant Respects?" (Proceedings for the Public Management Research Conference, November 19–20, 1979). Washington, D.C., Office of Personnel Management, OPM Document 127-53-1, p. 38.

6. Some fellow critics are Aaron Wildavsky, "The Once and Future School of Public Policy," *The Public Interest* 79 (Spring 1985): 25–41;

J. Patrick Dobel, review of *Impossible Jobs in Public Management, Journal of Policy Analysis and Management* 11 (Winter 1992): 144–47; and John Ellwood, "Traditional Organizational Behavior: What Can It Learn from and What Can It Offer Practitioners?" (Paper presented at Workshop on Practitioner Skill, Graduate School of Public Policy, University of California at Berkeley, January 19–20, 1990).

7. Lynn's diagnosis of the policy schools parallels, in an interesting way, Nathan Glazer's diagnosis in the "Schools of the Minor Professions" *Minerva* 12 (1974): 344–64. Lynn thinks policy academics suffer from their dependence on higher-status practitioners. Glazer thought that academics in the schools of such minor professions as education, city planning, and social work suffered from the higher status of faculty in such disciplines as economics and sociology, whom the minor schools sought to attract to their ranks. Lynn thinks the policy academics have lost their intellectual independence. Glazer thought the minor schools had lost coherence because the scholarship of the high-status academics they attracted had little relevance to the practices the schools had been created to serve.

8. Ibid., pp. 74–75.

9. Ibid., p. 76.

10. Ibid., p. 35.

11. Ibid., p. 91.

12. Ibid., p. 92.

13. See Lindblom, *Inquiry and Change: The Troubled Attempt to Understand and Shape Society* (New Haven: Yale University Press, 1991), p. 271.

14. Ibid., p. 272.

15. Ibid.

16. See, for example, his *Development Projects Observed* (Washington, D.C.: Brookings Institution, 1967).

17. Martin Rein and David Laws, "Knowledge for Policy and Practice," MIT, 1992. Mimeo.

18. Jane Tunstill, "The Children Act and the Voluntary Child Care Sector," in *Children and Society* 5 (1991): 374–84.

19. Martin Rein, *From Policy to Practice* (Armonk, N.Y.: M. E. Sharpe, 1984).

20. See Herbert Simon, 1977, cited in C. R. James, Sa. A. Mulaik, and J. M. Brett, *Causal Analysis: Assumptions, Models, and Data* (Beverly Hills: Sage, 1982).

21. See Donald Campbell, "Reforms as Experiments," *American Psychologist* 24, no. 4 (1969); and J. C. Stanley, "Experimental and Quasi-Experimental Designs for Research," in *Handbook of Research on Teaching* (Skokie, Ill.: Rand McNally, 1963).

22. For a fuller discussion of causal tracing and the background models on which it depends, see Donald A. Schön, "Causality and Causal Inference in the Study of Organizations" (Paper presented at the University of Southern California Colloquium on the Epistemology of the Social Sciences, 1990). In press.

23. This point is discussed more fully in Donald A. Schön, William D. Drake, and Roy I. Miller, "Social Experimentation as Reflection-in-Action: Community-Level Nutrition Interventions Revisited," *Knowledge: Creation, Diffusion, Utilization* 6, no. 1 (September 1984).

24. This contrasts with the process of hypothesis generation and testing in science as described by Sir Karl Popper in his *Conjectures and Refutations* (New York: Harper and Row, 1968). See chapter 4 in Schön, *The Reflective Practitioner* (New York: Basic Books, 1983) for further discussion of the logic of hypothesis and move testing in situations of practice.

25. Lynn, "Public Management," p. 76.

26. Ibid., p. 26.

27. Note that in all of these examples, the description of what is carried over is post hoc. Such explicit formulations tend to be made, if at all, after a process of reflective transfer has occurred. To assume otherwise is to yield to the ever-present temptation of instant historical revisionism.

28. The term *seeing as* is taken from Ludwig Wittgenstein, *Philosophical Investigations* (New York: Macmillan, 1953).

29. See Thomas Kuhn, postscript to the second edition of *The Structure of Scientific Revolutions* (Chicago: University of Chicago Press, 1964).

30. "But the greatest thing by far is to be a master of metaphor. It is the one thing that cannot be learned from others; and it is also a sign of genius, since a good metaphor implies an intuitive perception of the similarity of dissimilars." Aristotle, *Poetica,* in Richard McKeon, *Introduction to Aristotle* (New York: Modern Library, 1947), p. 657.

31. See Edgar Schein, *Professional Education* (New York: McGraw-Hill, 1973).

32. See, for example, C. Roland Christenson and Abby J. Hansen, *Teaching and the Case Method* (Boston: Harvard Business School, 1987).

33. See Donald A. Schön, *The Design Studio* (London: RIBA, 1984).

34. See Donald A. Schön, *Educating the Reflective Practitioner* (San Francisco: Jossey-Bass, 1987).

# References

Alexander, Ernst R. "Design and the Decision Making Process." *Policy Sciences* 14 (1982): 279–92.

Alker, Hayward, and Roger Hurwitz. *Teacher's Manual for Resolving Prisoners' Dilemmas.* Cambridge, Mass.: MIT Center for International Studies, 1980.

Allison, Graham T., Jr. "Public Management: Are They Fundamentally Alike in All Unimportant Respects?" In *Proceedings for the Public Management Research Conference,* November 19–20, 1979. Washington, D.C., Office of Personnel Management, OPM Document 127-53-1.

Arendt, Hannah. *The Life of the Mind.* Vol. 1, *Thinking.* New York and London: Harcourt, Brace, Jovanovich, 1971.

Argyris, Chris, and Donald A. Schön. *Theory in Practice.* San Francisco: Jossey-Bass, 1974.

Aristotle. *Poetica.* In Richard McKeon, *Introduction to Aristotle.* New York: Modern Library, 1947.

Balkovich, Edward, Steven Lerman, and Richard P. Parmelee. "Computing in Higher Education: The Athena Experience." *Communications of the ACM, ACM/IEEE* 28 (November 1985): 1214–24.

Bamberger, Jeanne, and Eleanor Duckworth. "The Teacher Project: Final Report to the National Institutes of Education." Massachusetts Institute of Technology, 1979. Mimeo.

Bardach, Eugene. *The Implementation Game: What Happens After a Bill Becomes Law.* Cambridge, Mass.: MIT Press, 1977.

Bassuk, Ellen. "The Homelessness Problem." *Scientific American* 251, no. 1 (July 1984): 40–45.

Bellush, Jewel, and Murray Hausknecht, eds. *Urban Renewal: People, Politics, and Planning.* New York: Doubleday Anchor, 1967.

Benhabib, Seyla. "Afterword: Communicative Ethics and Current Controversies in Practical Philosophy." In *The Communicative Ethics-Controversy,* edited by Seyla Benhabib and Fred Dallmayr. Cambridge, Mass.: MIT Press, 1990.

Berlin, Isaiah. *The Crooked Timber of Humanity: Chapters in the History of Ideas.* New York: Vintage Books, 1992.

Bershady, Harold J., ed. *Max Scheler: On Feeling, Knowing, and Valuing.* Chicago: University of Chicago Press, 1992.

Blanchard, Oliver; Rudiger Dornbusch; Paul Krugman; Richard Layard; and Lawrence Summers. *Reform in East Europe.* Cambridge, Mass.: MIT Press, 1991.

Bobrow, Davis B., and John S. Dryzek. *Policy Analysis by Design.* Pittsburgh: University of Pittsburgh Press, 1987.

Bouldilng, Kenneth. *Beyond Economics: Essays on Society, Religion, and Ethics.* Ann Arbor: University of Michigan Press, 1968.

Brach, Cindy. "The 707/Welfare Program Housing Homeless Families." Executive Office of Communities and Development Memorandum, July 1987.

Braybrooke, David, and Charles Lindblom. *A Strategy of Decision: Policy Evaluation as a Social Process.* Glencoe, Ill.: Free Press, 1963.

Burt, Martha. "Developing the Estimate of 500,000–600,000 Homeless People in the United States in 1987." In *Conference Proceedings for "Enumerating Homeless Persons: Methods and Data Needs,"* edited by Cynthia Tauber, U.S. Bureau of the Census, March 1991.

Butterfield, Fox. "Studies Find a Link to Criminality." *New York Times,* January 31, 1992, p. A16.

Campbell, Donald. "Reforms as Experiments." *American Psychologist* 24, no. 4 (1969).

Campbell, Donald, and J. C. Stanley, "Experimental and Quasi-Experimental Designs for Research." In *Handbook of Research on Teaching.* Skokie, Ill.: Rand McNally, 1963.

Campbell, Richard, and Laucig Sowder, eds. *Paradoxes of Rationality and Murdoch's Problem.* Vancouver: University of British Columbia Press, 1985.

Carpenter, Edmund. *Eskimo.* (Identical to *Explorations.*) Vol. 9. Toronto: University of Toronto Press, 1960.

Christensen, C. Roland, with Abby J. Hansen. *Teaching and the Case Method.* Boston: Harvard Business School, 1987.

Coleman, James. *The Asymmetric Society.* Syracuse, N.Y.: Syracuse University Press, 1982.

deLeon, Peter. "The Contextual Burdens of Policy Design." *Policy Studies Journal* 17, no. 2 (Winter 1988–89): 297–309.

Dewey, John. *Logic: The Theory of Inquiry.* New York: Holt, Rinehart and Winston, 1938.

―――. *The Public and Its Problems: An Essay in Political Inquiry.* Chicago: Gateway, 1946.

di Sessa, Andrea. "Learning about Knowing." In *Children and Computers,* edited by E. L. Klein. San Francisco: Jossey-Bass, 1985.

Douglas, Mary. *How Institutions Think.* Syracuse, N.Y.: Syracuse University Press, 1986.

Duckworth, Eleanor. *"The Having of Wonderful Ideas" and Other Essays on Teaching and Learning.* New York: Teacher's College Press, 1987.

Elster, Jon. *Ulysses and the Sirens: Studies in Rationality and Irrationality.* rev. ed. Cambridge: Cambridge University Press, 1984.

Forester, John. "Envisioning the Politics of Public Sector Dispute Resolution." Cornell University, 1989. Mimeo.

Fried, Mark, and Peggy Gleicher. "Some Sources of Residential Satisfaction in an Urban Slum." *Journal of the American Institute of Planners* 27, no. 4 (November 1961): 305–15.

Gamson, William A. *The Strategy of Social Protest.* Homewood, Ill.: Dorsey Press, 1975.

―――. "Political Symbolism and Nuclear Arms Policy." Paper delivered at Annual Meeting of the American Sociological Association, San Antonio, 1984.

―――. *What's News.* New York: Free Press, 1984.

Gans, Herbert. *The Urban Villagers.* New York: Free Press, 1962.

Glazer, Nathan. "Schools of the Minor Professions." *Minerva* 12 (1974): 346–63.

Gleicher, Peggy, and Mark Fried. "Some Sources of Residential Dissatisfaction in an Urban Slum," in *Urban Renewal: People, Politics, and Planning,* edited by J. Bellush and M. Hausknecht. Garden City, N.Y.: Doubleday, 1967.

Goodman, Nelson. *Ways of Worldmaking.* Indianapolis: Hackett, 1978.

Gusfield, Joseph. *The Culture of Public Problems.* Chicago: University of Chicago Press, 1981.

Habermas, Jurgen. *Knowledge and Human Interests.* Boston: Beacon Press, 1968.

―――. *The Theory of Communicative Action.* Boston: Beacon Press, 1984.

Habraken, John. *The Appearance of the Form.* Cambridge, Mass.: Atwater Press, 1988.

Hambrick, Ralph. "A Guide for the Analysis of Policy Arguments." *Policy Sciences* 5 (1974): 469–78.

Haveman, Robert, ed. *A Decade of Federal Antipoverty Programs: Achievements, Failures, and Lessons.* New York: Academic Press, 1977.

Heilbroner, Robert. "Analysis and Vision in the History of Modern Economic Thought." *Journal of Economic Literature* 28, no. 3 (September 1990): 1097–114.

Hirschman, Albert O. *A Bias for Hope: Essays on Development and Latin America.* New Haven: Yale University Press, 1971.

———. *Development Projects Observed.* Washington, D.C.: Brookings Institution, 1967.

———. *Exit, Voice, and Loyalty.* Cambridge, Mass.: Harvard University Press, 1970.

———. "Good News Is Not Bad News." *New York Review of Books* (October 11, 1990): 20.

———. *The Rhetoric of Reaction: Perversity, Futility, Jeopardy.* Cambridge, Mass.: Bellknap Press, 1991.

———. *The Strategy of Economic Development.* New Haven: Yale University Press, 1958.

Hopper, Kim. "Homelessness Old and New: The Matter of Definition." *Housing Policy Debate* 2, no. 3, 760–61.

Isaacson, Walter. *Kissinger: A Biography.* New York: Simon and Schuster, 1992.

James, C. R., Sa. A. Mulaik, and J. M. Brett. *Causal Analysis: Assumptions, Models, and Data.* Beverly Hills: Sage, 1982.

Jencks, Christopher. *The Homeless.* Cambridge, Mass.: Harvard University Press, 1994.

Jensen, Arthur R. *Straight Talk About Mental Tests.* New York: Free Press, 1981.

Kamin, Leon J. "Is Crime in the Genes? The Answer May Depend on Who Chooses What Evidence," review of J. Q. Wilson and R. J. Herrnstein, *Crime and Human Nature.* In *Scientific American* 254, no. 2 (February 1986): 22–27.

Kaufman, Nancy. "Helping the Homeless: The Massachusetts Experience." *Harvard Public Policy Review* 6, no. 1 (Spring 1989).

———. "Homelessness: A Comprehensive Policy Approach." *Urban and Social Change Review* 17 (Winter 1984): 21–26.

Keller, Evelyn Fox. *A Feeling for the Organism: The Life and Work of Barbara McClintock.* New York: W. H. Freeman, 1983.

Keyes, Langley. "Housing and the Homeless." Working Paper HP #15, MIT Center for Real Estate Development, March 1988.

Kingdon, John. *Agendas, Alternatives, and Public Policy.* Boston: Little, Brown, 1984.

Kohli, Martin, and Martin Rein (eds.). *Time for Retirement: Corporate Studies of*

*Early Exit for the Labor Force.* Cambridge: Cambridge University Press, 1991.

Kuhn, Thomas. Postscript to the second edition of *The Structure of Scientific Revolutions.* Chicago: University of Chicago Press, 1964.

———. *The Structure of Scientific Revolutions.* Chicago: University of Chicago Press, 1962.

Lasswell, Harold. *A Pre-view of the Policy Sciences.* New York: Elsevier, 1971.

Leibenstein, Harvey. *Beyond Economic Man.* Cambridge, Mass.: Harvard University Press, 1976.

Lindblom, Charles E. *Inquiry and Change: The Troubled Attempt to Understand and Shape Society.* New Haven: Yale University Press, 1991.

Lindblom, Charles E., and David L. Cohen. *Usable Knowledge.* New Haven: Yale University Press, 1979.

Lipsky, Michael. "Turning the Problem of Implementation on Its Head." In *American Politics and Public Policy: Essays in Honor of Jeffrey Pressman,* ed. Michael Lipsky. Cambridge, Mass.: MIT Press, 1978.

———. *Street-Level Bureaucracy.* New York: Russell Sage Foundation, 1980.

———. "Toward a Theory of Street-Level Bureaucracy." In *Theoretical Perspectives in Urban Politics,* edited by W. Hawley and M. Lipsky. Englewood Cliffs, N.J.: Prentice-Hall, 1974.

Lynn, Laurence E. Jr. "Public Management: A Survey." Draft paper prepared for presentation at the Fourteenth Annual Research Conference of the Association for Public Policy Analysis and Management, Denver, Colo., October 29–31, 1992. University of Chicago. Mimeo.

Mannheim, Karl. "The Ideological and the Sociological Interpretation of Intellectual Phenomena." *In Karl Mannheim,* edited and with an introduction by Kurt Wolff. New York: Oxford University Press, 1974.

———. "Letter to Kurt Wolff." In *Trying Sociology,* by Kurt Wolff. New York: John Wiley and Sons, 1974.

March, James G. "Model Bias in Social Action." *Review of Educational Research* 42 (Fall 1972): 413–29.

March, James, and Johan Olsen. *Rediscovering Institutions.* Glencoe, Ill.: Free Press, 1989.

Marin, Peter. "Helping and Hating the Homeless: The Struggle at the Margins of America." *Harper's* (January 1986): 19–30.

Marris, Peter, and Martin Rein, *Dilemmas of Social Reform: Poverty and Community Action in the United States.* London: Routledge, 1967.

Moore, Mark H. "A Conception of Public Management." In *Teaching Public Management,* Proceedings of a Workshop to Assess Materials and Strategies for Teaching Public Management, Seattle, Wash., May 9–11, 1984.

Murray, Charles. *Losing Ground.* New York: Basic Books, 1984.

Nagel, Thomas. *The View from Nowhere.* New York: Oxford University Press, 1986.

Nathan, Richard. *Social Science in Government.* New York: Basic Books, 1988.

Neuberg, Leland G. *Conceptual Anomalies in Economics and Statistics: Lessons from the Social Experiment.* Cambridge: Cambridge University Press, 1989.

Perry, William. *Forms of Intellectual and Ethical Development in the College Years.* New York: Holt, Rinehart, and Winston, 1970.

Piaget, Jean. *Play, Dreams, and Imitation in Childhood.* New York: Norton, 1962.

Pitkin, Hannah. "Justice: On Relating Private and Public." *Political Theory* 9, no. 3 (August 1981): 327–52.

Piven, Francis Fox. *Politics of Turmoil: Poverty, Race, and the Urban Crisis.* New York: Vintage, 1975.

Piven, Francis Fox, and Richard A. Cloward. *Poor People's Movements: Why They Succeed and How They Fail.* New York: Pantheon, 1977.

Polanyi, Michael. *The Tacit Dimension.* New York: Doubleday, 1967.

Polsby, Nelson W. *Political Innovation in American Politics.* New Haven: Yale University Press, 1984.

Popper, Sir Karl. *Conjectures and Refutations.* New York: Harper and Row, 1968.

Pressman, Jeffrey L., and Aaron Wildavsky. *Implementation.* Berkeley: University of California Press, 1973.

Raiffa, Howard. *The Art and Science of Negotiation.* Cambridge, Mass.: Harvard University Press, 1982.

Reddy, Michael. "The Conduit Metaphor." In *Metaphor and Thought,* edited by Andrew Ortony. Cambridge: Cambridge University Press, 1978.

Rein, Martin. *From Policy to Practice.* Armonk, N.Y.: M. E. Sharpe, 1984.

Rein, Martin, and David Laws. "Knowledge for Policy and Practice." MIT, 1992. Mimeo.

Rorty, Richard. *Philosophy and the Mirror of Nature.* Princeton: Princeton University Press, 1979.

Rossi, Peter. *Down and Out in America: The Origins of Homelessness.* Chicago: University of Chicago Press, 1992.

Sabel, Charles F. "Studied Trust: Building New Forms of Cooperation in a Volatile Economy." In *Industrial Districts and Local Economic Regeneration,* edited by F. Pyke and W. Sengberger. Geneva: Institute for Labor Studies, 1992.

Schein, Edgar. *Professional Education.* New York: McGraw-Hill, 1973.

Scheler, Max. *Die Wissenformen und die Gesellschaft; Gesammelte Werke,* band 8, ed. Maria Scheler. Bonn und Munchen: Francke, 1960.

Schön, Donald A. "Causality and Causal Inference in the Study of Organizations." University of Southern California Colloquium on the Epistemology of the Social Sciences, 1990. In press.

―――. *The Design Studio.* London: RIBA, 1984.

―――. *Educating the Reflective Practitioner.* San Francisco: Jossey-Bass, 1987.

―――. "Generative Metaphor: A Perspective on Problem Setting in Social Policy." In *Metaphor and Thought,* edited by A. Ortony. Cambridge: Cambridge University Press, 1978.

―――. *The Reflective Practitioner.* New York: Basic Books, 1983.

Schön, Donald A., William D. Drake, and Roy I. Miller. "Social Experimentation as Reflection-in-Action." *Knowledge: Creation, Diffusion, Utilization* 6, no. 1 (September 1984).

Schön, Donald A., and Glenn Wiggins. "Kinds of Seeing and Their Functions in Designing." *Design Studies* (Spring 1992).

Shahn, Ben. *The Shape of Content.* Cambridge, Mass.: Harvard University Press, 1957.

Simon, Herbert. *The Sciences of the Artificial.* Cambridge, Mass.: MIT Press, 1976.

Stone, Deborah A. *Policy, Paradox and Political Reason.* Glenview, Ill.: Scott, Foresman, 1988.

Susskind, Lawrence, and Jeffrey Cruikshank. *Breaking the Impasse.* New York: Basic Books, 1987.

Thurow, Lester. *The Zero-Sum Society.* New York: Basic Books, 1980.

Tunstill, Jane. "The Children Act and the Voluntary Child Care Sector." In *Children and Society,* 1991.

Turner, Victor. *Dramas, Fields and Metaphors: Symbolic Action in Human Society.* Ithaca, N.Y.: Cornell University Press, 1974.

Tversky, Amos, and Daniel Kahneman. "Judgment Under Uncertainty: Heuristics and Biases." *Science* 185 (1974): 1124–31.

Veblen, Thorstein. *The Higher Learning in America: A Memorandum on the Conduct of Universities by Business Men.* B. S. Huebsch, 1918. New York: Hill and Wang, 1957.

Vickers, Sir Geoffrey. *The Art of Judgment: A Study of Policy Making.* London: Harper and Row, 1983.

Vlastos, Gregory. *Socrates: Ironist and Moral Philosopher.* Ithaca, N.Y.: Cornell University Press, 1991.

Von Glasersfeld, Ernst. "Reconstructing the Concept of Knowledge." *Archives de Psychologie* 52 (1985): 91–101.

Wheeler, Michael. "Regional Consensus on Affordable Housing: Yes in My Backyard?" *Journal of Planning Education and Research* 12 (Winter 1993): 139–49.

Wildavsky, Aaron. "The Once and Future School of Public Policy." *The Public Interest* 79 (Spring 1985): 25–41.

Wilson, James Q., and Richard J. Herrnstein. *Crime and Human Nature.* New York: Simon and Schuster, 1986.

———. Letter to the Editors. *Scientific American* (May 1986): 5–6.

Wilson, William Julius. *The Truly Disadvantaged: The Inner City, the Underclass, and Public Policy.* Chicago: University of Chicago Press, 1987.

Wittgenstein, Ludwig. *Philosophical Investigations.* New York: Macmillan, 1953.

Wolff, Kurt. *Beyond the Sociology of Knowledge: An Introduction and a Development.* University Press of America, 1983.

Yates, Douglas. *The Ungovernable City.* Cambridge, Mass.: MIT Press, 1980.

# Index